Oriana Fallaci

NEW DIRECTIONS IN EUROPEAN WRITING

....

Editor: John Flower, Professor of French, University of Kent at Canterbury.

As the twentieth century draws to a close we are witnessing profound and significant changes across the new Europe. The past is being reassessed; the millennium is awaited with interest. Some, pessimistically, have predicted the death of literature; others see important developments within national literature and in movements cutting across frontiers. This enterprising series focuses on these developments through the study either of individual writers or of groups or movements. There are no definitive statements. By definition they are introductory and set out to assess and explore the full spectrum of modern European writing on the threshold of a new age.

ISBN 1350-9217

Previously published titles in the Series:

Allyson Fiddler
Rewriting Reality: An Introduction to Elfriede Jelinek

C. Davies
Contemporary Feminist Fiction in Spain: The Work of Montserrat Roig and Rosa Montero

Chris Perriam
Desire and Dissent: An Introduction to Luis Antonio de Villena

Mirna Cicioni
Primo Levi: Bridges of Knowledge

Alan Morris
Patrick Modiano

David Gascoigne
Michel Tournier

NEW DIRECTIONS IN EUROPEAN WRITING

Oriana Fallaci

The Rhetoric of Freedom

John Gatt-Rutter

BERG
Oxford • *Washington, D.C.*

PQ
4866
.A4
Z7
1996

First published in 1996 by
Berg
Editorial offices:
150 Cowley Road, Oxford, OX4 1JJ, UK
22883 Quicksilver Drive, Dulles, VA 20166, USA

Berg is an imprint of Oxford International Publishers Ltd.

Library of Congress Cataloging-in-Publication Data

A catalogue record for this book is available from the Library of
Congress.

British Library Cataloguing-in-Publication Data

A catalogue record for this book is available from the British Library.

ISBN 1 85973 069 8 (Cloth)
      1 85973 074 4 (Paper)

Typeset by JS Typesetting, Wellingborough, Northants.
Printed in the United Kingdom by WBC Book Manufacturers,
Bridgend, Mid Glamorgan.

To my children:

Nkemfuni Angelo Abanum
Roseanne Ifeanyi
Tessa Uche

Contents

{ vii }

Acknowledgements

Parts of this book originally took shape as papers delivered to the following conferences at universities in Victoria, Australia: La Trobe University, "Women in Italian Culture", 1992; Melbourne University, "Devouring the Text: Food and Drink in Literature and the Arts", 1992; La Trobe University, "Columbus Centenary Conference: The Consequences of 1492 in History and Literature", 1992; La Trobe University, "Europe at La Trobe", 1993.

Many sources used for this book are in Italian or other languages. Unless otherwise indicated, I have quoted these in my own English translation. Other sources, including most of Fallaci's works, have been quoted in the published English translation, except where there has been a particular reason to use my own translation, as indicated in the text or footnotes. I have quoted from Fallaci's texts in the Italian original only when its texture is important to my analysis. References are always given to her Italian text first, and then to the translation, and it is assumed that those studying Fallaci in the original will have the text before them. The issue of translation is frequently discussed, particularly in Chapters 5, 7 and 10.

Of the numerous friends and colleagues to whose knowledge and ideas the writing of this book is indebted, I must make particular mention of John Woodhouse in Oxford, John Hoyles and Jane Humphreys in Hull, England, Stephen Kolsky in Melbourne, Tim Prenzler in Brisbane, Mike Hanne in Auckland, and, at La Trobe University in Melbourne, Mirna Cicioni and the students of the "Narrare donna" honours seminar, and Richard Freadman. Mirna Cicioni, Dennis Costa of Boston University, Mike Hanne, Bruce Merry of the James Cook University of North Queensland, and Antonio Pagliaro, of La Trobe, provided invaluable practical advice and material help. At La Trobe, Consuelo Di Leo and Melissa Fisher lent their word-processing wizardry, the staff of the Borchardt Library were invariably supportive, and the University was generous with research funds and services. I also received kind help at the Biblioteca Nazionale Braidense and the Comunale in Milan, as well as the Mugar Library of Boston University. The University of Reading gave me full support while I was Visiting Professor there during 1995. I owe a special debt to Tara Kingston, of Dublin, who sent me a copy of her first-class honours thesis on Fallaci and material which it would otherwise have been difficult for me to obtain. I warmly thank all concerned. To my wife Esther and my children Nkemfuni, Roseanne and Tessa, who have lovingly and joyously sustained the writing of this book, my gratitude is unlimited, and I return their affection. I thank Oriana Fallaci for refusing to influence me, thus safeguarding my independence. The book's shortcomings are all my own.

John Gatt-Rutter

Part I

Outside the Texts

1

Reality and Rhetoric

How Many Fallacis?

Oriana Fallaci is the last person to make any sharp distinction between four spheres that might correspond to four Oriana Fallacis: her private history; her public figure; the interviewer and reportage writer; and the literary author. She has frequently screened off her private history (Fallaci One), and three times refused permission for films to be made about her (Ostellino 1990). She has also frequently claimed independent status for Fallaci Four (the literary author) from Fallaci Three (the journalist). But, reading Fallaci Four, we find it very difficult to dodge the other three Fallacis, as she figures prominently in her volumes of interviews (*Gli Antipatici* and *Intervista con la Storia*) and reportage (*Se il sole muore, Niente e cosí sia*), which means that we should add a fifth Fallaci – Fallaci the character, given as such, within her own writings. This fifth Fallaci will prove the most relevant to this book.

In the novels *Penelope alla guerra* and *Lettera a un bambino mai nato* the fictional protagonist cannot simply be identified as "being" Fallaci, nor can this or that discourse, fact, episode or character-trait be pinned to the real-life Fallaci. By the statutes of fiction it is also improper and irrelevant to do so. Nevertheless, a great deal about their protagonists corresponds to what Fallaci has stated elsewhere about herself and her circumstances, and readers tend to identify her with her textual protagonists.

It is because the fusion of fact and value, of fact and fiction, of the living person and the written artefact, is so close that I wish to avoid confusing the two. In exploring Fallaci's writings in Parts II–V below, I shall try to proceed as though no person of that name exists outside the body of writing that bears that name. As several of her works invoke real-world issues – the Vietnam war in *Niente e cosí sia*, feminism in *Lettera a un bambino mai nato*,

Greek politics in *Un uomo*, the Lebanese cockpit in *InsciAllah* – this is difficult. Fallaci has always committed herself publicly to everything she has written and to her struggle, through her writing, against all forms of what she sees as tyranny. My interest in studying her works is precisely that of gauging how quasi-fictional works at the narrowest remove from the world in which real people live and die can engage with ethical issues of freedom and justice.

Right away, then, we are in a thicket. Not only are Fallaci's works couched as judgements regarding social or political ethics and goals: she asserts her sense of identity and oneness, yet her narratives involve a breakdown of self-definition. This book will therefore also address the question of the coherence of the self as articulated in Fallaci's writings. The point of intersection in the literary work between problematical self-identity and public responsibility is the Author: a being as elusive of definition as any flesh-and-blood person, but radically different in being accessible only in the authored text. This "postulated author" within the text, now enshrined in literary theory (cf. Nehamas 1981), is thus not the same as the Writer outside the text, who can only report at second hand about the Author, nor is she the same as the "Writer" or, more usually, the "Narrator" within the text, herself a creation of the Author, though they may all carry the name Oriana Fallaci. The postulated Author is the same as the organizing principle of the work, its elusive intention, not necessarily identical with the avowed intention of the real-life Author outside the work, and certainly not identical with any component of the work, not even with the person within the work who says "I" and is identified with the real-life Author. This distinction between the various intra-textual and extra-textual Fallacis and the postulated Author specific to each text will be implicit throughout this book, and frequently explicit.

This chapter provides the biographical information which is legitimately expected in an introductory study such as this. My biographical account is based exclusively on what Fallaci has written about herself or said in interviews. Fallaci's projection of herself may not coincide perfectly with the postulated Author in any particular work. My brief contextualizing biographical narrative in this chapter will raise opportunely some of the issues to be developed in the body of the book.

Fallaci on Fallaci

One of the most informative of the numerous interviews of Fallaci (Carrano 1978)[1] begins with the question what it means to her to be a woman. Fallaci replied as Alexandros Panasgulis, just released after years of solitary confinement and torture, had replied to Fallaci's question: "What does it mean to you to be a man?" Being a woman, like being a man, meant having courage and dignity, and fighting, not necessarily winning: if there was any difference, it was that a woman had to fight harder than a man and have more courage.

This notion of women having to match or surpass male manliness, which Fetterley (1978: xx, quoted in Schweickart 1989: 26) has called "immasculation" and considers to be acquired especially through reading, runs right through Fallaci's work, though she always distinguishes between "maschio" (male) and "uomo" (man, an ideal humanity). (So also does the notion of lone endeavour.) As a young girl, Oriana was already going out into the country shooting with her father. In her masculine adventurousness, in her refusal to make women a special case, and in her cavalier treatment of feminism, as well as in her independence, Fallaci has something in common with the swashbuckling seventeenth-century writer Aphra Behn, who, Gallagher (1993) remarks: "took patriarchy too much in her stride and was therefore irrelevant to critics of the 1970s who were looking either for psychic damage or ideological ancestors. Indeed she was sometimes attacked as a mere male impersonator." Fallaci has always been close to current feminist revisionist attitudes such as those of Camille Paglia and Naomi Wolf and has often shown her distaste for "victim feminism" (P. Fallaci 1979b; Schalkäuser 1983).

Asked by Carrano whether her journalism was distinctively female in its "passion", Fallaci indignantly rejected the question as deriving from sexist behaviourist pseudo-science deterministically based on biological differences between men and women (Carrano 1978: 83). She always uses the Italian masculine forms for words like "writer", "author", "journalist"

---

1. I refer in this and the following sections to Carrano's interview with Fallaci *passim*, occasionally giving page references only. References to other sources are given in full.

("un giornalista"), in referring to herself, the grammatically iniquitous point being that the masculine is the unmarked or neutral form. (The mother in *Lettera a un bambino mai nato* comments on this and other sexist uses of language (O. Fallaci 1975a: 12; 12).) In her "male" self-assertiveness, Fallaci consistently presents a marked and consistent identity sharply opposed to Chodorow's portrayal of "female personality as relational and fluidly defined, starting with infancy and flowing through womanhood" (cf. Gardiner 1981).

Courage, Fallaci said, was the quality which she most prized, both in herself and in others: "I am obsessed by courage, both physical and moral" (Carrano 1978: 82). At the age of twelve, she had fallen in love with Jack London's *The Call of the Wild,* and with the book's hero, the dog Buck, from whom she learnt, as she was to write in an introduction tellingly entitled "*The Call of the Wild,* a Hymn to Freedom", that "life is a war that has to be fought over and over again each day, a ruthless, cruel struggle, from which you cannot allow yourself a moment's distraction, not even when you're asleep, not even when you're eating, or else you'll be robbed of your food and your freedom"; a struggle in which even love must be seen as a threat; a struggle which necessitates uncongenial survival strategies, tactical compromises with the oppressor. It was this book that made her understand the violence and enslavement of fascism, which she had until then taken for granted (O. Fallaci 1975b: ii–iii). Also, it taught her the tyranny of love, which the mother in *Lettera a un bambino mai nato* was to denounce so bitterly. "Nothing so enslaves Buck as does his love for his friend Thornton", Fallaci once remarked. "Not the thrashings of his captors, nor the harness that ties him to the sled" (Gerosa 1976: 16).

Beginnings

Oriana Fallaci was born in Florence on 29 June 1930, her sisters Paola and Neera followed in the 1930s, and Elisabetta was adopted around 1960. Oriana's anti-fascist father, Edoardo, a cabinet-maker, raised her in fascist Italy to share his "obsession with these words: freedom, democracy, dictatorship" – words which, she said, "were the milk that fed my mind". Edoardo was appalled when Mussolini declared war on France and Britain, countries that enjoyed freedom and democracy. He became the military commander in Florence of the *Giustizia e Libertà* Resistance contingents loyal to the *Partito d'Azione* (Action Party) and suffered imprisonment, torture and threats of execution at the hands of the fascists in March 1944 (P. Fallaci 1979a).

Thanks to her father, Oriana came of age when she was just thirteen and still wearing pigtails, on 8 September 1943, the day when Italy declared an armistice with the Allies and was promptly occupied by German troops (Carrano 1978: 70–1). When Florence was bombed, Edoardo stopped Oriana crying with a cuff across her face (Ostellino 1990). "Everything I am", she said, "everything I understand about politics, came from the Resistance." "I am a child of the Resistance," she would tell her US friends. Under the name "Emilia" she fought in the Resistance "like a little Vietcong", carrying messages, or a revolver, or bombs, or copies of the underground publication *Non Mollare* ("Stand Fast") across Florence on her bike, or smuggling escaped Allied prisoners past the German checkpoints, and received, upon her discharge as a private from the Freedom Volunteer Corps, 14,570 *lire* in pay, which she spent on shoes for the entire family (Carrano 1978: 70–1).

The men and women of the Resistance gave Oriana an education in "courage, disobedience, and dignity" and in the notion of "socialism-with-freedom", but her mother, Tosca, who had received only primary schooling and had battled against her own ignorance by reading everything she could, gave her a different sort of education. She was the daughter of an anarchist, Augusto Cantini, who prided himself on having refused to fight in the Great War, but for her politics was a luxury that her impoverished family could not afford, and she as a housewife and mother still less. Talk of fascists made her bang the saucepans around, sobbing, "Villains, cowards, murderers!" She "instinctively" realized that women would not be much better off under a democracy, that "she would continue to be a slave to the family, to society, to a system of taboos" (Carrano 1978: 70–1). She encouraged her daughters to escape domestic slavery by reading – books were the only luxury, "sacred objects" (ibid., p. 73), in the Fallaci household – doing well at school, and pursuing a career (pp. 75–6). Oriana was to be "totally and rigidly faithful" to each of the men in her life, but she never compromised with conventional domesticity and marriage except in the three years of her liaison with Alekos Panagoulis ("the great love" of her life) from their first meeting until his death and after, when she "sacrificed (her) work in favour of living" (pp. 76–7; 91).

Oriana took care to be always first in class ("except for conduct"), and found sweet revenge for her poverty in out-performing the wealthier children at school. "To be born poor means learning from the start to be courageous, to have dignity, to fight." She cited the experience of her school years as the cause of her *cattivo carattere*, her aggressive and quarrelsome personality, and her continuing vindictiveness (pp. 72–3; 101), but equivocated over this in her 1979 interview with Sabelli-Fioretti, and contradicted it in her 1991 interview with her sister Paola. She graduated from Florence's Liceo Classico Galileo Galilei with good marks in all subjects except mathematics (Ostellino 1990).

From the age of five or six Oriana felt she was a writer (Carrano 1978: 73–4), and her mother made her read Jack London's *Martin Eden* so as to see how hard it was for a poor person to succeed in that calling. The adolescent Oriana enthusiastically made the American writer and adventurer her model and dreamed of becoming a "Jacqueline London" (Gerosa 1976: 108; P. Fallaci 1991). Her journalist uncle Bruno, editor of the illustrated weekly, *Epoca*, pointed out to her that before one could write one must experience life. He recommended medicine as the best training for a writer (and Fallaci cited to Carrano the example of Vincent Cronin, creator of Dr Finlay, who was for decades very popular reading in Italy). In order to support herself for the six years of the medical course, Oriana, aged sixteen, "instinctively" tried her hand as a reporter, and was taken on by the Florentine Christian Democrat daily newspaper *Il Mattino dell'Italia Centrale* (having mistaken its office for that of *La Nazione*). Women journalists were then virtually unheard of in Italy.

She gave up medicine after a few months (P. Fallaci 1979b: 20), but worked for *Il Mattino* for six years (1946–52) – years of extreme tension between communists and anti-communists, especially Christian Democrats, who enjoyed near-hegemony – before being sacked for refusing to write a sardonic front-page report on a political rally addressed by the Italian Communist Party leader, Palmiro Togliatti (though, she remarked to Carrano, as an anarchist she was no more a communist than she was a

Catholic). To her editor's blackmailing pressure – "You don't spit into the dish from which you eat" – she replied, "I do spit into it, and I pass it to you to eat out of" (Carrano 1978: 79–80).

After a frustrating year or two working under her uncle Bruno for *Epoca*, Fallaci moved to Rome, working freelance at first, and living on next to nothing, for another of the illustrated weeklies, *L'Europeo*, before becoming part of the magazine's permanent staff in Milan and establishing first her Italian and then her international reputation as a journalist. She became a friend, around 1950, of the elderly writer and journalist, Curzio Malaparte (*nom de plume* of Kurt Suckert, a fellow-Tuscan of German descent), once a keen Fascist but later exiled for a while to a remote island. Fallaci acquired a flair for the dramatic style of his celebrated works, *Kaputt*, on the havoc of war and genocide in eastern Europe, and *La pelle*, on the aftermath of war in Allied-occupied Naples. Something of the Malaparte touch is visible in Fallaci's work right up to her 1990 novel, *InsciAllah*, in many images of the horrors of war.

The World, and the Tape-Recorder

In 1956 *L'Europeo* sent Fallaci to Budapest to report on the Hungarian uprising (Santini 1990a) and soon after made her New York correspondent. This led to her first two books of reportage – *I sette peccati di Hollywood* (which one might translate as "Hollywood Vices") in 1958, and *Il sesso inutile – viaggio intorno alla donna* (*The Useless Sex*), based on a trip round the world, in 1961. She was later to dismiss these early works as superficial (P. Fallaci 1979b: 16–17).

Yet Fallaci's journalistic experience feeds into her literary works and needs to be treated as seriously and positively as that of her childhood hero, Jack London. Her works of reportage present many interesting factors. Fallaci shows herself aware of the interplay between worldwide cultural differences and human communality and is one of the first writers to take the Italian novel convincingly outside Italy and focus on other societies with an unmistakably modern outlook. All this is connected with the cosmopolitanism of the roving foreign correspondent. Another sign of her originality as a professional journalist being turned to good literary effect is her personal involvement in her reportage.

She is not merely an observer or an investigator, but a catalyst, and something more than that, interacting energetically with the people she meets. Her own personality becomes a touchstone of the reality of others and of the material world in which they live.

The New York scene of 1957, along with "the idea of a feminism *avant la lettre*", fed into her first novel, *Penelope alla guerra* (*Penelope at the War*), published in 1962 and loosely based on her own experiences in New York at the age of twenty-six and including an episode "which borders on fact ... the episode in which Giò surrenders her virginity. That is exactly how it happened to me" – a valuable testimony to the autobiographical substrate and the relationship between fact and fiction in Fallaci's writing (Carrano 1978: 81; cf. Santini 1990a). Fallaci has confirmed also that the failed mother in *Lettera a un bambino mai nato* is barely distinguishable from her: both share the conviction, in the face of death, that "life doesn't die" (Bevilacqua 1980). The narrator's mother throwing away her contraceptive potion upon first feeling a new life stirring within her corresponds to Tosca Fallaci's reaction on finding herself pregnant with Oriana (Rossellini 1980). The series of houses and circumstances described in the three "fairy-tales" which the narrator recounts to the child she is expecting, including the magnolia, corresponds to the Fallacis' house-moves from their fourth-floor apartment within sight of Brunelleschi's cupola and Giotto's tower to a miserable basement and then again to an apartment in Via Mercadante. (Writing fairy-tales was, by the way, Oriana's earliest childhood literary activity.) "Anyone wishing to know more (about my private life) has only to read my other books carefully: everything is there between the lines, almost everything. Alas", she revealed (P. Fallaci 1979b: 23).

The roving correspondent Fallaci indulged her craving for adventure ("Adventure means risk and mystery: life's two most fascinating components") through journalism, which "stole" (or, hopefully, she said, "borrowed") her from writing for decades, but which also rescued her from poverty. Interviewing became Fallaci's journalistic speciality. *I sette peccati di Hollywood* and *Il sesso inutile* were structured around interviews, mostly reworked from those published in *L'Europeo*. The later volumes, *Gli antipatici* and *Intervista con la storia* are collections of interviews, selected from those published in *L'Europeo* and in the international press.

The title of *Gli antipatici* (1963) means something like "Beastly People", and the original series in *L'Europeo* included demolition jobs, or attempted demolition jobs, on such people as Anthony Armstrong-Jones (Lord Snowdon) and the highly successful young French writer, Françoise Sagan (neither of which appeared in either the Italian or English volume) (cf. O. Fallaci 1962b, 1962c), as well as Duchess Cayetana of Alba and Alfred Hitchcock (which did appear in both). Fallaci's preface explained that her title referred to the intrusive unpleasantness of celebrity as such, rather than to individual personalities, giving the title *Limelighters* to the British and *Egotists: Sixteen Surprising Interviews* to the US edition (1968). The Italian volume contains eighteen interviews, eight of them with Italians (ranging from the Communist leader Leonilde Jotti to the football star Gianni Rivera), while the US edition included six US personalities (including Norman Mailer and Sammy Davis, Jr.), and only two Italians (Anna Magnani and Federico Fellini).

Being interviewed herself by Jordan Bonfante in 1975, she provided his title "An Interview is a Love Story": "Each (interview) is a portrait of myself. They are a strange mixture of my ideas, my temperament, my patience. . .". As always, she dismissed the word "objectivity" as meaningless, preferring "honest" and "correct". (The pseudo-objectivity of "objective" journalism, especially in war situations, has been studied intensively by Pedelty (1995), whose conclusions abundantly vindicate Fallaci's position, as will be seen in Chapter 8 below.) Her interviewing could be notoriously aggressive. The equally tough Robert Scheer described interviewing her as being "like throwing two Bronx alley cats into a gunny sack and letting them have at it" (Scheer 1981). Fallaci clearly worked out an interviewing strategy in advance of each encounter so as to coax or cajole, browbeat or trap her subject into making unpremeditated disclosures. She was capable of giving an interviewee whom she found morally obnoxious a devastating final punch line. Hitchcock, who gloated over the real-life murders inspired by his films, she shut up with the retort that he was the most repulsive man she had ever known. She contrived to close her mammoth interview with Colonel Gaddafi in 1979 by getting him to feed her the cue for the remark: "I thought *you* were God" (cf. Bevilacqua 1980; O. Fallaci 1988).

The interview, then, is an intensely dramatic encounter for

Fallaci, an engagement of one personality with another. It provides one of the main structuring elements of her writing and of her way of knowing the world and other people. The first interview she tape-recorded was that with Ingrid Bergman in 1962, which opens *Gli antipatici* (Rossellini 1980; cf. Santini 1990b: 48), making her one of the first print journalists to make systematic use of the tape-recorder. This introduces an intermediary into the interview situation, intensifying its simultaneous intimacy and lack of intimacy. The tape-recorder supplants the reporter's notepad and makes the *tête-à-tête* a more self-conscious, inhibiting and impersonal affair, but also captures the speaking voice, the guarantee of the presence and authenticity of the person interviewed.

Fallaci thus began to spend long hours transcribing interviews, listening and re-listening to the interviewee's taped voice. Intonation, timbre, rhythm – the specifically acoustic and corporeal aspects of speech – thus become prominent means of access to the living person – an existential key. The linguistic aspects of speech – accent, lexis, syntax and style – which are familiar modes of literary characterization, providing a sociocultural key, are clearly more susceptible to study on a tape-recording. The living voice is characteristic of Fallaci's writing, including reportage, but she deploys it with increasing sophistication from the 1960s onwards. Two further turns derive from this. First, Fallaci, in listening to her taped interviews, hears not only the interviewee's voice, but her own also. She is thus able to perceive herself as other – object as well as subject. Second, Fallaci senses writing more and more as speech – as her voice speaking to other voices. Both these turns likewise become ever more evident in her literary works, even in an apparently unrelated one like *Lettera a un bambino mai nato* (see Chapter 5 below).

In the 1960s Fallaci reported on the US space programme, publishing in 1965 her long, ambitious, and widely read book *Se il sole muore* (*If the Sun Dies*), to be followed in 1970 by another volume of reportage on the Apollo project that put the first men on the moon in 1969, *Quel giorno sulla luna* ("That Day on the Moon"). This latter book has not been translated and is far more caustic about space exploration. During the interval between the two books, Fallaci had been radicalized by the US intervention in Vietnam and by the widespread perception that, under the banner of anti-communism, the United States had embarked on the quest for world hegemony and the repression of local liberties. This shift in Fallaci's attitude towards the role of the United States in the world is all the more striking in that she had established for herself a home from home in her beloved New York, where success was admired, and not resented as in Italy, dividing her time, when she was not travelling on assignments, between this nook and a country property in the Chianti area of Tuscany.

This renewed radicalism shifted Fallaci's attention to the international politics of liberation, justice and democracy and of warlike confrontations between States, as evidenced in her Vietnam war reportage and in her interviews with history in the making (Bonfante 1975), which was to give the title to her second collection of interviews. Fallaci was the first Italian woman war correspondent, reporting from Vietnam and other battle fronts, despite the fear that permanently froze her bowels, and as such held the rank of major in the US Army (Santini 1990b).

As with *Se il sole muore*, she reworked her Vietnam war reportage to produce in 1969 the even more successful and controversial volume, *Niente e così sia* (published as *Nothing, and so be it* in the USA and *Nothing and Amen* in the British version). Her none too veiled critique of the US intervention, and the bullets she received from the Mexican military as they gunned down hundreds of young demonstrators just in advance of the Mexico City Olympics in October 1968 (O. Fallaci 1968a, 1968b), made her one of the cult figures of the worldwide anti-war and radical youth and student movements. However, almost as soon as the book was out, she was disillusioned to find, on her first visit to North Vietnam, that Hanoi was not really interested in liberating the South, but only in extending its own autocratic power (P. Fallaci 1991; and see O. Fallaci 1990 (edn with 1977 additions and revisions) 72–3).

The radicalized Fallaci's *Intervista con la storia* in 1974 contained seventeen political interviews mostly dating from 1972 and 1973. Ten more, from the years 1974–6, were added in the 1977 edition and included in the English-language edition, *Interview with History* (1976). These interviews with world leaders from General Giap to Golda Meir and from Willy Brandt to the Shah of Iran, marked the acme of Fallaci's international reputation as a journalist. Several of them turned into political events in their own right, as Fallaci teased out compromising admissions – Yasser Arafat letting slip that his aim was the abolition of the State of Israel; Henry Kissinger suggesting that the US public admired him as a kind of Lone Ranger.

Fallaci was not unfailingly effective as an interviewer. She had surprisingly anodyne – though entertaining and intriguing – interviews with two Christian Democrat elder statesmen, Giovanni Leone, later disgraced as President of the Republic, and Giulio Andreotti, now being investigated on serious charges. Though mountainous evidence of widespread political corruption and mafia involvement and criminal conspiracy within the Italian political and State system has only recently been coming officially to light, the perception of it was widespread in Italy by the mid-1970s. It had been denounced by Pasolini shortly before his murder in 1975, and had been exposed in the mafia fictions of the Sicilian novelist Leonardo Sciascia. Fallaci, in her preface to the Andreotti interview, confessed her fear of the man and her sensation that his gentle courtesy, quiet humour, engaging stories, and piety masked the real and terrifying face of power. But though she pressed him hard on the question of Italy's political corruption, she got nowhere (O. Fallaci 1974 [1990]: 285–311).

The Personal Front-Line

Intervista con la storia was closely bound up with the figure of Alexandros Panagoulis, the opponent of the dictatorship of the Greek Colonels, who had been imprisoned in terrible conditions, for a long time under sentence of death, and subjected to mock executions and repeated torture since his attempt to assassinate Colonel Papadopoulos, the leader of the junta, in August 1967. On his release six years later, in August 1973, Alekos was interviewed by Fallaci, and immediately a liaison was established between them which still remains the great love of Fallaci's life. That interview is last but one in date of those included in the 1974 edition of *Intervista con la storia*, and is deliberately placed as the book's final liberating gesture. The English-language and the second Italian edition followed, almost as a farewell, after the death (or murder) of Alekos in a car crash in the small hours of May Day, 1976.

During those intervening three years, Fallaci put her journalistic career second, living with Alekos mainly in her house in Tuscany (Alekos being consistently denied a visa to enter the United States) and supporting his desperate endeavours to mobilize democratic opposition to the colonels' regime both in Greece and outside, and then his shortlived political career after the downfall of the junta in 1974. She spent four months shut away in Casole to work on a book project that she had started some years earlier, *Lettera a un bambino mai nato*, based on a previous miscarriage, in place of, and in preference to, a reportage on the abortion issue requested by *L'Europeo* (Gerosa 1976; Sabelli Fioretti 1979). The subject-matter – the presence of the Other within the female body – is still under-frequented even in writing by women.

This appeared in 1975, the year of the victorious campaign in Italy to confirm the legalization of divorce, the first great victory of the Italian women's liberation movement. Though it does not really deal with abortion, and, I think, is more readily interpreted as anti-abortionist than pro-abortionist, its strong generally liberationist thrust contributed to the successful abortionist campaign that brought about the most massive mobilization of feminist militancy in Italy, culminating in the referendum legalizing abortion in 1978. Literary and feminist circles received the book with a stony silence, most literateurs tacitly denying it literary status and feminists no doubt finding its defeatist ambiguities and individualistic emotionalism unhelpful to their cause. Yet it aroused enormous interest among the ordinary reading public and proved another major sales success for Fallaci, being the first of her books to sell over a million copies in Italy – a feat previously achieved only by Giuseppe Tomasi di Lampedusa's controversial (and posthumous) historical novel, *Il gattopardo* (*The Leopard*, 1958). It achieved similar success internationally with the English-language edition, *Letter to a Child Never Born*, and translations into other languages.

Carrano (1978) questioned Fallaci about the attacks by other journalists of which she had been a target. Indro Montanelli, one of the grand old men of Italian political journalism, attacked her after she had won a lawsuit in defence of her professional right not to disclose confidential sources regarding the murder of Pier Paolo Pasolini (*La Repubblica* 19.6.1977). Her worst detractors, she said, were women, even feminists, because "women are really the worst of enemies towards other women", out of the envy due to "the age-old oppression which has retarded their maturity" (pp. 86–7), whereas they should regard any achievement by one of their number as an achievement by women in general. She has always seen herself as instinctively and spontaneously feminist, and as living and acting accordingly, but she long resisted acceptance of the feminist movement, failing to recognize that it articulated much of what she thought and felt. She subsequently did support feminism with enthusiasm for several years, only to realize to her disappointment, she told Carrano, that feminists remained male-dependent, and that the feminist revolution could not be accomplished without men (Carrano 1978: 97–8). *Letter to a Child Never Born* marks the high point of feminism in Fallaci's writing, rejecting the family as microcosm of the societal power-structure and as the site and means of female subord-ination, and foregrounding woman as subject caught in the struggle to combine motherhood and career without committing herself to marriage.

Fallaci spent three years in seclusion, resigning from *L'Europeo* in disgust over a change of editor and of policy, and virtually renouncing journalism. The devastating shock of Alekos's sudden death had been compounded by her mother's long-drawn-out death from cancer early in 1977. She had docu-mentary evidence proving that Alekos had been murdered, which the Athens court had not cared to examine, and which she presented in *Un uomo* (*A Man*). During the eighteen months spent writing the first draft of the book, she slept with a loaded shot-gun beside her, in fear of being murdered in her turn. Fallaci felt (strangely, for an author of several previous volumes of reportage) "handcuffed" by the factual constraints to which she had submitted in writing about Panagoulis and (again strangely, for such an avid reader) even thought that she was inaugurating a new literary genre until her American publisher congratulated her on having produced a "faction novel" or *roman vérité* (Sabelli Fioretti 1979: 216–19).

She was bitterly disappointed with all the Italian politicians and political parties of the 1970s, except the Communists. She and her father had been particularly disgusted with the Socialists (for whom she had voted since the dissolution of the Partito d'Azione in 1948) over the handling of the kidnapping and murder by the Red Brigades in 1978 of the Christian Democrat party secretary, Aldo Moro, several times Italian prime minister. Her father resigned from the Party after forty-five years as an activist. She saw the Christian Democrats as the "bad guys" and the Radicals, whom she had briefly supported, as no better. Writing appeared to be the last remaining means of contributing politically to the cause of freedom and justice (ibid., pp. 224–33).

Manufacturing Bestsellers?

Fallaci's US reputation had been firmly established by the mid-1970s, and academic recognition came with an Honorary Doctorate from Columbia College, Chicago, on 10 June 1977 (who, however, have been unable to provide any further details) (Occhiuzzi 1977; Columbia College, Chicago 1994). She has been nominated a Community Leader of America, one of the Personalities of the Americas, one of the Men and Women of Distinction in America, and as one of the Two Thousand Notable American Women (Ostellino 1990). The Mugar Library of Boston University holds a Fallaci collection of autograph material (her Vietnam notebooks, correspondence, and such like) and interview tapes. In Italy, she was awarded the Bancarella Prize in 1970 for *Niente e così sia*, on grounds of the popularity and importance of the work, and the Premio Viareggio del Presidente in 1979 (a civic prize, different from the literary Premio Viareggio) for *Un uomo*. The 1991 Premio Hemingway for narrative went to Fallaci for *InsciAllah* (*Corriere della Sera* 26.5.1991).

Un uomo also attracted the sharpest attacks to date on Fallaci's literary reputation. Critics dismissed it as popular and distortive kitsch, exploiting and imposing the Panagoulis legend and Fallaci's own unbridled individualism (e.g. Guarini 1979; Marabini 1979; Rosa 1982, 1985). Kitsch or not, *Un uomo* was not dashed off in a hurry. In talking to Carrano in 1978, Fallaci emphasized the emotional stress which the book was costing her to write, describing it as a "cancer" (Carrano 1978: 96). She was to make similar declarations about *InsciAllah*, even through the narrator within the text, and did in fact develop breast cancer, which she felt was related to her literary labours (*Il Mattino* 3.12.1992; Leser 1993). Both these lengthy works underwent at least three major drafts over a period of three years or more (Rossellini 1980; Ostellino 1990), and of *Un uomo* Fallaci told

Carrano something which she was to repeat in *InsciAllah*, and which had been true also of *Lettera a un bambino mai nato*, that she was obsessed "almost to excess" with style, and especially with the "musicality" of the language, its rhythmic effects, phrase by phrase and page by page (Carrano 1978: 96).

The question of literary quality is posed in an unusual and acute form by Fallaci works, and partly coincides with the question of literary audience: most middle-brow writers are content to be such, and make no claims to literary excellence. Fallaci has repeatedly stated her literary ambitions, while making it clear that she wanted to communicate her ethical and political concerns to the widest possible readership. For this reason she settled for unusually low royalties for *Un uomo* (Rossellini 1980). However, Rizzoli's publication strategy for the book (though already common practice in English-speaking countries) marked a new stage in the bookselling trade and in the commodification of literature in Italy, creating a climate of expectation by massive advance publicity and pre-sale distribution of the entire first impression, and pre-publication excerpting of choice passages in *L'Espresso* and *Il Corriere della Sera* (Costantini 1979; Marabini 1979). This was called "manufacturing a bestseller", and no doubt helped in achieving sales of 800,000 copies in the first year.

Un uomo proved controversial also for its presentation of Panagoulis himself. His family and friends are reported to have questioned Fallaci's picture of his compulsive drinking, his wild behaviour in public, his harebrained schemes to provoke the dictatorial regime, and his physical violence towards Fallaci herself. Panagoulis's political associates are also reported to have complained that Fallaci misrepresented his political strategy and his views as regards the Greek oppositional parties and group-ings of the left. The film director Giuseppe Ferrara was widely reported as having refused to make a film on Panagoulis based on the travesty presented in Fallaci's book (cf. *Il Messaggero* 5.7.1979; *Il Giornale* 4.7.1979; Costantini 1979; Crimi 1980; Pat-tavina 1984).

The literary issue is not that of who accepts which more or less selective version of Panagoulis. Fallaci throws his heroic qualities into strong relief against his ordinary humanity, his own peculiar, private weaknesses, showing the coherence of his contradictions. The book makes and depends on strong truth claims in terms of privileged testimony – Fallaci having lived with Alekos for three years, having known him intimately, having heard his account of himself at first hand and in greater detail than any other person. Fallaci designates the work *romanzo* (novel, romance), making the issue, even more clearly than it would otherwise be, one of presentation and interpretation, the construction of particular meanings from the given "facts". This is implicitly to deny absolute privilege and precedence to even the most intimate testimony. Autobiography is based on the most intimate and privileged testimony – knowledge of oneself – yet can never claim exclusive truth-value in terms of judgement and meaning, but only as testimony still to be evaluated. No one is accepted simply and solely at his or her own evaluation. And since the autobiographical dimension is fundamental in nearly everything Fallaci has written, this issue applies to her work very broadly.

The selection or generation of "facts" is indistinguishable from the generation of meanings: both are formal and rhetorical effects. Fallaci's next novel, *InsciAllah* (*InshAllah* – Arabic for "if God wills"), presents a further problem. That novel too is based on documented public history which is well known to active participants and interested parties. But it grafts fictional private histories on that public history. This is itself problematical and provisional, since the private and the public are only two faces of the same reality. Fallaci's narrator throughout the text makes much play with the interchangeability of fact and fiction, compounding the indeterminacy of the documented facts with fictional elements which already have elements of evaluation built into them. Fallaci's fictive freedom also extends to altering the documented facts: thus, she has a contingent of the Italian peacekeeping force in Beirut destroyed by a speedboat suicide bomb, and she has some French nuns horrifically murdered by the followers of a Shiite Imam (cf. Giorgi 1990). Literary invention precipitates into political responsibility.

The massive, eight-hundred page *InsciAllah* is Fallaci's only book since *Un uomo*. It appeared in 1990, following an even more massive launch. Edoardo Fallaci had died, in February 1988, at eighty-four years of age. Oriana interrupted work on her book and returned to Florence from New York to nurse him through the last painful months of his life. Her memorial speech praises her father as an unassuming, ordinary yet extraordinary man who lived a life of inner freedom, whatever his circumstances; an everyday hero, whose heroism consisted in absolute fidelity to his libertarian and ethical ideals even in social and historical circumstances in which those ideals were denied or disappointed (Cecchi 1990; O. Fallaci 1990b).

Fallaci had returned occasionally to her journalistic role, with the two celebrated interviews with Gaddafi and Khomeini in 1979 and 1988 (O. Fallaci 1979b and 1988), and reportage from several battlefronts, from the 1983 international peacekeeping operation in Beirut which provides the subject-matter of *InsciAllah* to the 1991 Gulf War over Saddam Hussein's annexation of Kuwait. But for much of that time, from 1986, Fallaci hid herself away in her tiny Manhattan apartment, where she was busy writing her vast novel.

A thread that runs through this period, tying up with some of the encounters recorded in *Intervista con la storia*, is Fallaci's opposition to radical Islamic power, as represented in populist leaders enjoying massive support but intolerant of dissent or even diversity, and supportive of internal and international terrorism. Given her libertarianism and hatred of theocracy, her setting her mind against Islamic absolutism, however radical and popular, is understandable. However, Fallaci risks overlooking Western responsibility for provoking such uncompromising resistance, possibly the only effective resistance in Third World countries against the economic absolutism of the West. Her perspective (in common with that dominant in the West) begs this major political point. Is it an issue of Western pluralism against Islamic absolutism (cf. Parekh 1992, 1994)? Or is it an issue of the absolutism of the dollar purportedly based on humane values summoning up an oppositional absolutism purportedly based on the Koran? In Italy, the critical reception of *InsciAllah* has not addressed this point, which will be one focus of my discussion. Much of the literary establishment received the book in silence, and there was also negative criticism (cf. Giorgi 1990), but several highly respected critics praised its moral seriousness and its grand narrative energy and design (Gorlier 1990; Turoldo 1990; Vigorelli 1990).

The appearance of *InsciAllah* coincided with a widespread revival of the novel with the broad historical narrative canvas, both in Italy and internationally, ranging from Sebastiano Vassalli's *La chimera* and Dacia Maraini's *La lunga vita di Marianna Ucría*, both of 1990, to Norman Mailer's eleven-hundred-page *Harlot's Ghost*, of 1991, and Susan Sontag's *The Volcano Lover*,

Vikram Seth's thirteen-hundred-page realist romance of post-independence India, *A Suitable Boy*, Enzo Bettiza's two-thousand-page recreation of the 1930s Comintern, *I fantasmi di Mosca* ("Moscow Phantoms"), and Vassalli's *Il Cigno* ("The Swan"), all of 1993. In Italy, there had been antecedents in Elsa Morante's heavily publicized *La Storia* in 1974 and the massive novel *Petrolio* which Pier Paolo Pasolini had left half-done at his death in 1975. Fallaci's literary project, after two or three decades in which avant-garde Western literature busied itself preponderantly with the deconstruction of grand historical perspectives, and of the act of narration itself, is perhaps more at home in an emerging literary landscape where writers are concerned to define an intelligible history and the specific responsibilities within and for that history of individual human beings, social groups, institutions, corporate interests, nations, and international configurations (cf. Tani 1990; Caesar 1991 in Smyth 1991; Barański and Pertile 1993).

Rhetoric

Fallaci's public statements and her literary works invoke certain values – particularly courage, freedom and justice. These three values irresistibly generate a fourth: heroism. This fourth is rarely named by her, but often embodied – in the Italian Resistance and the Vietcong, in particular characters in *Insciallah*, and in the protagonist of *Un uomo*. When not named in Fallaci's literary discourse, heroism is silhouetted against its opposites. Along the personal axis, where it is synonymous with courage, it is thrown into relief by *viltà* – vileness, baseness, cowardice. Along the political axis, where it combines freedom and justice, its opposing negative is power.

In all this, freedom is the problematical middle term, where multiple antinomies collide: the personal and the impersonal; the individual and the social or political; existence and essence; the subject of thought and volition and the subject of the metaphysical or physical or discursive order of things. The status of the self as the source of ethical values and decisions is a central question in Fallaci's writing. Always, an autobiographical fictional counterpart of the writer is the vehicle for this ethical quest, interacting with other "characters" – one, as in *Un uomo*, many, as in *Insciallah* – who are the subjects of her literary enquiry. What Fallaci, when being interviewed, asserts with almost simple faith, is interrogated in her literary works from varying angles and with varying degrees of aperture.

The extratextual Fallaci's life-behaviour – risking her life on various front lines from the Resistance onwards, wedding a profession rather than a husband – encodes her values, and this behavioural code, or "rhetoric", inescapably affects readings of her literary works, as Fallaci the writer imports a selective version of herself as Oriana the character into *Se il sole muore* or *Niente e cosí sia*, as well as blurring the distinction between her extratextual and her intratextual authorial personae. The behavioural rhetoric is thus transformed into a quite different literary or narrative rhetoric, and it is at this literary level that I address Fallaci's works in the present study. The presence of the writer as a character within the text is a paramount rhetorical feature in Fallaci's works. An equally prominent rhetorical feature is the factual documentary authority invoked in varying manners and degrees in all her work, even non-documentary novels like *Penelope* and *Lettera*. Other rhetorical features range from narrative stance – who narrates? what is the narrator's status? who is the explicit and implicit narratee? – and timbre – sublime, ironic, mixed? cadenced or casual? – to disjunctions between the chronology of the events described and the order in which they are presented – beginnings and endings, flights into the past or future. Any other component of narrative, likewise, is not given but chosen, and, as such, has a rhetorical function – factual documentary as opposed to, or inserted in, a fictional fabric; multiplicity or singularity of discourses or discursive modes within the text; the scansion of events, deaths in particular; modes and degree of characterization; the incidence of ambience – cityscapes, prison cells, the womb.

Seymour Chatman (1989), discussing "The 'rhetoric' of 'fiction'" in terms of the "saliency" which Kenneth Burke defined as being the effect of formal techniques in fiction (cf. Burke 1968: 135), suggests that rhetoric consists not in techniques as such, but in the function to which a technique is applied in a specific text: "It is not concerned so much with the definitions of techniques . . . but in showing how they apply to the text's end – the set of explicit and implicit suasions of the implied reader" (Chatman 1989: 44). I follow this definition of Chatman's, but contest his distinction between "suasion to esthetic ends" ("something interior to the text") and "suasion to ideological ends" ("something outside the text, something about the world at large") (ibid., p.52) – (a distinction also asserted by Spinazzola (1987, and 1992: 141–2)). Chatman grants that "even non-didactic fiction radiates ideology", but argues that "the audience can be suaded in two different ways: toward an acceptance of the work itself or toward the investigation of some view of how things are in the real world" and encourages others to study that distinction (Chatman 1989: 55). This distinction between "ideological" and "aesthetic" suasion is perhaps more usefully defined by Ross Chambers (1984: 50–72) as the distinction between merely "narrative" (or informational) authority and "narrational" or "narratorial" (that is, discursive or artistic) authority, which exercises a subtle interplay between disclosure and non-disclosure, and which is clearly an important aspect of the narrative of fiction. That is, the art of story-telling can exercise an authority that then extends to the import of the story being told. My study of Fallaci's works examines the articulation in each of them of these two types of suasion – "aesthetic" or "narratorial" and "ideological" or "narrational" – and suggests that acceptance of the work is a condition of acceptance of the values promoted by the work, and vice versa, and that the same rhetoric has to do both jobs at once, because they are one and the same job. The way the values – courage, freedom, justice, heroism – are presented is in effect indistinguishable from the values themselves. The values are convincing or otherwise according to how they are realized in discourse. "Aesthetic" success or failure is indistinguishable from "ideological" success or failure. And, of course, it is the readers who decide.

Part II

Reports from Other Worlds

2

Hollywood Behind the Screen: "I sette peccati di Hollywood" (1958)

allaci's first published volume, *I sette peccati di Hollywood* (literally, "Hollywood's Seven Deadly Sins"),[1] was a reworking of reports which had appeared under the title of "Hollywood through the keyhole" in *L'Europeo*. This was (and, under the slightly changed title *Europeo*, still is) a high-circulation "quality" current affairs illustrated magazine addressed to an educated general readership, and thus roughly equivalent to *Time* or *Newsweek* magazines. Both the serial and the volume publication thus come under the rubric of "high" journalism and exhibit the skills which Fallaci had developed. A wealth of reliable information is selectively deployed within enlightening perspectives collectively offering a single coherent perspective on the Hollywood milieu. A corresponding wealth of correlations is established with other spheres of the social culture of Los Angeles and the United States. As will be selectively shown below, the reporter Fallaci's actual encounters with places and people are presented in lively and nimble narrative, with all the elements of difficulty, diffidence, suspense and surprise characteristic of an explorer's quest and with the quizzical gaze of the civilized outsider. A clean, brisk style negotiates rapidly shifting discursive modes and perspectives.

These strengths lift Fallaci's reportage above the merely ephemeral and documentary level, and *I sette peccati di Hollywood* does not lose by comparison with subsequent Italian writing about the Californian dream-factory (see for example Bernardini

---

1. This has not been translated into English. I quote in my own translation, giving page references to the 1958 Milan edition published by Longanesi. I quote the Italian original only where it presents stylistic features not apparent in the translation.

1985; Sapori 1989). As an encounter between a whole person and the United States film world, it has a living, experiential quality, an existential awareness of other human beings wagering their lives, and an ethical awareness of the real or imagined values for which they do so. Yet Fallaci's "discovery" of America has been ignored in Italian literary annals (see for example Affinati 1990).

Fallaci has always been outside the Italian literary circuit or any recognizable trends in Italian writing. By 1958, the dominance of *neorealismo* in Italy had been demolished, and Italian writers were moving in a variety of directions – from Bassani and Cassola's novels of private memory and affections to the philosophical pseudo-historical fables of Calvino and Sciascia's documentary or quasi-documentary investigations of the repressive or criminal machinations of political and mafioso power, to the postmodernist innovations of the "neo-experimentalists" and the "neo-avantgarde", with an increasingly strong tendency to dismiss narrative or discursive prose altogether as being simply the medium of the ruling ideology. Giuseppe Tomasi di Lampedusa's historical novel *Il gattopardo* (*The Leopard*), which was an immediate bestseller when it appeared in 1958, created a hullabaloo in literary circles, with most critical opinion dismissing it for a mixture of political and aesthetic reasons. Female writers achieved recognition only if they were well-connected within the literary world (cf. Merry 1990: 40–1).

The strengths of *I sette peccati di Hollywood* are accompanied by journalistic limitations, especially that of neat narrative and discursive closure. Yet, though the book displays no grand theory, no ambitious intellectual superstructure, whether along the lines of the "critical theory" or "negative dialectic" of the Frankfurt School, like Herbert Marcuse's *One-Dimensional Man*, or of a systematic approach analogous to that applied to the media in the works of Marshall McLuhan, and though the style makes no affectation of "literariness", Fallaci's novelistic, quasi-autobiographical inside view of Los Angeles was not to be rivalled by an Italian writer until Andrea De Carlo's caustic *Treno di panna* (*The Cream Train*) in 1979.

The writer presents herself as participant observer, a "character" interacting with the others portrayed, thus co-opting the reader through the use of the first-person subject in her own expectations and emotions. Fallaci shows herself already a considerable way along the road towards what was to be called the

"New Journalism" and theorized as such by Tom Wolfe in terms of a convergence between journalism and narrative fiction. Wolfe identifies and recommends as features of the New Journalism, as practised by writers such as himself, Gay Talese, Truman Capote, Norman Mailer and others: the dramatic involvement of the reporter in the reality being reported on; scene-by-scene construction; dialogue as the essence of characterization; presenting experience through the eyes of other "characters". All these features are calculated to enhance the liveliness, immediacy and authenticity of the reportage and to give reportage a literary status supplanting that of the novel (Wolfe and Johnson 1973).

This method is already visibly well advanced in *I sette peccati di Hollywood*, independently of and before the theorization of the New Journalism by Wolfe and others, and Fallaci was to extend it in her subsequent volumes of reportage and non-fiction novels. The one major respect, however, in which she did not follow the New Journalism's hybridization of reportage and fiction until as long after as 1990 in *InsciAllah* is that of going imaginatively inside another character and presenting reality as seen by that character. The writer thus runs the risk, in all her reportage and non-fiction novels until *InsciAllah*, indicated by Wolfe: "Journalists had often used the first-person point of view – 'I was there' – just as autobiographers, memoirists and novelists had. This is very limiting for the journalist, however, since it can bring the reader into the mind of only one person – himself – a point of view that often proves irrelevant to the story and irritating to the reader" (Wolfe 1972: 33–4).

This risk is to grow in successive works as the authorial voice grows more intrusive and peremptory. In *I sette peccati*, as will shortly be seen through detailed analysis, there is still a saving distance between Fallaci's authorial voice and the figure of Oriana: it is the latter who occupies the space denoted by the first-person pronoun "I"; the former maintains a relatively detached, impersonal stance, and the movement from one to the other, from participant observer to detached informant, a movement articulated by modulations of style, is an inconspicuous but seductive rhetorical structure of the book. This is a quality of much good travel writing. It is less sustained in Fallaci's next work, *Il sesso inutile*, and she wilfully abandons that delicate equilibrium in her later books.

The titles of Fallaci's books are often provocatively unliterary. This first title slyly drops the gossipy (and inapt) "Hollywood dal buco della serratura" ("Hollywood through the keyhole") of the original serialization, and deliberately raises expectations of stark revelations of glamorous vices. Instead, the book displays the unglamorous banality behind the celluloid world. The "vices" turn out to be those of terrified conformity and religiosity, coupled with narcissism and ambition, or sheer greed. An arch preface by Orson Welles sets the tone.

The book is structured differently from the serialization, and this, too, signals a more serious, and a more literary, intention. The long "Preludio" (O. Fallaci 1958: 45–72) again raises false expectations: Oriana's quest to meet the most fascinating Hollywood personality of them all, Marilyn Monroe, more than ever a living legend then, with her marriage to the playwright Arthur Miller. Here the suspenseful vicissitudes of Oriana, more the active participant than the observer, beginning with the expensive talisman of a dozen silk shirts which she offers the insouciant millionaire Jean Negulesco in his Hollywood home once owned by Greta Garbo, hoping to secure an entry to Monroe and Miller through him, and moving on to the evasive tactics of her quarries and the failure of the quest lend themselves to effective narrative – the rhetorical procedure of delaying a revelation by narrating the steps taken and the obstacles overcome in approaching that revelation, in arriving at a truth. Truth, having thus been constituted as a narrative construct, is then aborted, revealed as absent or unavailable. This anticlimax prefaces the main Hollywood quest, suggesting another narrative likely not to reach its goal, enhancing the aura of elusive mystery that surrounds the deities of the film world, but giving a strong hint of their human vulnerability.

This is low-key, delayed-effect reportage, a literary strategy, working on the mystique of Hollywood as it affects the psychology of Hollywood personalities themselves, as well as a dazzled public, and the unbeliever, Oriana, in pursuit of that mystique and what lies beneath it. Early on, the narrator recalls the "long unbearable summer" which she has previously spent in Hollywood, using the present perfect ("Sono stata a Hollywood più di una volta, vi sono rimasta una lunga insopportabile estate" p. 15), as she does periodically through the book to close the distance between the investigating Oriana (locked in the

passato remoto, or preterite) and the reporting Fallaci (commanding the present).

In the opening scene of Chapter 1, Oriana and the reader are
plunged straight into the Hollywood mystique at a gala dinner
attended by the stars. But Oriana sees it as an exhibition of
waxwork dummies, pathetic grotesques. One of these "statues"
is Bette Davis. Another, who loses an olive in his suit, is Gregory
Peck. Each portrait is followed by an identical exchange: "'Who's
that?' I enquired. – 'Bette Davis, can't you see?' I was told." . . .
"'Who's that?' I enquired. – 'Gregory Peck, can't you see?' I was
told", etc., several times over. And the passage continues:

> No, I couldn't see. There was a little woman with a flattened body,
> her bones concealed beneath a mantle of Titian-red hair, and her
> name, I was told, was Rita Hayworth. There was a blonde with fat
> arms and the face of a dead doll, and her name, I was told, was Kim
> Novak. There was another blonde with a ruin of a face and a
> disfiguring scowl on her lips, and her name, I was told, was Lana
> Turner. There was an old man with silver hair and a moustache and
> his name, I was told, was Clark Gable. And they all seemed older or
> uglier, and their faces, which are capable of expressing and eliciting
> so many emotions when they assume the lineaments of a character,
> were now totally devoid of life. They bore no resemblance to our
> image of the stars. I felt sorry for them, or occasionally amused, for
> they were comic, and I had a vague feeling that I'd been let down.

> (O. Fallaci 1958: 46–7)

Serial repetition of syntactic structure, and of identical phrases,
works visibly enough here as a rhetorical effect, suggesting a
series of puppets manufactured to the same basic design, and
imparting a mocking tone and a seemingly irresistible emphasis
to the grotesque caricatures. This is writing that (mildly enough)
draws attention to its status as writing, visibly superimposing a
deforming lens over the reality. But it is not postmodern *écriture*,
which deconstructs itself before the reader's eyes: rather, it is a
traditional, not to say an archaic, rhetoric, more characteristic of
the age of Manzoni or Dickens. It is an adequate and an effective
device here in representing a personal impression, if cruel to
named fellow human beings. Similar stylistic means remain part
of Fallaci's literary armoury right up to her latest work, and will
be applied to varying effect. Such devices operate a discursive
closure, leaving no alternative to the specific logic which they

support, brooking no argument. Such peremptoriness will also be a permanent characteristic of Fallaci's writing, which guides thought along clearly defined lines or into categorical alternatives.

In the passage quoted above, the inescapable conclusions are, as always in Fallaci's writing, explicitly drawn. Here, the rhetoric and the conclusions are justified as avowedly a subjective impression ("I had a vague feeling that I'd been let down"), and suasion is furthered by a far less prominent, more natural-seeming, and thus more powerful, panoply of rhetorical moves. The final phrase of the passage quoted is immediately followed by a rejoinder from Oriana's companion in direct speech – "I felt I'd been let down, too, when I moved down here" – which converts the preceding passage from an implied address to the reader, as in any writing, to an account of a conversation with another person actually present at the gala, picking up the previous shift from "'Don't you see?'" to "No, I didn't see". This almost imperceptible, typically novelistic, shift in perspective – a narratorial suasion – recaptures and disarms the reader and begins to corroborate Oriana's subjective impression.

The corroborating second opinion is that of a writer called Bill. In sharp contrast to the waxwork figures of the film stars, he is a "lean and lively young man" whose "pained irony" is only enhanced by his "hooked nose and glasses". Fallaci's text thus spins authority out of the elements it has itself posited – lifelessness and liveliness, waxworks and irony, each bodied in actual observed persons – to deliver a judgement from which there can be no appeal. These judgemental poles – authenticity, vitality and intelligence as the positives, and their corresponding negatives – operate throughout the work, and, indeed, throughout Fallaci's other works as well. Whereas Oriana is an outsider, a short-term visitor, Bill has become an insider. But if he is an "egghead", "an intellectual through and through", he is not to be taken seriously when he says that "there is no such place as Hollywood", because all "intelligent and proper people" in America "are ashamed of Hollywood" (where even the rocks in the film sets are fake) and therefore claim that there is no such place (p. 48). Having thus debunked the Hollywood mystique, the author has cleared the way to presenting the real Hollywood as one of the nineteen suburbs of Los Angeles.

The travelogue proper now begins with the first overwhelming impressions that Los Angeles makes on a visiting Italian of the later 1950s: first, of course, the sheer sprawling expanse of the city and the related number of vehicles – well over one on average for every resident (excluding Orson Welles). This much is common knowledge, and features prominently in every account and every image of the city, and, along with the film industry itself, is the foremost emblem of its modernity, of the American dream in one of its fullest realizations. Fallaci's text concentrates effectively on sensory impact and factual inform-ation without superimposing any interpretative or evaluative overlay on the emblems of the real. Rather, the concrete elements in the picture provide their own commentary, and here there are surprises. Journalistic, literary or cinematic presentations of Los Angeles (even Raymond Chandler's or De Carlo's) rarely if ever show two features which are foregrounded in *I sette peccati di Hollywood*: one is the ubiquitousness of oil-rigs, active or disused, which explains the rule of the automobile and which gives the city its characteristic, all-pervasive odour of petroleum, barely mitigated by the abundant greenery (pp. 50–1); the other is the rats which infest the dense tree-cover of Beverley Hills – "the fattest and most insolent rats in the world" – and which all the desperate measures of the resident millionaires can do nothing to remove (p. 60).

These emblems of the underside of affluent modernity are reinforced by a third, introduced directly after the petroleum fumes and shortly before the rats, opening up a recurrent leit-motiv for the book, and hinting at a reticent metaphysic: this third emblem is the commodification of death, displayed in publicity hoardings flanking the ubiquitous freeways (pp. 52–3). These reassuringly advertise the services offered by the vast Forestlawn cemetery. Under the name of Whispering Glades, this was the subject of Evelyn Waugh's satirical novel *The Loved One*, of ten years earlier.

If the first vice of Hollywood is that of being a fake waxworks world behind its glamorous façade, the second is revealed in the terror aroused by the presence of Oriana, a journalist, at a highly exclusive reception given by Joseph Cotten (pp. 73–93). Fallaci cheerfully admits having broken her promise to Cotten that she would not write about the occasion: "The stars are scared of the public, scared of the producers, especially scared of journa-lists" (p. 80). The scandal-mongering gossip journalism of Los

Angelene publications such as *The Lowdown* and *Confidential* has cowed Hollywood society into abject conformity and respectability, and this second vice connects to the third – the utter banality of the stars' domestic lives, discovered by Oriana during an evening spent at home with the Hathaways and friends (pp. 100–2). This conformity is evidenced on Sundays by the star-thronged church of the Good Shepherd, nicknamed "Our Lady of the Cadillacs", because of its congregation of millionaires who sit, perfectly obedient Catholics, through hellfire sermons against the Sodom and Gomorrha which is Hollywood (pp. 95–9). And it is further evidenced in Hollywood's powerfully matrimonial values and the consequent ostracism of Véronique Passani for her intrusion into the marriage of the long-suffering Gregory Peck (pp. 115–17).

All of this clearly coincides with a reaction against the invasion of the Italian cinema by Hollywood-produced films (cf. Forgacs 1990: 116–19) and the values or ideology which they promoted; and also with an anti-clerical Italian's reaction against the continuing hegemony of the Christian Democrats and the Catholic Church in Italy. It might also be a comment on the US film industry after the McCarthyite anti-leftist purges of the early 1950s, which had reduced it to a bromide. Thus the argument of *I sette peccati* carries on to the next "vice", a long-standing theme in the literature on Hollywood – the neurosis of repression induced by the film world and amounting to "a streak of madness". Fallaci presents the tragic consequences for Judy Garland and Gene Tierney, among others, whose humanity could not be contained within fabricated stardom: "The Hollywood star, in short", the author sums up, "is not a human being, but a synthetic product, fabricated by the make-up department, by publicity, by the press-agent, by the cameraman, by the producer, and by the press" (p. 131).

This judgement is illustrated in the chapters which follow. Chapter 5, on how a star is fabricated, with Kim Novak as its subject, is challengingly contrasted with Chapter 6, "on the most appealing girl in Hollywood . . . the only one who hasn't let me down", one who made herself a star by dint of "courage, imagination and sheer face". She is Jayne Mansfield, who flouts Hollywood's hypocritical prudery by flaunting her femaleness, acting dumb, and fully preserving her autonomy and integrity. These large-scale female portraits are followed by two series of male portraits: the established idols of the system – Frank Sinatra, William Holden, and "the star of stars", who "acts himself", the "Self-Made Mystery Man", Yul Brynner; and the younger "rebels" – Montgomery Clift, Marlon Brando, Anthony Perkins, Elvis Presley – typically inhabiting a horizon wider than Hollywood's, though working within it.

Though detailed, well-informed and lively, most of these portraits lack the intimacy of close-ups, and rely on the writer's skill in achieving psychological and even existential penetration through publicly available information on her elusive subjects. The brief scene with the accessible, yet most elusive of all, Yul Brynner is one exception (pp. 187–91). A consummate confidence man, he has Oriana fooled with an emotional confession followed by a dramatic exit, until Richard Brooks, directing Brynner in *The Brothers Karamazov*, reveals that he has just gone off to the toilet – something that Jean Cocteau had advised him a star must never let the public imagine him doing. The judgmental clockwork of *I sette peccati* seems to miss a beat in the face of this authentic faker.

Ironically, Oriana's or Fallaci's overt judgement seems to prefer the authentic man of the Bible, Cecil B. De Mille, known as "the King of Hollywood". In the first of her two concluding chapters, Fallaci relates her interview with him (the only one other than the brief encounter with Brynner). She is as interested and as interesting in relating the circumstances of the interview as the interview itself, making once again for a more novelistic approach to her subject. She is, after all, approaching the very heart of the system, the holy of holies. Yet she has the effrontery to seek an audience with the great man at the height of the success of *The Ten Commandments* without having seen the film. But, despite her suspicion of his power and of the industry over which he rules, and despite her hostility to revealed religion, Oriana appears disarmed by the man's charm and sincere fervour for the Holy Book and for his vocation as a film-maker (pp. 215–28).

The final chapter might suggest that De Mille represents the naïve and enterprising faith of the passing generation, now being overtaken by actors turned producers, like "the detested superman", Burt Lancaster, who can command huge percentages of the profits for their performances and invest the proceeds in their own film ventures. Not all stars remain passive products of the system. Hollywood never dies, Fallaci concludes: the achievers, the tycoons, keep restoring its myths and its vices. She had ended the main section of the book (Chapter 8) with Elvis Presley portrayed as a sinister figure, "because he is genuine", a totally self-assured and conscienceless hooligan, indistinguishable from a gangster. "He is terrifying", writes Fallaci, slipping in a magisterial "us" ("ci fa paura"), "because of the power which he enjoys, not just materially but, above all, by his appeal." He evokes, to her, the criminal side of US society, "[which is] so modern and so ferocious that it sweeps aside every human constraint and bound, which plans the production of artificial life, while it keeps death in the icebox" (pp. 210–11). Death and waxworks, amid Hollywood's eternal life, return at the very end of the book. Hollywood, whose celebrities seem to exist in a timeless dimension like wax statues, also churns out its corpses, its failures: "In Hollywood, where everything recalls a cemetery and reeks of faded flowers, no one ever dies" ("non si muore mai": p. 243).

That is the end, and yet not the end, for Fallaci adds a curious appendix which brings her to the brink of postmodernist, almost Warhol-like, collage, but remains straightforwardly illustrative. It contains reproductions of pictorial and composite advertisements from the Los Angeles gossip and scandal magazines. These, she says, are clues to the massive economic infrastructure of which the film industry is only the crowning mystique: foundation garments and prayer are equally promoted as means to personal charisma and the power and success which it brings. The dream factory appears as the ultimate advertising fantasy. Though apparently the least ambitious of Fallaci's works, *I sette peccati di Hollywood* is the only one in which she displays people's human destinies being played out as part of a system which they sustain but which transcends them.

3

The Female Hemisphere: "Il sesso inutile: viaggio intorno alla donna" (1961)

*J*ournalistic imperatives weigh more heavily on Fallaci's "circumnavigation of woman" than on her venture into Hollywood. If in *I sette peccati* the author–narrator Fallaci chose to override the notion that "Hollywood doesn't exist", in *Il sesso inutile*[1] the narrator–character Oriana herself (now defined in blasé tone as "a journalist accustomed to visiting distant lands", using the masculine form "un giornalista" in Italian) starts by denying that women constitute a separate hemisphere ("as if they live on another planet"), that women exist as women rather than simply as human beings. For this reason, Oriana is at first disinclined to take up her editor's invitation to report on women, mostly in Asia. Her resistance has a seemingly excessive emotional charge:

> Whenever I possibly can, I always avoid writing about women or about problems concerning women. I don't know why, but the notion makes me feel ill-at-ease, I find it ridiculous. Women are not a special kind of fauna ... So whenever I'm asked "Do you write articles for women?" or "Do you write about women?" I get terribly angry.
>
> (pp. 7–8, both versions)

Only when a friend of hers, a young, successful and independent career woman, talking to her *tête-à-tête*, breaks down in tears, confesses her misery precisely because she is successful, and

---

1. Quotations in English are from the translation by Pamela Swinglehurst (1964b). Page references to the original Italian are followed by those to this edition.

complains "Ours is a useless sex, anyway", does it occur to Oriana "that, whereas men's basic problems spring from economic, racial or social issues, women's basic problems spring also – and mainly – from the very fact of being women", and particularly from the social "taboos" superimposed upon women's biological difference from men, and that even words, such as "virgin", are applied differentially and, in some societies, with dire consequences for women. This perception decides Oriana to embark on her new quest for the sources of women's happiness or misery (pp. 8–10; 8–9).

So Oriana travels round the world's women in thirty days. She has a few days each for Pakistan, India, Malaysia, Hong Kong, Japan, Hawaii and New York: an apparent journalistic absurdity of instant illumination and glossy jet-hopping travelogue. Her itinerary-driven text necessarily takes the shape of a series of brilliant fragments, arbitrarily juxtaposed: in literary terms, the traditionalist, non-ironical counterpart to the collage presentation in alphabetical order of each State constituting the United States in Michel Butor's *Mobile* (1962). In the book's final pages, Oriana and her photographer, Duilio, have reached New York on their way back to Italy. Fallaci devotes five pages to the proposition that women rule America, being a majority of voters, share-holders, teachers and media people, and of insurance and pension beneficiaries; being exempt from war service; outliving their menfolk, and domineering over and exploiting them mercilessly. "The American woman is a man," pronounces the author. "She is a man with many advantages" (pp. 247; 178). (She fails to mention the virtual absence of women in institutional decision-making and social command structures.) Duilio, whose amorous inclinations towards women round the world have been frustrated so far, looks forward to seeing his regular New York girlfriend, Laureen, but recoils when he discovers that she is planning to organize not only his stay in New York, but also the rest of his life. Oriana finds herself having to comfort a disconsolate Laureen "so very like my Italian friend who cries and blows her nose". By this quasi-novelistic sequence, the author closes the circle of her quest: all over the world, women are moving from repression to emancipation, yet all over the world women are marching "around an abysmal [*cupa*], utterly stupid unhappiness" – the book's final words (pp. 245–55; 177–83).

That glib conceptual closure hardly fits this remarkably open-ended text. Episodes cover radically non-Western situations, like Islamic Pakistan, where the chador and rules of purdah prevail, and the matriarchs of the Malaysian jungle, who regard men as being of little importance or, worse, an encumbrance; as well as rapidly Westernizing or modernizing societies, like India, the various Chinas, and Japan; and submerged societies like Hawaii, whose past lingers on in the form of chemically preserved relics and a few ageing survivors beneath the obliterating gloss displayed to tourists.

The book's discursive opening and finale move from a denial to an affirmation of a female difference in essentialist terms, without confronting real power relations between the sexes. Fallaci includes an episode where she is very nearly detained, and her photographic equipment confiscated, by the Indonesian authorities, who see her as a threat to the visit by the Soviet leader, Khrushchev. She is rescued by an American – male, of course. Fallaci's pinprick contribution to the Cold War perhaps inadvertently instances male supremacy.

Yet the book's impoverished conceptual framework does not account for the key "character" in the narrative, Oriana herself, who appears as self-sufficient and immune to the anguish which she diagnoses in women generally (apart from that emotional charge with which she reacted to the notion of women's difference). Nor does it account for the presiding (female) deity of the work, the medical doctor and distinguished testimonial writer Han Suyin, who acutely chronicled the relationship between China and the West in the 1940s and 1950s. That conceptual framework does even less justice to the great variety of women's differential histories, which make up the body of the book, and which often throw gendered power-relations into strong relief. (The episode of the Malaysian matriarchs – "the happiest women in the world" – draws an explicit contrast between their social code and that obtaining in Europe (pp. 104–18; 76–85)). The fragmentation of the text speaks against the factitious and vacuous unity offered by the enclosing discourse of women as the weaker sex.

The writer's vividly communicative style may be gauged in part by the unavoidably brief snatches that appear in this chapter. Lacking the narratorial agility (or suasiveness or authority) evidenced in the book on Hollywood, the writing of *Il sesso inutile* does not draw attention to itself or prompt the suspicion that "reality" is in the process of being linguistically and textually constituted. It approaches a maximum of clarity and directness combined with unaffected, informal elegance. It displays no self-conscious literariness, not even that of the coming New Journalism, but pursues the ideal of transparency. The kaleidoscopic interplay of self-presentation, argumentation, narrative, description, dialogue and dramatic confrontation is extended on several occasions by a newly developing and increasingly confident interviewing technique. Oriana develops her potential as catalyst, at times eliciting from her various interlocutors a considerable degree of self-characterization, and revealing striking historical self-awareness on the part of women ranging from royal rank to the humblest. In one case, a long monologue on footbinding is recorded. Textual space is used to give autonomy to other voices in a procedure which is natural to journalistic reportage but is teasingly problematic for literary conceptions of authorship in which all voices are ultimately emanations of the authorial voice. Here the "author" is more visibly and therefore less absolutely the editor of others' voices than is the "author" of narrative fiction. The interlocutor's speaking voice in *Il sesso inutile*, more than in *I sette peccati*, appears increasingly (even across other languages, through English, and into Italian) as the guarantee of another's individuality, of the existential self.

Finally, a male "character", Duilio, provides another novelistic element running longitudinally through Fallaci's travelogue, as his eagerness for congenial female company is repeatedly frustrated and culminates suspensefully in the anti-climax of his reunion with Laureen. Lightly and inconspicuously sketched, Duilio functions as a male foil to Oriana's indulgently female humour, and illustrates a slyly understated point – that female anomie results also in male anomie; or that anomie is for both males and females the outcome of the sexual divide.

Fallaci appears most palpably awry in pronouncing upon the society, of those she visited, which she knew best – the United States. Her presentation of less familiar societies is necessarily limited. Her strictures on the disabilities of women under Islam implicitly dismiss the notion that different civilizations may have equally tenable, though apparently opposed, codes, or that Western women may simply labour under a different set of disabilities. But, overall, *Il sesso inutile* effectively documents aspects of the state of women across the world and the perceptions of an emancipated Italian woman.

This was the period of the big sleep of bourgeois feminism, in between the historic appearance in 1949 of Simone de Beauvoir's exposition of the subordination and alienation of women's subjectivity in *The Second Sex* (the very issue which gives *Il sesso inutile* an obscure visceral impetus), and the mass feminism that was born out of the ferment of 1968. *Il sesso inutile* marks the beginning of Fallaci's feminist re-education, which was to reach its maximal expression with *Lettera a un bambino mai nato*. Yet at no time does Fallaci's underlying value-system change. *Il sesso inutile* corroborates and extends the values evident in *I sette peccati*. Autonomy, self-determination, and authenticity, self-awareness and moral self-sufficiency – whether of individuals or of whole cultures – constitute the hallmark of Fallaci's identification of modernity with freedom. Yet female emancipation, which would appear to coincide perfectly with these values, is found wanting, in its effects at least. One of the author's more explicit formulations of the reason for the misery of modernity and female emancipation is that which closes Chapter 2, the chapter on India, and comes as a Leopardian comment on a conversation between female Indian intellectuals such as could have taken place between intellectuals anywhere in the Western world: ". . . all the world is spoiled nowadays. With our progress we have destroyed our only weapon against tedium: that rare weakness we call imagination."

This apparent contradiction on Fallaci's part obscurely voices the basic dual dilemma of feminism: that female emancipation cannot properly be so called if, on the one hand, it entails women moulding themselves into the patterns laid down by patriarchal society, and, on the other, it forces on women the choice (as stressed by de Beauvoir (1972: 705)) between either participation in the public polity and the formal economy or child-bearing and family life. This dual dilemma is explored in Fallaci's two strikingly unorthodox but uncontestably feminist novels, *Penelope alla guerra* and *Lettera a un bambino mai nato*. By contrast, *Il sesso inutile*, despite some interesting articulations, remains distinctly underwrought.

Part III
Woman's Body

4

The Self-Repleting Text: "Penelope alla guerra" (1962)

or 1962, when it was first published, or 1959, when it was first drafted (cf. O. Fallaci 1962: prescript),[1] *Penelope alla guerra (Penelope at the War)* is a precocious novel at least in terms of its subject-matter. The title indicates a reversal of gender roles. The virgin Giovanna (not a matronly Penelope) goes adventuring across the ocean to New York. This at a time when the female subject within the Italian novel was virtually locked into familial or male-dependent gender roles, whether in the work of female novelists (Natalia Ginzburg, Alba De Céspedes, Elsa Morante) or of male novelists (Cesare Pavese, Alberto Moravia, Armando Meoni's *La ragazza di fabbrica*). The exceptions emphasize Fallaci's forward leap towards female autonomy: Clelia in Pavese's *Tra donne sole*, of 1949; Mirella in De Céspedes's *Quaderno proibito*; Anna Banti's transhistorical Artemisia Gentileschi. Even *L'età del malessere*, of 1963, by Fallaci's younger contemporary Dacia Maraini, still portrays the young female protagonist as passive victim – typical of Italy's social reality, but less in touch with historical changes already afoot. Fallaci's novel also virtually inaugurates the expatriate theme in Italian fiction, the encounter between Italy and elsewhere. Anguilla's emigration to the United States in Pavese's *La luna e i falò* (1950) and the episodes set in Switzerland and Yugoslavia in Pasolini's *Il sogno di una cosa* (1962) are among the few tentative precedents.

Penelope also stands out when compared to contemporary writing in other Western countries (though engulfed by the

1. Page references in this section are to the Italian original, followed by the English translation by Pamela Swinglehurst (London, Michael Joseph, 1964).

newly emerging postmodernist *nouveau roman* of Marguerite Duras and Nathalie Sarraute, Alain Robbe-Grillet, Michel Butor and others, which was followed by parallel developments in Italy). Françoise Sagan, the girl prodigy whose early novels were all the rage internationally in the latter 1950s, and who at eighteen had won the 1954 Prix des Critiques with *Bonjour, tristesse!*, presents quite a different face from Fallaci. The naughtinesses of the affluent French bourgeoisie, unconcerned by France's disastrous wars with Indochina and Algeria, are spiced by the sharp existential awareness of Sagan's heroines. But, though women are generally the losers in the game of love, there is no gender war, personal or political.

The closest mirroring of *Penelope alla guerra* comes in a novel by an established American male. This is Irwin Shaw's *Two Weeks in Another Town*, which appeared in 1960. Shaw had written the brilliantly modernist anti-war one-acter *Bury the Dead* in 1936. An acclaimed master of the short story in the 1930s, he had become a prolific novelist, achieving greatest celebrity with his Second World War epic *The Young Lions* in 1948. This was the subject of an equally successful Hollywood production starring Dean Martin, Montgomery Clift and Marlon Brando. Shaw is mentioned in *Penelope* when Francesco, Giovanna's soul-mate and prospective husband, tries to dissuade her from going to New York to script a film. Rooted in Italy's past, he exclaims: "half an hour with a peasant from Agrigento enriches me more than an afternoon with Irving [*sic*] Shaw or Joe Di Maggio" (pp. 15; 11).

While *Penelope alla guerra* relates the twenty-six-year-old Giovanna's two-month mission in New York, *Two Weeks in Another Town* is the account of a visit to Rome, also on film business, by a thrice-married middle-aged American ex-actor, John Andrus, now working at NATO headquarters in Paris. Apart from an Italian starlet surrounded by gigolos and an aura of venal decadence (a male chauvinist image of women's liberation), the female characters in Shaw's novel are contained within the matrimonial paradigm, and Andrus's resolution of his mid-age crisis involves reacceptance of a normality itself centred on NATO and marriage. He delegates to the youthful fire of another American, Bresach (the reincarnation of his own long-expired youthful idealism and the counterpart to his estranged son's fierce radicalism), his bid to infuse authenticity into a movie spawned by Hollywood out of Cinecittà. Contrary to Fallaci's novel, Shaw's accommodates generational change to the prevailing hegemonic structures – social, political, and even military – of the Western world in the Cold War era.

Fallaci's Giovanna is also assigned to an Italo-American co-production, and *Penelope alla guerra* is the matrix for the screenplay she will write out of her experience in New York. Fallaci's novel is thus retrospectively (and sometimes directly) projected through the filmic eye, yet is too self-effacing, too modestly self-reflexive, to be called postmodernist, quite unlike the avant-garde and experimental novels of the time. Sagan and Shaw are skilled and strict practitioners of the conventions of what Belsey (1980: 7) has called "expressive realism" (the projection through the "transparency" of language and of an individual viewpoint of a reality taken as given). As will be illustrated more concretely below, Fallaci's text displays similar traditionalist skills, tending, like Shaw rather than Sagan, towards an over-explicit articulation of the novelistic fabric, of its thematic, psychological and existential concerns, and of its plot-contrivances. Fallaci, however, switches between various modes of subjectivity and occasionally focuses on other characters besides Giovanna – Richard, his mother Florence, and Bill. Subjectivity is conveyed with the urgency of the speaking voice: in the abundant use of dialogue, often strongly patterned; in an indirect free style approximating to stream of consciousness technique; in direct address by the protagonist to herself; and even in the narrative or descriptive moments, which are never detached or impersonal. The stylized voice-print is pitched to magnify the vibrations of the psyche in the existential instant. Fallaci, building on the novelistic skills deployed in her books of reportage, displays in *Penelope* a narrative technique and style quite unlike those of the *nouveau roman*, tending more towards the popular novel.

Penelope also transgresses against consistent realism, hovering on the brink of the Gothic novel, or "the fantastic". But the transgression appears "naïve" rather than systematically sub-versive, showing some affinity with Alberto Moravia's earlier *Il conformista*, where the realist mode is likewise disturbed by antirealist elements – implausible coincidences, startling revel-ations, dreamlike scenarios, metaphoric landscapes, the textual patterning of recurrent motifs and geometrical plotting of relationships, and the enigmatically apprehended phenomenology of androgyny and homoeroticism – which can be collectively subsumed as "the uncanny", the *Unheimliche* (see Todorov 1970; Apter 1982; Jentsch 1906 in Ceserani *et al.* 1983). In both texts "conformity" is the screen against which the uncanny appears in obscure opposition. That obscurity denotes an unresolved problem in the fictional mode and psychic address of the two writers.

The fantastic in *Penelope* appears from the opening scene, a monologue by Giovanna's boss, to which Giovanna replies absently, her mind on childhood memories of a wounded US serviceman, Richard, hiding in her parents' house in Nazi-occupied Florence and occupying her bed, and on the sinister phantoms floating out of the grandfather clock and the photographs of deceased relatives on the mantelpiece. She will later recognize a bewhiskered one of those phantoms in a key character of the novel, Bill. Moreover, Bill will perceive himself as such in his mirror (pp. 293; 212).

Uncanny coincidences rule the plot. Francesco, seeing Giovanna off in Rome, warns her against the dead, who are more alive than the living, and can destroy them (pp. 17; 13). The undead person turns out to be Richard, who represents her childhood romance and her apocalyptic vision of the United States: "Together with Richard she would climb the skyscrapers whence angel trumpets would herald the Last Judgement on the damned gathered in the Vale of Jehoshaphat. Then the skyscrapers would crumble like sandcastles and the next chime of the clock would surprise her in this state of abject terror" (pp. 9; 7). Richard had been reported killed while trying to get through the German lines – yet Giovanna catches sight of his red head from a distance at her first New York cocktail party, only to lose him ("'It was a ghost'" (pp. 50–2; 37–8)). She tries in vain to trace him through the telephone directory or to recognize him in the men she sees, never renouncing her senseless quest, until, at the house of her closest New York friend, Martine, she meets, accompanying Martine's current lover, a playwright called Bill, his friend Dick, who is Richard (pp. 59; 44). A less prominent coincidence occurs when, amid a million-strong crowd thronging to see the Queen of England (wearing an orange-coloured hat) on her visit to New York, Giovanna gets pushed against Bill and Richard's mother, pointedly named Florence (whose black hair associates her with Giovanna's own mother).

The uncanny or Gothic element also appears in other guises. One is the pacing to and fro of footsteps on the floor above Richard's room during Richard and Giovanna's first night (Chapters 4 and 5) and repeatedly thereafter, eventually revealed to be those of the tyrannical Florence. Another is the sensation experienced by Giovanna as she walks beneath Niagara Falls and Richard attempts suicide: she senses the massive wall of water of the Falls – deafening, impenetrable, irresistible – as the manifestation of an overpowering force dividing her from Richard. The mystery of this force that drives Richard to attempt suicide or escape constitutes the novel's controlling narrative rhetoric, its suasion of the reader towards the signifying system of the novel both as textual artefact and as constructed "truth" about the world, at once "narratorial" seduction of form and "narrational" seduction of content. Eventually, in a blinding revelation, Giovanna recognizes this overpowering force in Bill.

The chain of relationships, and their geometrical configuration, shows the same oneiric excess, forcing surface realism in a dramatization of the unconscious, "the unseen", "the unnameable", suggestive of the literature of the uncanny (cf. Jackson 1981: 38–9). Giovanna's ally, Martine, is a wealthy divorcee, a former girlfriend of Francesco's, and now Bill's. Richard, whom Giovanna ardently woos but cannot quite win, turns out, after strongly foreshadowed yet anguishingly suspenseful vicissitudes, to be himself Bill's dependent lover, and equally in thrall to his mother Florence, who makes common cause with Bill to keep her son away from Giovanna. The all-conquering Bill then turns his irresistible attentions to Giovanna herself, who can only escape by returning back to Francesco in Italy and the prospect of a conventional relationship. Francesco, however, rejects her as he had rejected Martine, and Giovanna has independence forced upon her.

This obsessive plot signifies the paradox of freedom through the text's unfolding: freedom amounts to the female subject's exclusion from relationship. Exclusion is her only alternative to subjection, or to her fruitless attempt to deliver the male partner from prior subjections, embodied in Florence and Bill. The characters in this post-Freudian "family romance" are abstracted from the quotidian web of social relationships, from any recognizably real social fabric, but projected against the New York media scene as against a cinema screen. Most of the characters are involved in media, with an illusory power over people's perceptions of the world: Richard is a magazine photographer; Bill, a playwright, discusses writing with Giovanna; both men hold forth in lofty and sprightly style about the masses leading their banal, unreflecting, predictable lives.

Giovanna's entry into womanhood is doubly marked in the novel. One marker is her virginity. Much is made of this by Francesco, Martine, Bill, and especially by a needlessly conscience-stricken Richard. The prior marker is menstruation (possibly, for 1962, a novelistic first). The twelve-year-old Giovanna has her first menstruation during her grandfather's funeral, with only her father to attend to her. He exclaims that, unlike any other girl, she remains dry-eyed, so that "she must have turned into a little man [*ometto*] and not a woman at all" (pp. 24; 18). Richard calls her a "little man", and Giovanna is consistently presented in androgynous terms. This is marked early on: Giovanna has shortened her career name to Giò (Gio in the English translation), sounding like "Joe", both American and male (pp. 27; 19). Looking at herself in the mirror, she is disappointed not to see a robust figure but a boyish one ("efebico" (pp. 10; 7)), and when, for the first time, she wears trousers (still a historic act for an Italian girl in the late 1950s), Martine remarks "Sembri un efebo" ("You look like a boy" (pp. 200; 146)). The word "efebo" indicates a youth just entering into manhood. This boyish appearance appeals homoerotically to Richard and to Bill, who nickname her "Funny Boy", and Gio's gender ambiguity is central to the gender politics of the novel.

In *Penelope*'s sex war, patriarchy appears as being doubly subverted in the double subjection of Richard: to matriarchy through Florence; and to a homosexual order through Bill. It is hinted that Richard's father has been driven to death by Florence (pp. 86; 63), who is divorced and lives comfortably on her inheritance from her first husband and alimony from her second, following the paradigm of female dominance proposed in *Il sesso inutile* (pp. 246–7; 177–80). Bill, by virtue of his age, his protective role towards Richard, and his complicity with Florence, appears as a homosexually incestuous pseudo-father to Richard, intent on sharing Richard's female partner, Gio. Richard sees New York (uncanny-sublime emanation of the patriarchal order) as a city built on corpses: its dark underside is the Mortuary, filled with the victims of capitalist or gangster greed (*Penelope* pp. 143; 105).

Gio presents a third threat to the gender hierarchy of the phallocratic order, but this is read within the text (pp. 261–71; 191–7) either as the threat of female ascendancy, or, alternatively, as a threat to the system of gendered differences as such, by the fact that, first, she partly elides those differences in her own person, and, second, that she elides power relations in favour of relations of equality.

In this latter view, Gio's stance is antithetical to that of Florence or Bill: neither of the latter subverts power relationships between individuals: they divert them into other configurations of power (female over male, male over male). However, Gio rejects the option of sharing Richard with Florence and Bill (neither of whom Richard can give up), seeking mutual sole possession. She fears domination both by Bill and by Florence, and rejects the possibility of a polymorphous relationship with both Bill and Richard simultaneously. She competes for Richard with Florence and Bill, and, when she does make love to Richard, finds herself in the physically and symbolically superior position. Full and exclusive mutuality – that is, the professed social norm, the romantic heterosexual paradigm – remains her goal, though she also seeks equality in the relationship. Failing with Richard, she falls back on Francesco, but he applies the male double standard and rejects her for her involvement with Richard, though this corresponds symmetrically to his own previous involvement with Martine.

In the final confrontation between Gio and Bill in Chapter 14, Gio is equated with Bill and Florence: all three accept each other as united in their love for Richard. But there are still two complications: Gio discovers that she is now under Bill's spell, and withdraws; while Richard discovers that he is drained by the love of others, and would rather be free. Gio's New York producer, Gomez, assures her that three to a bed is no big deal, but fails to keep her in New York. Gio's sexual liberation through the reluctant discovery of homoerotic love and acceptance (verbally, at least) of its legitimacy (pp. 267; 195) does not extend to bisexuality and sexual and emotional sharing. Yet, though individual possession remains her norm, she does not wish to be possessed, to fall into the male power of the quasi father-figure, Bill, embodiment of the law beyond the law. This leaves Giovanna–Penelope dangling in a void (of which the uncanny is the novel's aesthetic correlative). Committed to the social norm of exclusive heterosexual mutuality, yet drawn to men who are drawn by what is other than female in her, she finds herself excluded from all relationship.

The absence of the mother is decisive in *Penelope*, though made visible at only one point: the first onset of Gio's menstruation. That this takes place at her grandfather's funeral in her father's presence indicates the continuity of the paternal role. The mother's unexplained absence and the father's reluctant takeover of the maternal role in this rite of passage are given salience: "Terrified she had looked for her mother, but her mother wasn't there"; "'I hope your mother's at home.' Mother wasn't home"; "if he [the father]'d ever thought it would be up to him to deal with such matters he'd have run straight to the station and fled" (pp. 23–4; 17–18).

Thus, while father figures in the novel (Gio's boss in Rome, perhaps the traditionally-minded Francesco, Gomez, Igor – the Russian psychiatrist in up-State New York – and, of course, Bill) appear positive, mothers figure negatively: the domineering unhusbanded Florence, and Martine, who has lost her male partner and her walnut-sized, minutely described, unborn child (pp. 233–5; 169–71). Gio's mother is expunged from the novel, denied the status of a "character", and reduced to a vivid, but merely memorial, trace in Gio's psyche in the opening pages, where Gio reflects upon her own reflection in the mirror as not being masculine enough:

> The only thing she liked about the girl in the mirror was the hair, because it was blonde and so enabled her to forget that she belonged to a country where women had dark hair,[2] like her mother, and counted for nothing, like her mother, and wept, like her mother. Once, when she was a child, she had seen her mother weeping. She was ironing shirts and weeping, and her tears were rolling down on to the iron and sizzling against the hot metal; they left slightly opaque little marks on the iron, as if they had been drops of water instead of tears. But then even the little marks faded away, as if their grief had never existed, and from that moment on she had sworn never to iron shirts and never to weep.
>
> (pp. 10–11; 7–8)

---

2. The *capelli neri* of the Italian at this point link Gio's mother in Florence to Richard's mother named Florence, who also has black hair.

(The weeping motif runs through the novel and becomes prominent towards the end. The very last line reads: "There now: here was a tear. And it had the taste of salt.") Italy is established as the country of mothers' subservience and misery, yet the black hair of Gio's mother in Florence returns in Richard's mother, Florence, in New York.

There are other fleeting recollections of Gio's mother, most saliently during Gio's first day with Richard in New York: "that night they were children again", and, as children, they retrospectively throw off maternal authority which equates Gio's mother with Richard's, eagerly devouring nut brittle (*croccanti*), which both mothers had denied their children (pp. 69; 51). Richard never succeeds, however, in freeing himself from his mother's love and power, as Gio fails to establish her own autonomy against American matriarchy. The mother is converted from victim into tyrant.

Two other emblematic mother-figures acquire prominence in the book. One is the gigantic figure of "the great iron lady that they call the Statue of Liberty", surrounded by the "cries of grief" ("urlare un lamento") of the seagulls, which Richard displays to Gio in overwhelming close-up by telescope (pp. 67; 49). This iron lady reappears when Richard has disappeared for a second time after Gio's confrontation with Florence, and Gio, going to have a closer look at her on the "tiny island where the steel giantess, towered, vulgar, on her stone pedestal", "mounted the spiral staircase inside the huge empty body, up into the huge empty head, looking out from the empty halo and seeing nothing but emptiness: the emptiness of the sky, the emptiness of the sea, the emptiness of her own disappointment" (pp. 253–4; 184). The Goddess, in her dual aspect of Freedom and Motherhood, remains standing as the gigantic emblem of the United States ("America") and of emptiness.

The other emblem of matriarchy in Fallaci's novel is the Queen of England in her orange-coloured hat on her visit to New York "with her husband", hemmed in by the throng of New Yorkers lining her route, a "vice of jackets and elbows" which grips Gio as she attempts to make her way to her appointment to meet Richard and his mother, and which turns into a "solid wall". The Queen, as female power, is closely juxtaposed to Gio's encounter with Florence. Gio accidentally kicks a woman in the crowd who is talking to Bill: "swiftly a high heel bit down on the guilty foot, and then, quick as a whiplash, the head of black curls turned, two brown eyes bored into her face and a metallic voice froze her: 'How dare you? How dare you?'" At her rendezvous with Richard and his mother a few minutes later, Gio discovers that the latter is the woman who has just used her stiletto heel on her foot (pp. 239–42; 174–6). (This rejection of the mother partly explains the uncanny in the novel and the author's reluctance to publish the book, mentioned in her prescript.)

Both icons – the Statue of Liberty and the Queen of England – are associated in Fallaci's text with the conformist masses, the great American public from which Richard and Bill and Gio so sharply dissociate themselves – the crowds who throng to see the Queen, the crowds who visit the Statue of Liberty or Niagara Falls. This is the mass of Americans whom Richard, in a long tirade to Gio in Chapter 10 (pp. 186–93; 136–41), preannounced by Bill, identifies with the "hurricane", whose voice is the radio, which is the voice of God "equals America equals Business equals America equals God". Echoing Giovanna's original vision of Richard passing judgement, Richard equates the millions of patient American commuters with "the damned in the Valley of Jehoshaphat", and ends lamenting the tragic isolation of those few souls who do not serve this God and who are swept aside by the hurricane.

The novel thus seems predicated on the rejection of the mother, and this rejection in turn excludes the daughter from the gendered order of conventional society. The female subject, Gio, as she enters womanhood and libidinal relationship, is helplessly torn between acceptance and rejection of that social order. But she encounters an alternative that she can barely conceptualize as the "hermaphroditism" of snails referred to by Bill (pp. 109–10; 79–80). We may see this hermaphroditism as corresponding to the "polymorphous perversity" which Freud attributed to the infant and which was later championed by the women's liberationist Shulamith Firestone (1970), or the "androgyny", transcending male–female gender distinctions, studied by Heilbrun (1982).

Gio's revulsion against hermaphroditism or polymorphism confirms her refusal to recognize herself as androgyne (or *efebo*) in the mirror and her preference for the powerful physique which the reader readily recognizes in Bill. She recognizes the power of the father, and wishes to share it, is unable to, and flees the sex war to give battle on the career front: the historic dilemma of the bourgeois feminist project of entering a world structured and defined in male terms. Within such structures, the female can never be accepted as equivalent to male. Yet Gio does not question the values subtending those structures. Rather, she sees them on the one hand as "homosocial" (to use a term coined by Kosofsky Sedgwick (1985) which I return to shortly) and therefore subordinating the female, and on the other hand as matriarchal, in effect blaming what is irreducibly female – the potential mother – in herself, as represented in her physique. Gio embodies the limits and the failure of immasculation, the elimination of the mother in herself. In this, Gio appears remote from the left-wing Italian feminism of the Unione Donne Italiane after the Second World War, which consistently campaigned for the economic, social and political empowerment of women not only in the field of employment, but also in their domestic roles as housewives and mothers.[3]

The converse is Richard, presented as less than fully male, with a falsetto voice, subject to maternal power and a quasi-paternal male partner, prone to tears, ready to embrace and kiss the twelve-year-old Gio and beside himself with guilt when he breaks the hymen of the twenty-six-year-old Gio, unable to determine his personal and sexual relationships and ineffectually wishing to take his own life. There is no entry in the New York telephone directory under his (and his father's) surname, Baline. His mother uses her (divorced) second husband's surname.

By contrast, Bill is the supermale, seemingly omnipotent. He displays both physical and moral strength and courage: in Chapter 9, he pilots Gio with Richard to a Harlem religious service and, supported by a pugnacious Gio, faces violent blacks, while Richard cowers inside the car; then, after the fight, comments that, whether black or white, "Poor people aren't bad but they have the bad taste to be quarrelsome with the rich" (pp. 164; 120); in Chapter 12, Bill's voice, "full of dignity", suddenly rings out above the panic of other American voices over the Soviet Sputnik satellite that has just appeared passing in orbit over New York and bringing the threat of nuclear annihilation: "We've nothing to fear except fear. And anybody who's afraid is a coward!" (pp. 225; 164).

3. I am indebted to Mirna Cicioni for this point.

This is the heroic voice of America in the novel (echoing Franklin D. Roosevelt's inaugural speech), the voice that conquers Gio, and before which she has no other choice than to surrender or to flee. It is the authoritative voice within the novel, an imperious discourse, expressed in Bill's conversations with Gio and in his final letter to her, apparently incontrovertible and irresistible as Niagara Falls, combining the authority and power of the successful writer (as a playwright, Bill writes roles for others), with the resultant power and authority of wealth and influence. Bill also delivers the discourse on hermaphroditism, and in his undifferentiated desire for Richard and for Gio (having discarded Martine), he also embodies sexual polymorphism as the central presence of the novel. Yet any such transcending or transgressing of gender boundaries is strongly rejected by Gio and by the postulated Author's novelistic rhetoric. Bill's discourse is not that of the novel as a whole, whose strenuous job it is rather to transfuse it with ambiguities. Rather along the lines argued by Ross Chambers (1991) for "reading (the) oppositional (in) narrative", these ambiguities open up interstices within the text which allow for considerable play.

What is "oppositional" in the narrative of *Penelope* is not simply that Gio escapes into the isolation that Richard had assured her was not tolerated in the United States. Much less is it that she opts for Hollywood as a scriptwriter in pursuit of the financial success that Richard and Gomez have assured her are the real God in America (and the God that Bill so patently embodies), or that she does so exclaiming, as she sheds her first salt tear, "Oh, God! God! God: why don't you exist?" In doing these things, Gio is admitting her unfreedom, accepting the terms imposed on her, while competing for the power to which she succumbs. It is the figure of Bill himself that opens up a subversive space by the ambiguity already hinted at that, as male rival, he is also the father.

Fallaci's narrative rhetoric achieves a double effect, setting up Bill as a pole of simultaneous attraction and repulsion, an embodiment of qualities that are at once most desirable and most unacceptable. The revelation of Bill's relationship with Richard is managed with the suspense and surprise of a mystery thriller, and with a build-up of tension until near the end of the novel. Agnello-Modica (1992: 77) remarks that this is a thriller without a corpse, but there is a corpse – Giovanna, whose life-project collapses. The homosexual bond between Bill and Richard is strongly foregrounded by the narrative through this delayed recognition on Gio's part. It comes, then, as an explanatory revelation, but, in fact, is nothing of the sort – or rather, it simultaneously explains everything and nothing, being a discursive displacement.

Whereas Gio's relationship with Richard is fully relayed and evidenced both through her own subjectivity and Richard's, the same is not true of Bill's relationship with Richard, which is only hinted at from time to time in limited focalizations of Bill and Richard themselves and of Martine, and eventually declared by Bill to Gio. This is the rhetoric of narrative preterition, a partial silence within the text. By contrast, Bill's attempted takeover of Gio is forcefully transmitted through Gio's subjectivity, and is what really precipitates the narrative denouement in that Gio is forced to escape precisely because she feels attracted to Bill and fears falling under his power.

The narrative preterition – the fact that the relationship between Bill and Richard is not rendered evidential in the way that Gio's relationships are – acts partly to reinforce a sense of taboo, of the uncanny and sinister, the unnameable and forbidden, or *Unheimliche*, and partly also to represent that relationship's otherness to Gio as unknown, as an area of male experience unavailable and alien to her. Homosexuality thus remains an empty space in the narrative discourse, a void highly charged with narrative tension. The solid space that surrounds this empty space, the evidential fabric of the relationship between Bill and Richard, is in fact paternal and homosocial, rather than homosexual. Bill is protective towards Richard, whom he regards as a child, to the extent that Richard's career as a photographer is claimed by Bill to be his own creation. Eve Kosofsky Sedgwick (1985), following up insights by Gayle Rubin and Luce Irigaray, has argued for the ambiguity or variability of homosexuality, which, she observes, is defined in some societies (say, Judaeo-Christian) as antagonistic to male hegemony, and in others (say, classical Greek) as supportive of it. What is common to all male hegemonic systems is "homosociality" – social bonding between males, with females acting as a medium of exchange between males.

Penelope at War presents the powerful figure of Bill in terms that slide between a homosocial and a homosexual relationship with the filial figure of Richard. While Florence, as the over-possessive mother and predatory wife, is spectacularly characterized through her recurrent and sinister footsteps overhead and her furious encounter with Gio in the pizza-dive, Bill emerges as a far more convincing embodiment of power, and he envisages co-opting Gio in a relationship with himself and Richard which smacks of ductile exchange transactions controlled by Bill himself ("I was mad too, to delude myself that throwing you into his arms would be of any use. I was mad too, to give you to him in the hope of doing him a favour" (pp. 266; 193)). The exchange transaction is masked by the discourse of love. Herself powerfully drawn to Bill, Gio's dignified reply to him is: "your love for him . . . matters a good deal less to me than you think. Every kind of love is permissible so long as it's real love. This goes for you, for me, and for Florence. It would go for Richard too if he was capable of loving anybody. But he's only capable of being loved. And since we love him, we simply have to accept him as he is; and go on loving him" (pp. 267–8; 195). Richard responds with a more serious suicide attempt, after driving aimlessly around New York, "weeping, thinking that he had never asked to be so fiercely loved by everyone". His thoughts are dramatized with the evidential intimacy, the quasi-vocal vibrancy, of indirect free style: "They loved him, yes; but they didn't understand that just as loving someone filled you, so being loved emptied you: because the one who loved you fed on you, taking what was best in you, and day by day consumed you, robbed you, sucking your secrets, your lymph, your life out of you, until you were just an empty shell" (pp. 281; 204).

"Love", then, is possession, vampirism, and power-struggle; possession as a sort of investment claimed by Gio and contested by Bill, who pits the claims of maternal gestation and his own long years of devoted protection against the "capital" of Gio's "miserly virginity" (pp. 262–3; 191). Bill defines their unrecipro-cated love for Richard as "the most ancient form of masochism, and the most stupid" (pp. 268; 195). It is from this "maso-chistic" power-struggle, love as possession, possession of Richard or pos-session by Bill, or both together, that Gio withdraws, just when Richard eagerly waits to apply the psychiatrist Igor's advice to save himself and achieve normality by committing himself to her.

In withdrawing from these asymmetrical engagements (Gio as

the androgynous female overmastering the androgynous male Richard but being overmastered by the bisexual supermale Bill), Fallaci's protagonist is registering the unreality – within the given social world – of the symmetrical androgyny of the "male/female double" and the "journey beyond gender", of which Joanne Blum concludes that "its 'natural' place (is) somehow more mythically than socially realizable". Male–female inter-subjectivity between Gio and Richard and Gio and Bill is centred by the psychic rhetoric of the "uncanny" and by the narra-tive rhetoric of implausibility, of extraordinary encounters, as the novel's most prominent concern, only to be revealed as yet another doomed site of power conflict. Blum's remarks are sug-gestive: "As these fiction writers strive to 'journey beyond gender,' they also attempt to transcend numerous other cultural divisions which separate being from being, being from nature, even being from deity. . . gender emerges finally as a metaphor for division, for separateness, and for polarity in human life generally" (Blum 1988: 77–8).

New York in 1957 comes across in *Penelope* as a geography and history of the psyche, and not as documentary topography or history. The novel recaptures the atmosphere of that autumn when Americans were stunned to see the Sputnik in their skies and charmed to see the Queen of England in their streets, and this topicality may well have led to the novel's being read for its surface discourse about America and modernity and mores. The interface between actuality and fiction, between journalism and literature, is always at play in Fallaci's book publications, the one aspect exploited for its real-world authentication and up-to-the-minute historicity, the other for its signifying potential. But the frequently banal or bogusly brilliant conversations and the touristy sights – from the Niagara Falls to the Statue of Liberty – and cocktail party milieu are, in Barthesian terms, "reality-effects", which have been semiotically translated into an imagery of gender politics. New York functions as "another place", simply and effectively counterbalancing Rome as "new" against "old", but also as an *outopia*, a nowhere place, beyond the scope of censorship, where homosexual love may dare to speak its name and patriarchy or matriarchy, the entire social and sexual order, may with impunity be rewritten.

American matriarchy in the New York of *Penelope* is susceptible to the same Jesuit and Papal influence then predominant in Rome under Christian Democrat hegemony. At the "Sputnik party", a nuclear shelter salesman assures a Catholic lady that his Jesuit confessor has advised him that it is fully permissible to shoot outsiders trying to enter one's shelter during a nuclear attack (pp. 225; 164). In the next chapter, Richard tells Gio in his mother's presence that she found Cardinal Fulton Sheen rather more appealing than her own husband (pp. 246; 179).

But this is the journalistic small change within the semiotic economy of *Penelope*, whose historic discourse is about the unfreedom of a woman who aspires to autonomy, to speak "man to man" (pp. 303; 220). Just as the Statue of Liberty turns out to be vulgar and hollow, so the foetus in the womb is not free to ordain the length of his legs or the colour of his eyes. And as for Gio: "It wasn't she who'd chosen this men's clothing . . . It wasn't she: yet she wore it and she couldn't have changed it because you can't go against the decisions of the Invisible Player without asking yourself whether or not you agree with him" (pp. 307; 223).

Her revenge is (mis)representation, playing the joyless – the alienated and alienating – game of inauthenticity: tearing up Bill's letter, she decides to make a book – or, easier and quicker, the screenplay for a film – out of her encounter with America, with Bill's part perfect for Burt Lancaster. Penelope has achieved transformation from "she" to "I" (before the final self-apostrophizing, self-splitting "tu" of the book's close):

> Of course she would have to modify the plot otherwise there'd be trouble with the censors: perhaps she ought to stick in a woman instead of Bill, or else turn him into a kind of father figure. And the ending? Well, maybe I'll change it: the public doesn't like sad stories and I can almost hear the commendatore saying "What's this story? It's not possible, there are some things that just don't happen. And then, little mouse, don't you see that this way nobody gets saved? Get them married!" All right, then, I'll get them married. Now let's see, if I get up at seven I can do a ten page synopsis by midday . . .
>
> (pp. 305; 222)

This way Penelope–Giovanna means to show that though she's a woman she's better than a man. To use Ross Chambers's phrase, in ironically representing the fictional Gio's ironical readiness to adjust the fictional mode to consumer demand and moral censorship, Fallaci as postulated Author has found "room for manoeuvre".

5

The Self-Depleting Text: "Lettera a un bambino mai nato" (1975)

t is a long leap in time across many intervening works and experiences from the publication of *Penelope alla guerra* in 1962 to that of *Lettera a un bambino mai nato* (*Letter to a child never born*) in 1975.[1] These works are viewed consecutively here, since they are the only two works in which Fallaci focalizes the female subject in her private and bodily dimensions as well as in her public role in the working world, and both works particularly problematize motherhood. *Lettera a un bambino mai nato* has been little more discussed, in analytical literary terms, than *Penelope alla guerra*, and never, as far as I have been able to discover, in terms of its overall narrative strategy. This is worth baring. The text consists of the monologue which a career woman, finding herself pregnant, addresses to the embryo, foetus or child within her womb, whom she decides to keep. She lectures the child on the world "he" is due to enter – a world dominated by male power and fraudulent or unrealized values such as love, family, progress and liberty. Swaying from defiance to despondency in the face of the power nexus, the expectant mother illustrates her theme and her moods by informing the child of the progress of her pregnancy and accompanying incidents and encounters, describing the development of the embryo and foetus from a photoreportage, recounting auto-biographical "fairy-tales" and dreams and experiences, running from her own conception through childhood and on to her recent past.

1. Page references are to the Italian (O. Fallaci 1975a) followed by the revised English translation, by John Shepley, London, Hamlyn Paperbacks, 1982. I quote from John Shepley's translation, except where indicated otherwise.

A couple of months into the pregnancy, the mother is confined for a considerable period to her bed. Allowing her up again, the doctor expresses his doubts about the supply of blood to the placenta (pp. 57; 54). Not long after, the mother sees a warning spot of blood, but, after a week in hospital under sedation, can stand confinement no longer, and walks out, to undertake a business trip. Her doctor tells her that this is tantamount to murdering her child (pp. 63; 60), but neither mother nor child appear to suffer any ill effects from the journey. The mother's elation at this is short-lived, however: the rough roads of the foreign country bring on further bleeding, and the foetus is pronounced to have died two or three weeks earlier (pp. 75; 71).

In hospital again, and herself near to dying, the mother dreams that she is on trial for murdering her child. The male doctor, the child's father, and the mother's employer, each combining the roles of legal counsel, witness, juror and judge, find her guilty. Alternating with them, the female doctor, the mother's female friend, and the mother's parents, find her innocent. The surprise last witness and judge is the child itself, who confirms this hung verdict.

The mother awakes to be told that she might herself die if the dead foetus is not removed from her womb. After this operation, once more she awakes, to find a glass beside her bed, and, inside it, "you" – the child:

> At last, I am looking at you. And I feel cheated, because you have absolutely nothing in common with the child in the photograph. You're not a child: you're an egg. A grey egg, floating in pink alcohol, in which no features can be distinguished. You ended long before anyone realized: you never got as far as having fingernails and skin and the infinite riches which I bestowed upon you. A figment of my imagination, you barely managed to realize the desire for two hands and two feet, something that resembles a body, the outline of a face with a tiny nose and two microscopic eyes. In effect, what I loved was a tiny fish-fry. And out of love for a tiny fish-fry I conjured up for myself a calvary which threatens to end me too. It's unacceptable.
>
> (p. 98; cf. pp. 92–3. My translation)

If the mother has had a trick played on her by the fact that the child died as an embryo, far earlier than had been suspected, the reader has likewise had a trick played on her in that the terms of the book's central debate, its "action", in effect, are suddenly transformed before her eyes. She has been led into a double narrative trap, a self-deleting text, addressed to a discursively constructed interlocutor – the child – who is then abruptly dissolved in retrospect.

We have here a placental text ingested via the umbilical cord, not by the fictive "tu" ("thou" or "you"), the child, but by the virtual, or potential, "tu" – you, the reader. The child tells his mother: "Along with the water in which I was immersed, I drank in your every thought. . . . my drafts of light and awareness were you". Subsequently, however, he goes on to say, his mother's doubts, the collapse of her courage, her delegation of the choice between life and death to the child in her womb, destroyed his will to live: the placental sustenance turned to poison, killing him: "To wash away your fear one day you bestowed on me the decision to exist, Mother. You claimed you had obeyed an order of mine, not your own choice. You actually accused me of being your master: you my victim, not I yours" (pp. 89–90; 84–5). The text is turned against itself, and becomes self-deleting.

But, since it turns out that the child was a fantasy of the mother's "letter", already dead before progressing much beyond the embryo stage, that is, almost all the way through the book, the child has existed purely as a textual figment: or rather, by an elementary *mise-en-abîme*, as a textual figment (of the narrating mother) within a textual figment (of the published book): "My body was only a plan that developed in you, by virtue of you; my mind was only a promise that was realized in you, by virtue of you," says the child (pp. 89; 84). It is this textual figment that has been poisoning the mother from the inside. What at first sight reads like a simple monologue, turns out to be a complex of self-deleting textuality, whose very source, the narrating mother, is herself deleted in death. The text survives, therefore, only as a series of deletions, as a toxin, the perfect semiosis of a mis-carriage followed by the death of the gestatrix. But, of course, whereas the text consumed in its fictive status by its fictive recipient, the child, acts as toxin, when consumed as a real instance of discourse – that is, when it is ingested by actual readers – its function is to act as anti-toxin or *controveleno*, immunizing the recipient against the poisons it contains. The mother in the text may die, poisoned by the results of her own discourse, but the mother of the text, as Author, continues to live as text. The mother in the text may have been guilty of the capital sin of *viltà*, cowardice ("È una bestia che sta sempre in agguato, la viltà" – "A beast always lying in wait, is cowardice" (pp. 15; 14. My translation)), a sin against life: the mother of the text has her confess this sin, accept the consequence of death, and, in the text's dying words (quoted below), proclaim the triumph of life.

Throughout the mother's monologue, the issue foregrounded was the clash between the interests and rights of the foetus, as a potential person, and the interests and rights of the mother herself, as an actual person. The final revelation that the pregnancy had ended long before the mother took any risks with the health of the foetus thus ironically deletes all the discourse centred on that issue. But the irony of the self-deleting discourse is even more far-reaching than that, since the embryo to whom it is addressed has ceased living at the point when the discourse itself begins. The discourse thus ends by thematizing its own virtuality.

This self-deleting discursive structure is obliquely reinforced in several ways. Before the mother has seen her tiny egg, the nightmare of her murder trial climaxes with the testimony of the child (vocalized as a grown man), who asserts that he has accepted his mother's lesson that "life is a death sentence" (pp. 91; 86) and therefore refused life. He ends, however, by forgiving his mother, in the expectation that he will be born again. "Splendid words, Child", she replies, "but only words." No individual is ever reborn (pp. 92; 87). So the Child appears to have the last word, only to have it annulled. It is the mother who really has the last word, but hers too is annulled. Possibly dying, she dreams of her child grown to manhood, now bearing her up as an old woman and leading her to where he will pick the magnolia flower (which, in one of her "fairy-tales", she had told him could never be reached), only for the vision to disappear, for the man-child to become a dead egg in a glass of alcohol once again. "You're dead. Maybe I'm dying too", she says, in the closing words of the book. "But it doesn't matter. Because life doesn't die."

These, too, may well have sounded like "splendid words, but only words," to the readers of 1975 and for fifteen years after, when the global military strategy of MAD – the thermonuclear balance of "mutually assured destruction" – governed the world. Still today, though less immediately, the peril of ecological disaster threatens our planet, and highlights how desperate is the mother's vitalistic faith in life as something indestructible and ever triumphant. Those final words also lay bare one of the central tensions that run through all of Fallaci's texts: on the one hand, individual existence is a supreme value, individual non-being an absolute negative; on the other hand, the individual is insignificant, it is the continuity of life in general that counts.

But words, however splendid, carry less weight than other effects of discourse. The competing discourses that make up the text of *Lettera a un bambino mai nato* tend to neutralize one another, as regards their propositional or constative content, their power to persuade. The mother frequently emphasizes the impossibility of arriving at any final truth ("Child: our logic is full of contradictions . . . " (pp. 11; 11)). The polemical rhetoric on one side is as effective as that for the other side, and the text explicitly enacts this by the hung verdict on the mother. The jury of witnesses is evenly split, and the decisive testimony of the child himself is: "you killed me without killing me" (pp. 89; 84). At this level, the text is open-ended and pluralistic. Again, the child explicitly affirms that both accusers and defenders of the mother are right, and that she herself had warned him that truth is never simple, but complex, multiple, and contradictory. Italian critics and reviewers have cited this plurality of conflicting voices as a reason for the book's almost unprecedented sales success (e.g. Medail 1976).

This is also true as far as it goes, but it does not go very far. *Lettera* does more than present a representative array of conflicting arguments on the right-to-life issue. It works above all by its semiotic structure – a narrative structure that approximates (as closely as the printed page will allow) to a dramatic, even to a theatrical (perhaps an over-theatrical) structure. It is not primarily the content of discourse that articulates the rhetorical effect of Fallaci's text, but the instance of discourse.

Apostrophe Kills

The master instance of discourse in *Lettera a un bambino mai nato*, its controlling mode, is self-evidently the direct address to the child in the womb by the mother. The second person singular "tu" used throughout to address the child posits the latter as interlocutor within the text. Though the book is called a "letter" and uses the written word, its basic fiction is that it is spoken directly to the child, who is thus linguistically "created" as a person. This grammatical move is all the more effective in that the book's real addressee is you or I – the reader, whose existence as former foetus is thus bound up with that of the foetus as possible person, suspended between non-being and being.

This invites a question, which was put to the writer by Nazareno Fabbretti soon after the appearance of the book in 1975: "But Catholics, some Catholics, will object that if Fallaci doesn't believe in God or in the soul, how is it that she's addressed a foetus as if it were a child, a human being?" To which Fallaci replied that it was a necessary literary device: "How else could I have written the book? Sure, so as to use a foetus as an interlocutor, I've accepted, in a literary way, the Catholics' basic concept of the human person" (Fabbretti 1975a, 1975b).

This answer does not quite dispose of the matter, however, as the grammatical "thou" retains its rhetorical impact even after it has been revealed, at the end of the book, that the embryo died at just about the moment when it was brought to life as "thou". So much so, that the mother, having conceived of the embryo as a person, concludes: "You belong neither to God nor the state nor me. You belong to yourself and no one else" (pp. 30; 28); and when, finally, the child speaks to her, it is to confirm that he chose for himself in opting out of life.

All this coincides with what Barbara Johnson has written about apostrophe – the speech-act of addressing as "thou" an entity that is absent, inanimate or dead – as a rhetorical trope, and especially about apostrophe as applied to the ambiguous status, the problematical personhood, of the human embryo. Apostrophe, she writes, is "both direct and indirect: ... it manipulates the I/Thou structure of *direct* address in an indirectly fictionalized way. The absent, dead or inanimate entity addressed is thereby made present, animate and anthropomorphic. Apostrophe is a form of ventriloquism through which the speaker throws voice, life and human form into the addressee, turning its silence into mute responsiveness" (Johnson 1986 in Warhol and Herndl 1991: 631).

Johnson observes of Shelley's "Ode to the West Wind" that the poem attempts to "animate", or attribute life to, the west wind in order that the west wind may in turn animate the poet, restore his failing sense of life. And she continues: "One of the bridges this poem attempts to build is the bridge between the 'O' of the pure vocative, Jakobson's conative function, or the pure presencing of the second person, and the 'oh' of pure subjectivity, Jakobson's emotive function, or the pure presencing of the first person" (p. 632).

While "O" and "oh" do not appear in Fallaci's text, the functions which they represent in Shelley's poem – conative and emotive – are very markedly present in *Lettera a un bambino mai nato*, as is the vitalistic impulse towards reciprocal animation. Johnson relates apostrophe to poems by mothers who have aborted or lost "children" – poems which use apostrophe in an analogous attempt to determine the uncertain animate status of the mother-poetesses who address their offspring who might have been, and of those offspring themselves: "The uncertainty of the speaker's control as a subject mirrors the uncertainty of the children's status as an object." Gwendolyn Brooks's poem "The Mother": "attempts the impossible task of humanizing both the mother and the aborted children while presenting the inadequacy of language to resolve the dilemma without violence . . . It is impossible to tell whether language is what gives life or what kills" (ibid., p. 635). Johnson links this ambiguity of language to the "mother-tongue" learnt by the infant from its mother, and its first word, "mama", through which the child becomes subject of, and subject to, discourse.

This ambiguity of language applies in more than one way to Fallaci's book. Much of the text is concerned with the difficulty of defining the starting-point of personhood on the one hand, and, on the other hand, the status of the embryo or foetus in relation to that of the seeds of trees or the young of various animals wasted in nature or devoured by their own parents. Dilemmas are at the heart of the language of *Lettera*. Also, as I have shown, the text repeatedly deletes itself, and annihilates the child which it has itself created. The title ambiguously prefigures this deletion, announcing the death of the foetus, but not that it dies so early in the pregnancy. More broadly, while being is repeatedly asserted to be infinitely preferable to non-being, however bad the terms on which the former is available, the values associated with being – love and liberty – are so assiduously negated as to lead to the child's rejection of life, which, in turn, may possibly lead to the mother's own death at the moment that the text dies into silence with a paradoxical affirmation of life.

The text as a whole hinges on the question of whether the mother wishes the death of her child. She even accuses herself of this, and acknowledges that the voices of her accusers are also the voice of her own conscience: ". . . you had judged me guilty because I had judged myself guilty" (pp. 92; 87). That the mother of *Lettera* has not in fact aborted her child makes little or no difference. Johnson remarks that mothers who miscarry also feel guilty for the loss, and she talks of "the indistinguishability between miscarriage and abortion" in Lucille Clifton's "The Lost Baby Poem", which refers to a miscarriage (Johnson 1986: 641). There is some clinical basis for this: Agnello-Modica (1992: 100) cites Verny (1981: 215) to the effect that the mother's condition early in pregnancy may produce adverse hormonal changes which may lead to the death of the embryo, and indeed the doctor in *Lettera* warns the mother of this, and even talks of "a thought that kills. At the unconscious level, of course" (pp. 57–8; 54–5). Anxiety as a cause of miscarriage had been discussed by Simone de Beauvoir (1972 [1949]: 516). The Italian word *aborto* covers both "abortion" and "miscarriage" (which has to be qualified as *spontaneo*).

If apostrophe finds itself at home in the no-man's-land between being and non-being, second-person address is not an unprecedented innovation of *Lettera a un bambino mai nato*. It is a traditional feature of the poetic ode and other writing from classical times. More recently, Fallaci's fellow Florentine and older contemporary, the well-known novelist Vasco Pratolini, had used it tellingly and movingly in the memorial to his dead brother, *Cronaca familiare* (1947), and Fallaci herself had applied it to structure *Se il sole muore*. Several critics complain that she has overused the device, and that it becomes overbearing. (This, with its corollaries, is the only explicit criticism levelled at *Lettera* by hostile intellectuals.) After a detailed analysis of certain passages, Milani (1971: 47–9) finds fault with the oratorical effect, in *Niente e cosí sia*, of the narrator's speaking voice with its "schemi iterativi" and "enfasi cantilenante" ("schematic iterations" and "singsong rhetoric"), and sums up with a general attack on Fallaci's use of the one-sided dialogue (even though this is far less marked or systematic in *Niente* than in other works of hers): "the dialogue-form also sounds oratorical . . . in its continuous, overpowering address to the reader, who is forever assailed, harangued, cajoled by that omnipresent *tu*, to which there is no right of reply, since that *tu* is also and primarily *io* [I]." (The mother within Fallaci's text asserts that her one-sided dialogue is really a monologue, since the child has no awareness (*coscienza*) independent of the mother's (pp. 62; 59)). Rosa (1982: 63–4) argues that a "sfumatura ultrapatetica" ("hyperemotional over-tone") invades *Lettera* and *Un uomo*, not merely involving, but overwhelming the reader: for, whereas in *Se il sole muore* and *Niente e così sia* it was only geographical distance that separated the narrator from the addressee, in the two later works, the addressee (as also, we may note, in Pratolini's work) is dead. She talks of the author–narrator's "narcissistic self-projection", and remarks:

> In *Lettera*, that provocation was effective in that the dialogue form aimed at endowing with speech a potential being, allotting to it the task of disentangling the emotions attendant upon freely chosen motherhood: in this ambitious endeavour, the style was inflated in the alternation between visceral impulses and cynical reflections. Armfuls of that very "melodramatic rhetoric" and "silliness from popular songs" for which the mother-to-be yells her detestation [pp. 53; 51] were in fact devoted to browbeating the reader, who was never given the chance to stand back.

Natalia Aspesi (1975) also writes more sweepingly of "the strident rhetoric, the embarrassing over-writing" of *Lettera a un bambino mai nato*.

Rhetorical overkill is central to the book, and lends itself to the charge of "divismo" – "stardom" or self-idolization – which Aspesi, like many others, lays against Fallaci. Fallaci lays herself open to this charge, in *Lettera* as in others of her books, by inviting identification between her real-world person and her textual protagonist, and by gearing her narratives close to self-dramatization. *Lettera* does not escape this charge, as, though Fallaci keeps the mother and all other characters and places in the narrative anonymous, yet numerous of the mother's circumstances and characteristics and of the "fairy-tales" and other anecdotes which she relates transparently belong to the writer herself. To some readers it has appeared as the unprincipled self-affirmation of competitive self-aggrandizing individualism; others may read it as principled anarchism or libertarianism. (The reasons for Fallaci's ostracism by literary critics, feminists, and most politically committed intellectuals, and for the generally enthusiastic reception of most of her works by the public and the reviewers, offer an elusive though intriguing subject of study which cannot be allowed to interfere with the internal analysis which is the focus of this present study.) Whatever the valuation placed on it, "I", the subject as immediate presence, prevails over the impersonality of "he" (or "she") as absence and distance.

The anti-novelistic "I" – inescapably linked to the second-person "thou" – signals Fallaci's implicit challenge to Literature as institution, her anti-literariness. This distinction between "I" and "he" was opened up in Barthes's *Writing Degree Zero* (Barthes 1953: 53–8 [1984: 30–3]), in which the "he" is presented as (along with the preterite, the French narrative past tense, not used in speech) one of the two key conventions, or "masks", of narrative, common to the writing of both novels and history, fiction being in fact predicated on a "History" which is the product of a social order. In reading Fallaci, the hypothesis must be entertained that her intrusive "I" marks a disbelief in such a social order, in its constricting and interested rationality. Since the rationality of "History" has been, historically, a male rationality, in which woman, in so far as she differs from man, is seen as Other, it is no accident that, where Fallaci writes most incontrovertibly as a woman – from the most distinctively female position of pregnancy – she collides against that male rationality, that "History", and against that institutionalized "Literature" which is part of that history, and against the Novel as an institution. In *Lettera a un bambino mai nato* the mother's revolt against the male-ordered world, its grammar, and its theogony (God the Father as an old man with a beard) is quite explicit, in the name of a more inclusive rationality: "Child, I'm trying to tell you that to be a man doesn't mean to have a tail in front: it means to be a person. . . . *Person* is a marvellous word, because it sets no limits to a man or a woman. . . . The heart and the brain have no sex" (pp. 12–15; 11–14). The mother's critique of the sexism of Italian grammar closely matches that made by Italian feminists and analysed by linguists (cf. Lepschy 1991), and she selects, out of the available linguistic options, that of applying the "unmarked" masculine forms ("man", *bambino*) to include females also, redefining them by detaching their linguistic gender from gender as social construct. This smacks of "immasculation", but it is one of the options which Italian women have consistently taken.

The Placental Text

One way of looking further into Fallaci's *Lettera* is to inspect the foetus bottled up in other texts. Fallaci seems to have had no predecessors, but several successors, in interpellating the foetus – to have opened up, in fact, a theme hitherto closed to writing. Agnello-Modica (1992: 95) dismisses Phyllis Chester's diaristic *With Child* (1979) as "constantly echoing if not plagiarizing Fallaci", and Fallaci's book is also strongly echoed, even in its title, in Lidia Ravera's *Bambino mio* (1979). This uses Fallaci's I–thou structure and unnamed characters, and divides in two parts – pregnancy and infancy. Self-consciously literary in style, and at least as rhetorical as Fallaci's, though very different, in its use of iteration and other verbal devices, Ravera's book has everything comfortably both ways: rapturous motherhood and murderous post-Freudian readings: "The child's death is unbearable, it fulfils our deepest, most secret aspiration" (from a book by Serge Leclaire entitled, in Italian, *Si uccide un bambino*); and, from Helene Deutsch: "Mrs Smith had numerous abortions (or mis-carriages?) because she was afraid she was unable to be a good mother. This appeared clear when we discovered that she refused to identify with her mother" (Ravera 1979: 12, 130. My re-translations). Both quotations, along with much of Ravera's book, seem to be in dialogue with Fallaci's text, while wholly lacking its tension.

Susan M. Squier (1991) discusses the mutually problematical relationship between mother and foetus presented in two stories – Jayne Anne Phillips's "Bluegill" (1987), and Laura Freixas's "Mi mama me mima" – "My Momma Spoils Me" – (1988). The latter probably predates *Lettera*, as it refers to the Biafra war, but interestingly develops a similar situation: the marginalization and mutual dependence of mother and foetus will lead to the child's not being born and to both being laid in a specially shaped coffin. Here it is the foetus that speaks, refusing to be born into the dangerous and uncomfortable world outside. Kathy Lette's novel *Foetal Attraction* (1994) starts from a similar situation to that in *Lettera*, being narrated by a young woman whose lover dumps her when she decides to keep her baby, but is more interested in satirizing the London literary scene than in the ethics and the metaphysics of gestation.

Degrees of Écriture

Lettera a un bambino mai nato has all the appearance of being traditional in style and literary address, and indeed of hardly being literary at all, but of being geared to straightforward communication, in keeping with the political urgency of the radicalism of 1968 and after, and the temporary marginalization of the literary. But, as has already been seen, the instance of discourse of the book is deceptive, even if remote from the ostentatious foregrounding of textuality practised by the writers of the *neoavanguardia* and *neosperimentalismo* in the 1960s.

Syntax and lexis – the raw materials of style – in *Lettera* are likewise almost purist in their almost reductive logic, with barely even an inflexion of Fallaci's demotic Florentine. But, in keeping with the development of Fallaci's prose visible at least as early as *Penelope alla guerra*, it is the existential urgency of the speaking voice that dominates the text, with its insistent emphasis, vehemence even, even to excess, its rhythms performing a mimesis of the emotions, playing on the pauses between breathgroups (to talk in linguistic terms). Though it may be a monologue, it is always a dramatic monologue, primarily in its life-and-death address to the foetus, but also in encounters and exchanges with others. The discourse of *Lettera* never comes from a sociolinguistic distance, it is never the flat recording of casual speech. It has the curious effect of great intimacy broadcast with great amplification, as if over the radio, corresponding fictively to the mother's voice being conveyed to the child in her womb not via vibrations in the air, but directly through the body tissues and fluids. The suppression of proper names for the "characters" and places, syntactic simplicity, the deliberate recall and re-use of the same phrases and images spanning the book – these characteristics also serve the fiction of an elemental discourse with a potential person as yet unsocialized. Rhythm, tone, and the stylistic features visible on every page (no matter who the putative speaker, whether it is the mother or one of the other characters) thus amount to a rhetoric of the speaking voice, of the bodily self, of the biological and existential present, which exclaims, proclaims, urges, pleads, complains, browbeats, and which many aesthetically oriented critics have condemned – a rhetoric, which, as has been seen, is undercut and counterbalanced not only by its own internally and explicitly contradictory messages, but by its multiple deletion within the structural rhetoric of the narrative.

Some general considerations about literary style are called for before sampling Fallaci's writing in *Lettera*. One of the demolition jobs attempted against Fallaci on grounds of sub-literariness came in 1979 in the form of a newspaper review by Ruggero Guarini of Fallaci's just-published *Un uomo* (*A Man*), under the title "Come si fabbrica un romanzo di stagione" ("How to manufacture a potboiler novel"). This slyly takes the form of a Socratic dialogue between two book-lovers, of whom one persuades the other not only that Fallaci's would-be literary creations are not worth reading, but that they are positively pernicious in debasing cultural standards. Referring back to *Lettera a un bambino mai nato*, Guarini picks from it what he sees as a damning sample of Fallaci's style: "'Aghi d'angoscia mi trafiggono il petto': un perfetto esempio di quella prosa *kitsch* che i profumieri e i *mannequins* scambiano per poesia, e che induce i critici di mezza tacca a parlare di 'struggente lirismo'" (Guarini 1979: "'Needles of anguish pierce my heart': a perfect example of that kitschy prose that perfume manufacturers and fashion models mistake for poetry and that leads halfbaked critics to talk of 'poignant lyricism.'" – My translation, but *petto* (chest, breast, bosom, heart) does not quite translate here into today's English).

The fact that I have hunted through the relatively small haystack which is *Lettera* without finding any such needles does not mean either that the phrase quoted by Guarini does not appear in the book nor that it is not indeed a "perfect example" of its style. Nor does the fact that Guarini rather simplistically or reductively dubs the work "un libro autobiografico" and mis-reports its title as *Lettera a un figlio mai nato* take away the force of his criticism. On the contrary, judgement of Fallaci's stylistic register – usually too disdainful even to be dignified by print, and thus marked by the worse than infernal damnation of consignment to the limbo of critical silence – is one of the central aspects in the literary evaluation or dismissal of Fallaci's work.

The burden of this refrain, on the rare occasions when it

surfaces (particularly in connection with *Lettera* and *Un uomo*) is that Fallaci's style is of the kind associated typically with the Italian *romanzo rosa*, sentimental romance or romantic novel, as most signally exemplified in the best-selling "sub-literary" works of women writers from Carolina Invernizio to the enormously successful and prolific Liala (the Italian Barbara Cartland). The difference, and the danger, according to Guarini and others, is that, while the other writers more or less avowedly serve the consumer demand of a particular market without claims to literary or artistic merit, Fallaci presents stylistic vulgarity and intellectual superficiality with spurious pretensions to the prestige and authority of high culture, usurping the aura of the literary.

This critique resides in traditions of literary taste whose aristocratic disdain of petty-bourgeois kitsch finds renewed theoretical support from the self-styled revolutionary left. Barthes's dismissal, in *Writing Degree Zero*, of the prefabricated literary style of a Maupassant or a Daudet, whose "bien écrire" is "un signe littéraire enfin détaché de son contenu" ("fine writing" as "a literary sign at last detached from its content"), and which relies not on lexical effect, but on "expressive" syntax and rhythm to foreground certain words, making a myth of expressivity itself, might appear remarkably apposite to Fallaci's style, and indeed (as we shall continue to see in later chapters) her rhythmic expressiveness is recognizable in books as different and far removed from one another as *Se il sole muore* and *Un uomo*. Likewise (and this is what I now propose to examine), Barthes's scorn for the metaphorical style of "écriture petite-bourgeoise" beloved of writers in the (pseudo-)realist line up to Roger Garaudy might with equal plausibility be directed at Fallaci, and at *Lettera a un bambino mai nato* in particular (cf. Barthes 1953: 98–102 [1984: 56–61]).

A glance at the opening of *Lettera a un bambino mai nato* will show that categorical dismissal of Fallaci's writing on these grounds is inappropriate, and that criticism needs to address her literary project far more attentively. Fallaci gives us no would-be omniscient narrator embellishing a banal image of a supposedly objective reality with fancy metaphorical and rhythmic effects of style and self-conscious narrative "prose". Narrative is conducted through dramatic monologue. The first-person narrator constructs herself, through her discourse, as a subjectivity, with a marked stylization of the speaking voice which belies the pen-and-ink implications of the title and far more strongly suggests the acoustic medium of the tape-recording (and indeed in 1993 Fallaci did publish a tape-recording of her own reading of the text). The prosodic features of the "mother"'s Italian are largely lost in the English translation, which is obviously unhappy with the "un-English" emphasis of the original (excessive even to the Italian literary ear). Here are Fallaci's opening lines, reproduced in breath-groups:

> Stanotte ho saputo che c'eri:
> una goccia di vita scappata dal nulla.
> Me ne stavo con gli occhi spalancati nel buio,
> e d'un tratto, in quel buio,
> s'è acceso un lampo di certezza:
> sí , c'eri.
> Esistevi.
>
> (Fallaci 1975a: 7)

[Last night I knew you were there:/ a droplet of life which had leapt out of nothingness./ I lay wide-eyed in darkness,/ and suddenly, in that darkness,/ there was a flash of certainty:/ yes, you were there./ You existed. – (My translation is nearer to the words of the original than John Shepley's, but makes no attempt to match Fallaci's prosody.)]

The transcription of the original given above shows that the first four lines vary between two and four beats per line with a markedly anapaestic rhythm (two weak syllables preceding each stressed syllable), matching the excited suspense at the intuition of a discovery. This anapaestic rhythm is cancelled by the heavy iambic rhythm (one weak syllable preceding each stressed syllable) of the four beats of the fifth line, expressing the finality of certainty. This finality is emphasized by the two following short lines, a near-rhyming micro-couplet. The verbal echoes of "c'eri" (also approximated in "Esistevi") and "buio" reinforce this phonic patterning.

Prosodic effects are visible right through Fallaci's text, often reinforced by the insistent syntactic patterning (binary and ternary structures with elaborate variations), of which Fallaci's critics have often complained as of a kind of verbal artillery barrage (see especially Milani 1971: 45–9). This phonic dimension leads one to talk of the text in terms of prose-poetry or poetic prose (braving kitschiness!), and many other poetic dimensions are consistently visible throughout the text. Let us therefore pass now to the metaphorical dimension which was the object of Guarini's scorn.

The lines quoted above show two "poetic" metaphors of the type indicated by Guarini's phrase "Aghi d'angoscia mi trafiggevano il petto", namely – "goccia" and "lampo", both of which appear dangerously trite. In fact, "goccia" turns out to be the precisest possible image for the embryo, as taken up again at the end of the first page: "La tua goccia di vita è soltanto un nodo di cellule appena iniziate." ["Your droplet of life is only a cluster of new-formed cells."] Likewise, in the lines immediately following the passage quoted, the "lampo" rapidly turns into the flash of a rifle and of artillery:

> È stato come sentirsi colpire in petto da una fucilata. Mi si è fermato il cuore. E quando ha ripreso a battere con tonfi sordi, cannonate di sbalordimento, mi sono accorta di precipitare in un pozzo dove tutto era incerto e terrorizzante. Ora eccomi qui, chiusa a chiave dentro una paura che mi bagna il volto, i capelli, i pensieri. E in essa mi perdo.
>
> (Fallaci 1975a: 7)

> [It was like a bullet hitting me in the chest. My heart stopped. And when it started beating again with a dull thudding, a cannonading of consternation, I realized I was hurtling downwards in a well where all was uncertain and terrifying. Now here I am, locked inside a fear that soaks my face, my hair, my thoughts. And I lose myself in it. – (Again, my translation aims to give some idea of the verbal effects, and something near the precise meanings, of the original, rather than an aesthetic English rendering.)]

The "well" of uncertainty turns into the prison of fear in which the mother finds herself "locked in", linking up with the original "darkness" which was momentarily lit up by that lightning-flash of realization.

We are still in the realm of trite, obvious and transparent, imagery, marked by its communicative immediacy rather than poetic preciosity, originality, or suggestiveness, and this is in keeping with the character of the speaking voice, which is the text's instance of discourse. And yet, we have already seen that the metaphors interconnect, indicating one level of elaboration.

Another level of elaboration is evident in the fact that they
suddenly cease at this point: no others are to be found in the
remaining two pages of the novel's opening section, unless we
count, a few lines below the end of the last quotation, the barely
perceptible metaphors of: "È paura di te, del caso che ti ha
strappato al nulla, per agganciarti al mio ventre." ["It is fear of
you, of chance which has plucked you out of nothingness, to fix
you to my womb."] This metaphorical style is therefore not
uniform, not at all an *écriture* in the Barthesian sense, a ready-
made pseudo-literary cloak draped over the "facts" of the
narrative. Rather, it contrasts strikingly with other styles that are
applied functionally at specific points of the text: in this opening
section we have the sententious discourse on the fear of life as
being all war and work; the metaphysical discourse of being and
non-being; and the bare factual narrative of the mother's
mother's (the "child"'s prospective grandmother's) attempts at
ridding herself of an unwanted pregnancy.

That Fallaci (in her function as postulated author-within-the-
text, categorically distinct from the narrating "mother" of the
text) is exercising a specific and unusual type of control of her
style – a control approximating to that of poetry but quite distinct
from any prefabricated false poeticism – is further suggested by
the fact that the metaphors not only interconnect with one
another, forming a web, or metaphorical "system" or "language",
but also interconnect with other language systems within the
text. That metaphorical "flash" of certainty interconnects with
the literal "darkness", the "last night", in which the mother lay
wide-eyed, and this literal, physical level is in immediate
communication, from the very first line of the book, with the
metaphysical level of "il nulla" – nothingness or non-being as the
metaphysical correlative to the darkness of night.

These webs of interconnecting and mutual reference in fact run
through and constitute the entire text. (They are not always
visible in the English translation: the "caso" quoted above, for
instance, becomes "circumstance", while the next page, more
faithfully, gives "even by chance" for "sia pure per caso": the
verbal link is lost, and with it some of the text's cohesion.)
Already, the first few lines spell out the to-be-or-not-to-be
polarity, hint at slaughter as one of life's constants, oscillate
between certainty and uncertainty, define mental confusion as
the mode of the text's discourse, and fear as its root. Critics may

or may not like it, but a firm principle of composition is very much in evidence, foregrounding, if not positively flaunting, its own internal problematic. Explicitness is a paramount feature of this principle of composition, and if such criticism as there has been of *Lettera a un bambino mai nato* has missed the import of a problematic so explicitly stated, that is because such criticism is itself the prisoner of an aesthetic grounded in the subtle or implicit, in the hidden suggestion or ambiguity.

Existence and Existentialism

The first page – indeed, the very first line – of *Lettera a un bambino mai nato*, then, immediately establishes, with remarkable speed and economy, the existential terms of the narrative: an absolute "I" and an absolute "thou" catapulted into the moment between "stanotte" and "il nulla" (Heidegger's existential historicity of the self). The starting-point of individual life is death, existence is rooted in (or thrown out of) non-being. But the existential anguish or *Angst* ("paura") here is that of the self, the "I", not in the face of non-being, of death, but in the face of *another* existence, "tu". This is existentialism unprecedentedly translated into the feminine. The dilemma is the dilemma of conception and gestation, whether to accept on behalf of *another* the terms of existence, whether to make the existential choice on behalf of another. This dilemma is subsequently further translated into that of the competing claims of "I" and "thou", self and other, mother and foetus, no longer at an existential level, but at an everyday experiential level, morally insoluble, and susceptible only of political resolution. This "other", present in its grammatical absoluteness and anonymity from the very first line of the book, is kept present as the instance of discourse and the cue for the speaking voice throughout, explicitly invoked as interlocutor from time to time with perlocutionary forms such as imperatives ("Cerca di capire . . ." ["Try to understand . . ."] "vedi" ["see"]) or vocatives ("bambino" ["child"]), not always rendered in the English translation.

Whether or not Fallaci herself read Sartre's *Being and Nothingness* or Heidegger's *Being and Time* or other texts of existentialist philosophy is not at issue. Existentialism was in the air during the formative period of her adolescence and early adulthood in

the latter 1940s and through the 1950s, and was virtually man-
datory for a non-believing, anti-Marxist, libertarian individualist
as she was. She has stated that in her second year at *liceo* "mi
beavo di Sartre" ["I revelled in Sartre": Fallaci 1963: 99]. Existentialism articulated the inescapable problems of individualism
in terms akin to those of Fallaci's novelistic production.

In *Lettera a un bambino mai nato* what is striking from the very
opening is the fusion of the physical and the metaphysical.
Existence is tied to the body: the "chance" that plucks a new life
out of nothingness fixes it to the mother's womb. The mother's
anguished fear in the face of the existential choice between being
and non-being expresses itself in a sweat that soaks her face and
her hair and also her thoughts. The flash of certainty that a new
life has started within her is like a bullet in her heart. Existence
starts as a droplet, a tiny cluster of cells. Existence has to come to
terms with the body: "we get used to (suffering) just as to the fact
we have two arms and legs" (pp. 8; 8). The bodily dimension is
paramount from the beginning – with conception – to the end –
with the deaths of foetus and mother. Fallaci's book thus gives
one possible version of an *écriture féminine,* a distinctively female
mode of writing, as postulated by the French feminists, Cixous
and Irigaray, from the early 1970s. The female body is the
protagonist and speaks with a "bodily" voice. Fallaci literally
articulates the inarticulate of the existential divide between
mother and foetus, anticipating the remarks by Hélène Rouche,
when interviewed in Luce Irigaray's *Je, tu, nous,* about the "placental economy". Rouche observes: "It seems to me that the
differentiation between the mother's self and the other of the
child, and vice versa, is in place well before it's given meaning in
and by language" (Irigaray 1993: 42; quoted in Ward 1994: 326,
footnote 22).

Lettera a un bambino mai nato is internally structured in two
main ways: first, by the conflicting moods and views of the
mother herself and of the other people that she encounters; and
second, by the variety of discursive modes and hypotexts
adopted – not only the diaristic mode of introspection and
recollection, the effusion of attitudes, views and emotions, the
narration of day-to-day incidents within the narrative time
dictated by the pregnancy, but also several sub-genres within the
pseudo-genre of the "letter". There are the three third-person
"fairy-tales", experiences recalled from the mother's past; there

are dreams and anecdotes; and there is the mother's running commentary on a photoreportage on the development of the foetus, which she keeps coming back to right up to the end of the book. This internal structuring of the text gives it not only great variety, but, within a bare hundred pages, a very considerable reach, and a rhetorical suasion in both the senses that I have used in Chapter 2 above, again indissolubly: a suasion that commands the reader's attention both to the text as artefact and to the text as argument.

Within this economy, Fallaci's refusal to create "characters" emerges as strictly functional to the quasi-dialogue between mother and child, though a US reviewer thereby found the novel "flawed by the dominance of a passionately engaged narrator over a subsidiary cast of sloppily limned two-dimensional characters and a strident brand of feminism that makes a cardboard villain of every man with whom she comes in contact during her pregnancy" (du Plessix Gray 1977). In this respect, *Lettera a un bambino mai nato* belongs to a sub-genre of the novel which has always been more important within the ambit of the Italian novel than in other countries (with the significant exception of the eighteenth-century French *contes philosophiques*) – the *romanzo saggio*, a cross between narrative and essay-writing. All Fallaci's books (some more explicitly than others, and the more so the more closely they approximate to reportage) present concepts or issues as structuring elements of narrative. Dramatizing a thesis, problem, argument or issue is more important than illusory realism of character or milieu. The Italian *romanzo saggio* goes back to Manzoni's historical inquiry into justice in *Storia della colonna infame*. It is a prominent aspect of the *oeuvre* of Moravia, Sciascia and others in the twentieth century, and it is visible in Svevo and Pirandello also. The refusal of rounded characters and realist conventions indicates the postulated Author Fallaci's disbelief (within this work) in the Novel as an institution and as part of a preconceived "History", an agreed reality, as theorized by Barthes ("L'Écriture du roman", Barthes 1953: 45–60).

The "characters" in *Lettera*, then, are not only, as the narrator–mother admits, voices within herself: they are also (and perhaps primarily) the conflicting voices of the society which has formed her. And, in so far as even hostile critics have allowed that Fallaci has captured within her text the terms of the debate about the respective rights of mother and foetus, it is justifiable to speak of a "discursive realism" in the book. The concept of "character" as a coherent plenitude, a "stable ego", had been demolished by the end of the nineteenth century, and the disintegration of the central "character" in *Lettera* – her dissolution in delirium and possibly death at the end of the novel as a direct result of the confusion of voices within her – marks the most far-reaching and critical outcome of the work. The presumption of the integrity and autonomy of the individual is absolutely central to the life-values of the narrator–mother, and yet (as in *Penelope*) this presumption has been shattered by the end of her narration.

Lettera a un bambino mai nato re-enacts the crisis that has always beset individualism, the crisis of its origin and the origin of its crisis – the essential abstractness of individuality, in that there can no more be an individual without society or species than there can be society or species that is not composed of individuals. It is not only the fact of being a career woman that destroys the mother, but also the fact that she is an isolated individual, outside the traditional matrimonial structures of society and without an alternative supportive social network. She utters the discourse of feminism but stands outside the social and political network of the feminist movement. Feminist solidarity is as yet only vestigial, limited to the support which the mother receives from her female friend and from the female doctor. Thus isolated, the individual, in her experiential moment of choice for or against motherhood, enjoys a freedom which is largely illusory. As Petchesky (1980) shows, such a woman is subject to the multifarious pressures of the prevailing social order, and her individual "choice" is really the outcome of her particular situation. Fallaci's text represents this in two ways. First, the mother finds herself unable to make the choice, and delegates it to the foetus. Second, against her illusory mothering of the foetus, her deep rejection of the terms of social existence, of what she sees as its false values and radical unfreedom, determines the child's "choice" not to be, and the death of the foetus. In both instances, it is the overwhelming adversity of social pressures that negates the will, choice, and freedom of the individual whose project it is to combine career with motherhood. Real choice for the individual in such a matter is dependent on a social dispensation supportive of such a project and annulling the psychic costs of combining rather than splitting the two roles. The mother's friend's experiences of abortion concisely encapsulate the argument (pp. 24; 23).

The shadowy characterizations, their lack of names (just as the child, being yet unborn, is nameless) and their designation simply in terms of their relationship to the child and his mother – the list is brief: mother, father, female friend, boss, male doctor, female doctor, mother's parents, with fleeting appearances by a dressmaker and a nurse – clearly suits the fiction of direct address to the pre-social foetus. These characters are each defined by little else than their discourse about child-bearing. The male characters are negatively marked by their dogmatic or hypocritical concern for the child at the expense of the mother. The white-overalled doctor is further marked by his metaphorical iciness and the father by his snivelling. It is species and gender being – the modes of being which are primary to gestation and reproduction – which are, appropriately, the primary modes of being addressed in *Lettera a un bambino mai nato*.

Nevertheless, a concreteness, and even a historical specificity, is fleshed in via the diversity of hypotexts included within the main text. The mother's three "fairy-tales" reinstate the preterite (in place of the present perfect which dominates *Lettera*) and convert the "I" into the third person, visibly constituting before the reader's eyes a new history (or "herstory") in opposition to the official histories institutionalized by male society, just as the fairy-tale stands in opposition to conventional novelistic narrative. They are tales of unfulfilled desire (the woman who touches the flowers of the magnolia tree only by plunging to her death), of the arrogance of wealth (the poverty-stricken girl who is denied the luscious *gianduiotti* chocolates), of the unattainability of freedom and justice (the girl who finally loses faith in tomorrow when she finds herself condemned to washing the underwear of her liberators). The first two provide an intimate girl's-eye-view of the conditions of social and economic life in Fascist Italy; the third does the same for the political history of the transition from Fascist to post-Fascist Italy through the Resistance struggle and the Liberation. The episode of the moon-rock (in effect, another fairy-tale) which the mother is promised but not given again illustrates human – and especially male – fickleness and arbitrariness and re-states the cosmic dimension of human desire. The dreams about fishing frogspawn out of the pond and about the minuscule infant kangaroo link the psychic unconscious to the theme of species survival and pro-creation, with the human species as one among the innumerable varieties of life on the planet. The "cluster of cells" mentioned on the first page leads to the scientific discourse about DNA and the development of the embryo and the foetus within the womb. Always, personal history, political history, species history and natural history generally, back to the first explosion of matter in empty space, are held in relation to the theme of being and non-being as such.

Within this variety of discourses, another medium of repres-entation – the photoreportage on the development of the foetus – provides one of the structuring elements that runs through the text. This relates to the scientific discourse which is one of the book's main components and sites of contestation. It also serves the mother to give some greater sense of solidity and reality to the "character" of the child, making "him" visible, lending him the objectivity vouchsafed by photography and science. Petchesky has written on such photographic representations of the foetus as strategies tending to personalize the foetus while depersonalizing the mother by leaving her invisible. It is through thus "seeing" her child's photograph, in fact, that the mother decides to keep him (pp. 9; 9; cf. Petchesky 1987: 265). This visual strategy was adopted for the video-film *The Silent Scream*, which dramatized abortion as murder. The photoreportage in *Lettera* appears to support the same strategy – the fundamental dis-cursive strategy of the whole book – of constructing the foetus as a person, but with two differences which radically subvert that strategy. First, the child is "created" by the voice of the mother: he is a child of her text and cannot subsist independently of her text any more than the biological child can subsist independently of her womb. Secondly, the photographic construct of the child is subject to the same ironic retrospective deletion as the rest of text when it turns out that the foetus was already dead virtually from the beginning of the photographic sequence. The effect of irony – that of simultaneously stating and negating – is therefore visible here as everywhere else in the text.

The same applies in reverse. *Lettera* contains the mother's caus-tic demolitions of the values or myths of love, family, freedom, work. Yet it is these very same radical negations which determine the death of the foetus and, consequently, that of the mother herself. They are eloquently and vehemently stated, their suasive rhetoric is overwhelming, and turns out to be the rhetoric of death, a suicidal discourse and the suicide of discourse. But since discourse always differs from itself, the text of *Lettera* also contains its own difference, perceptible in the difference between the fictive instance of discourse – the mother's address to her unborn child – and the real instance of discourse – Fallaci's address to her readership. If the instance within the text is the abdication of motherhood and childhood, the suicide of discourse and the demise of its interlocutors, the instance of its publication is the problematization of that very discourse and its implicit rejection or transcendence (*Aufhebung*).

Pickering-Iazzi draws out of *Lettera* a pedagogical distinction between the institution of motherhood as social imperative (systematically undermined by the "mother") and "the mother's regenerative notion of motherhood", "the meanings of mother-hood in its personal and social dimensions". She affirms: "Central to Fallaci's reconceptualization of motherhood is the right of choice" (Pickering-Iazzi 1989: 337–9). However, the "mother" in *Lettera*, in shifting the onus of choice from herself to her child, in negating authoritarianism in the name of liberty, somehow manages to negate liberty itself, and presents mother-hood as a contradiction. She, the mother, will herself strip her child of freedom, for the irony in conceiving of freedom in individualistic terms is that one discovers constraints every-where. "Free" in the confinement of the womb, "outside", the mother says, "you'll have countless masters". And she continues:

> And the first will be myself who, without wishing it, maybe without knowing, will impose things on you that are right for me but not for you. Those nice little shoes, for instance. To me they're nice, but to you? You'll yell and scream when I put them on you. They'll bother you, I'm sure. But I'll put them on all the same, even telling you you're cold, and little by little you'll get used to them. You'll yield and be tamed, to the point of suffering when you don't have them on. And this will be the beginning of a long chain of servitude whose first link will always be represented by me, since you won't be able to do without me. . .
>
> (pp. 35–6; 34)

Where "Penelope" rejects the mother, the mother here rejects her-self. Child-bearing and -rearing are posited as radical and mutual unfreedom. In terms of narrative suasion, *Lettera a un bambino mai nato* works through a paradoxical inversion of Ross Chambers's connection between "narratorial" and "narrational" authority. Fallaci's narrator within the text gets her story fatally wrong, imaginatively endowing with life a foetus that is already dead; but her fatal error only enhances the authority of the text and of its postulated Author.

Part IV
Other People's Voices

6

Fallaci and the Tape-Recorder: "Gli antipatici" (1963) and "Intervista con la storia" (1974)

Whose Interview?

The journalistic interview has something of the nature of the chess-game, though the collaborative aspect is usually more prominent than the adversarial. Both take place in "real time" only once, but can be transformed into text (print, audio or video) and "played back" any number of times. Both are also played out between two participants whose control over each other's "moves" is limited. But there is also a fundamental difference: the interviewer always has the first move, and always has the initiative throughout the "game", and also always has the last move, or the last word (which may be silence), studying her or his subject in advance, preparing questions and interview strategy, remaining basically in command of the interview situation, and then (except in interviews broadcast live) having control also over the editing process, over the choice of end-point, and over all the introductory material and commentary, subject only to legal checks on misrepresentation.

Can the interview, then, be viewed as a literary form? Can another person's discourse constitute a literary creation authored by the interviewer? This proposition seems preposterous. But, given the considerable textual control exercised by interviewers, there is at least a degree of orchestration on their part of the voice of their interviewees: the two may work in harmony or in counterpoint, and at times the stronger (institutionally, the interviewer) may overwhelm the weaker.

The game-playing metaphor suggests that the interview belongs to journalism rather than to what we fetishize as "literature". But the distinction is one of gradation more than opposition. If "New Journalism" writing and high reportage lay claim to literary status, and if they straddle the borderland between the two territories or discourses, they make no apology for incorporating other people's voices – often in interview situations – into their "factual" artefact. The "factual" and the "artefactual" are not so very distinct, and fiction, even at its least "factual", is always "quoting" speech of one sort or another, what varies being rather the degree of avowed elaboration and control exercised by the author over the linguistic fabric, over what is directly or indirectly quoted, rather than fidelity to the presumed non-authorial authority of the documentary record.

Another way of defining this continuum is in terms of lesser or greater approximation to the author's own first-person discourse. Even when this authorial element is at a minimum, as when the interviewee is talking, the interviewer's presence as silent Author is always the precondition of the interview, presiding over it and mediating between the dialogic discourse of the interview and the audience or public of its eventual recipients. The presence of a listener is what Mukařovský, defining the three "necessary and thus omnipresent aspects of . . . dialogue", has called the second or "situational" aspect. Mukařovský's first aspect is that of the relationship between the two alternating participants, which in our case relates to Fallaci's own personality and values and her interaction with those of her interviewee. His third aspect is that of the "specific character of the semantic structure of dialogue", by which he means the unity of theme or textual coherence of the discourse of the two alternating participants (Mukařovský 1977 [1940]: 86–8).

Interestingly, however, Mukařovský argues that the characteristics of "dialogic speech" can suffuse monologue and that dialogue, if one of the speakers predominates, can have a "monologic quality", concluding that "monologic and dialogic qualities comprise the basic polarity of linguistic activity . . . whether formally monologic or dialogic" (ibid., pp. 108–12). Critics of Fallaci's *Lettera a un bambino mai nato* and *Un uomo* and other texts of hers have indeed often complained that though such texts are ostentatiously structured in dialogic form and addressed to a real (i.e., supposedly extra-textual) person as "tu" ("thou" or "you"), the "addressee" is a textual construct rather than a genuine interlocutor. The "surface" dialogic structure does not necessarily coincide with a "deep" dialogic structure.

In discussing Fallaci's two volumes of interviews, and her two major works of reportage which deliberately straddle the discursive practices of journalism and literature, I propose to trace the articulations of dialogue as a major innovative aspect of narrative rhetorical suasion both towards the instance of discourse (whether "factual" or – in the later developments represented by *Un uomo* and *InsciAllah* – as "fictional", or "factional", with an ever more slender distinction between the two) and towards the argument or "ideology" contained in that discourse.

Fallaci developed as an interview journalist just when television was becoming the dominant medium of mass communication, and when, therefore, the television interview was coming into prominence. Yet she has always remained committed to print journalism, thus keeping to a minimum her distance from the parameters of literature, though she was among the first to make systematic use of the tape-recorder to capture her material. In eschewing the live broadcast media, Fallaci maximizes authorial authority by hiding it, the interviewer's face and voice (and those of the interviewee) being abstracted from the published interview, translated into a transcript in which they remain invisible, except for the occasional photograph. This concealment coincides with a literary effect which has passed under the name of "the death of the Author" and the apparent autonomy of the text – the opposite of the journalistic effect whereby the person of the author is inseparable from his text and responsible for it. The literary author is the text's invisible authority, and yet not "responsible" for his "fiction" (though legal, and especially religious, authorities have often, up to the case of Salman Rushdie, held writers of "fiction" responsible for the moral and theological valence of their texts (cf. Hanne 1994: 189–243)). The writer as journalist is visibly responsible for her text, yet, by this very visibility, her authority is far more vulnerable. Fallaci combines these two divergent effects in her more "journalistic" as in her more "literary" works. The autonomy of the printed text, especially in book publication, also keeps to a maximum the autonomy of authorship, which would be severely circumscribed by the institutional and industrial constraints of radio or television broadcasting, but it retains this autonomy by restricting its address to people who read books and quality journals – a definable social class.

These authorial effects have been much commented on by readers and reviewers of Fallaci's interview collections. Guiducci (1970) reads Fallaci's volume on Vietnam, *Niente e cosí sia*, metaphorically as one long one-sided interview in which Oriana's narrated self plays a purely receptive role, with a building of tension in the search for meaning, like sensitized audiotape. This metaphor of Oriana as an audiotape (reminiscent of Isherwood's "I am a camera") suggestively links Fallaci's experience as an interviewer with the large-scale enterprise of portraying or "interviewing" Vietnam. This sort of "negative capability", this receptivity and sensitivity, if it can be demonstrated, would certainly constitute an important quality common to both the best journalism and the best literature. Altomonte, using the literary terms *personaggio* ("character") and *narrativa* ("fiction"), regarded it as true also of *Intervista con la storia*, but he associated with Fallaci's receptive sensitivity a more active purposiveness:

> . . . what can be sensed as fundamental is the quest for what the character can give away; indeed, many interviews are one long reiterative portrayal of the interviewee. The interview then moves more along the lines of narrative fiction than of journalism. So that, paradoxically, it may happen that, while striving to illustrate and to inform, what is most surprising – what in the end takes over – is a sense of astonishment at a certain elusive something, at an aura of mystery surrounding the character, like a sort of recurrent hiatus in the discourse by which Fallaci "displays" that character.

(Altomonte 1974)

Prisco (himself a fiction-writer of note) dwells on the novelistic skills of Fallaci as *narratrice* in pursuit of a deep and not merely journalistic characterization of her interviewee, identifying two features that explain her success in discovering the secrets of the interviewee's personality. One is that "she is the first to turn herself into a character", interacting dramatically with her interviewee especially by her strongly held moral and political values and her keen scent for cant of any kind, and especially for the cant rooted in political power. This, says Prisco, is what provides the thread that runs through each interview and that links the various interviews together, giving each of her published volumes its unity. The second instrument by which Fallaci penetrates the psyche of her subjects is the introductory narrative which prefaces each interview, setting the scene and describing the behaviour of the interviewee (Prisco 1974).

Prefacing *Intervista con la storia*,[1] Fallaci described her passionate involvement in her interviewing in the much quoted phrase: "Su ogni esperienza professionale lascio brandelli d'anima" ("In every job I do, I leave behind a piece of myself" – my translation: *Intervista*: 7; cf. *Interview*: 9). Her interview techniques – essentially of moral and psychological engagement – have been illustrated by Aricò (1986b). Reggiani, however, reviewing *Se il sole muore*, accuses Fallaci of using "literary" techniques and her personal involvement in such a way as to overwhelm her subject rather than illuminate it. He writes of her "overbearing character that drives her, even when using a tape-recorder, to take over the interviewee", so that the various personages presented in that book "were, between the lines, so many little cameos of the Oriana Fallaci in question" (Reggiani 1965). Fallaci herself has repeatedly pronounced herself to be fiercely and unashamedly subjective and judgemental, a partisan for what she sees as right, and has scorned those who pretend to objectivity.

The degree and kind of subjective intervention therefore become an issue, and Mukařovský's linguistic reflections on the relations between the dialogic and the monologic can be related to Bakhtin's privileging of the dialogic imagination over the monologic in the novel genre. Fallaci may be in danger of swamping other voices with her own, pre-empting the possibility of intersubjectivity and the autonomy of others' subjectivity by imposing her own and thus operating an anti-novelistic discursive closure, a denial of pluralism. Her control as interviewer over the voice of the interviewee is considerable. Milani (1971: 30) quotes Fallaci saying in an interview: "I transcribe the entire interview, then I work on what I publish in the same way as a film-maker does on a reel of film: I omit, I cut,

---

1. References are to the extended 1977 Italian edition, shown first, and to the 1976 English translation by John Shepley (London: Michael Joseph, 1976). Quotations are from Shepley's translation unless otherwise indicated.

I splice."[2] The rhetoric of freedom in Fallaci's works depends in very large part on the speaking voice – hers and the voices of others. The quality of her voice and the autonomy which she allows to the voices of others will be a precise measure of the real freedom carried by that rhetoric. This applies not only to the interview collections of *Gli antipatici* and *Intervista con la storia*, but also to the two intervening works which are largely structured around connected series of interviews, *Se il sole muore* and *Niente e cosí sia*.

Gli antipatici – *The Beastly and the Nice*

Fallaci's various notes and prefaces to the original and translated versions of *Gli antipatici* – "beastly people"[3] – jauntily explain that journalistic, provocatively publicity-seeking, title as defining celebrity as such. But she also defines those celebrities as either actual or potential friends or enemies, and unapologetically declares her subjectivity, particularly as expressed in the introductions to the individual interviews. The transcription smoothed out the kinks in the discourse of both interviewer and interviewee, says Fallaci; and the visual blank of the tape, the loss of all the non-acoustic signals which can so greatly modify the impact of what is said, was filled in by her introductory scene-setting and narrative. Fallaci thus declares the extent and judgemental nature of her intervention, partially contradicting another of her remarks: "Rather than interviews . . . they are conversations recorded on a tape recorder, then transposed into written dialogue. Rather than conversations, I would add, they are monologues provoked by my questions and opinions . . ." – which rather understates the degree of Fallaci's "provocation" and interventionism.

The "Preface", then, establishes Fallaci herself as a "character", the controlling character, who links together all the others and

2. Milani refers to *L'Europeo*, n. 1205, 1968, p. 20.
3. Oriana Fallaci, *Gli antipatici*, Milan, Rizzoli, 1963. References are to the 1970 edition, followed by the English translation by Pamela Swinglehurst, *Limelighters*, London, Michael Joseph, 1967, or *The Egotists: Sixteen Surprising Interviews*, Chicago, Henry Regnery Company, 1968, as indicated. Quotations in English are from these published versions unless otherwise indicated. Most of the interviews with Italians published in the original are not, however, included in the British or US versions.

who has the authorial prerogative of commenting on them. This "character" subsequently develops in the course of the various interviews and preceding introductions through the diverse situations and interaction with the diverse personalities. *Gli antipatici* is thus as much a matter of self-construction and self-projection on Fallaci's part as it is on the part of her interview subjects, and as such becomes a remarkable account of the encounter between self and others.

The lack of intimacy of the interview situation poses severe limits on the nature of the interaction and the personal revelations that can take place – limits which Fallaci makes it her business to overcome, exploiting the presence of the other as the essential avenue to intimate revelation. Where interviewer and interviewee are tacitly agreed on the limits of discretion or the interviewee's self-assessment, the interviewer's presence is felt in the warmth of the initial description and the unemphatic empathy of the questioning. This applies to most of the female interviewees, from Ingrid Bergman and Anna Magnani to Natalia Ginzburg, and to a few of the males – the Spanish aristocrat Don Jaime de Mora, the Italian soccer star Gianni Rivera and – in *The Egotists* – Norman Mailer, among others. Otherwise, the adversarial model of the chess tournament is more in evidence, as Fallaci provokes and her subject responds or parries.

In some cases, the duel is one-sided. The duchess of Alba, with her affectation of simplicity and her scores of titles, her tenderness for little birds and her taste for bull-fighting, her enormous wealth and her disdain for money, and her numerous other patrician inconsequentialities, is an easy target for Fallaci's caustic questioning and presentation. In many others the results are interestingly ambiguous. The interview with Fellini reads like a revenge for the "great Italian director"'s previous exasperating disruption of Fallaci's professional arrangements, which her introduction describes with narrative verve. She persistently attacks what she sees as Fellini's self-regard, encouraging him to see his fame as equal to Verdi's and pressing him to acknowledge his latest film as self-indulgent autobiography, and provoking him, at the very start and at the very end of the (edited) interview, to insult her cordially as: "Disgraziata. Screanzata. Ballista. Maleducata." Yet Fellini's cordiality emerges as genuine, he addresses her throughout by the affectionate "tu", while she has, since their previous clash, changed to the coldly polite "lei".

His mild obsession with his own celebrity and his other weaknesses and misdemeanours, both with the truth and with women, come across as ingenuously and engagingly boyish. This is quite different from the interview with Hitchcock ("Mr. Chastity"), in which Fallaci shows the great man every deference, encouraging him to indulge his complacency to the point where he ends by saying that he feels sorry for her because she has to write an article about him and yet knows nothing about him: he has laid a trap for himself, giving Fallaci an entry to retort that she has seen through his genial humour and innocent paunch and finds him the nastiest and cruellest man she has ever met.

Another ambiguous case is that of Nilde Jotti, the Communist parliamentarian and life-companion of Palmiro Togliatti, leader of the Party across the tumultuous period from the 1930s to the 1960s. Here again, Fallaci's questioning is aggressive, suggesting that Jotti's celebrity is merely a side-effect of Togliatti's, positing their domestic ménage as that of two political institutions, hinting at the Party's disapproval of their union, repeatedly charging the Communists with intolerance and fanaticism, and closing by mocking Jotti's political faith as a substitute religion: "La prego, onorevole Jotti: preghi per me." ["I pray you, Right Honourable Jotti, pray for me."] And yet, Jotti responds to all Fallaci's provocations with good humour, spontaneous warmth, and dignified composure, and emerges as totally admirable.

This is all the more remarkable in that Fallaci's introduction to the interview with Jotti revolved around Fallaci's none too fantastic fantasy of the Communists as a latter-day Holy Inquisition, busily hauling dissidents, among them Fallaci, before the firing squad, and of Jotti herself as an "abbess" earnestly persuading Fallaci that it was perfectly right that she should be shot. Not for nothing is Jotti's office described as being meticulously spick-and-span, with sparse, almost Spartan, furnishings, and the precision of her office routine and the punctuality of her appointment-keeping as being matched only at Cape Canaveral (now Cape Kennedy) and in the Vatican.

Several of these introductions go well beyond simple factual information of a journalistic kind, combining a variety of other features. One of these is usually an initiation into a startlingly unfamiliar milieu: here, the Communist Party's Rome headquarters; elsewhere, a bull-fighter's ranch; or a working-class soccer star's humble home. Another is a "reading" of a face, a physique, and accompanying apparel, of which one instance is the split soul of the USA being read out of Norman Mailer's good eye and bad eye in *The Egotists*. Fallaci's own psychic state is always one of these key elements, sometimes reaching high levels of fantasy, as in the case of "abbess" Jotti brainwashing Fallaci before the firing-squad.

One of the most elaborate and lengthy introductions presents Giancarlo Menotti, the moving spirit of the Two Worlds festival at Spoleto. The interview is entitled "Il demonio di Mount Kisko" ["The demon of Mount Kisko"], "demon" being Menotti's own self-definition, and Mount Kisko being his residence in the depths of the country, almost a wilderness, outside New York. Fallaci begins in quasi-novelistic style: "That autumn I often went from New York to visit Mount Kisko, where Giancarlo Menotti has been living for I don't know how many years together with another composer, Samuel Barber" (my translation). Although Menotti is away, his presence fills that environment, where Fallaci feels perfectly at home, though the only people around apart from the impeccably be-suited Barber are jeans-clad male music students, and the only other female present is a great black bitch called Fosca, who attaches herself to Fallaci and then plunges into the lake for a swim. Fallaci at last runs down Menotti for an interview in Spoleto during festival time, when the small and ancient central Italian hill-town is invaded, to use Menotti's own phrase, by people wearing "pink shirts and gold sandals". Fallaci and Menotti seem to be alluding warily to a gay life-style, at a time when it was still taboo in Italy and subject to persecution. In her introduction, Fallaci weaves two dizzily intricate pages around the host of ambiguous characters and intricate double and triple relationships among these invading festival people who mill around her. This culminates with a nightmare she has in which she has turned into a great black bitch and is led by the demon into the lake, where she is saved from drowning by the same demon turned into an angel. Fallaci's interview fails to solve any of the enigmas of Menotti's personality: he emerges as too saintly for his own liking, too much the musical philanthropist, so that he corrects the image of saint into that of devil. Fallaci concludes that one thing is certain: "that as a man he is courageous and honest. As a man he is chic." [My translation.] Thus the discourse and the

images of the introduction interweave with those of the interview, compounding the ambiguities of both in a markedly
"literary" way and preventing discursive closure in any simple
message, any straightforward moral arithmetic. The judgemental
rhetoric here is neutralized, and a libertarian space is opened up.
Though Fallaci's own values and attitudes are always clearly
visible, those of her interlocutors also come through, and the
dialogic integrity of the interview genre is preserved.

Gli antipatici thus does not appear to bear out the criticism
that Fallaci's personality overwhelms that of the interviewee.
Speaking styles – idiolects – come across as markedly distinct,
Ingrid Bergman's and Don Jaime de Mora's as well as Alfred
Hitchcock's and Federico Fellini's or Leonilde Jotti's and
Giancarlo Menotti's. Not only that, but Fallaci's own idiolect
varies considerably, either sympathetically, as with Natalia
Ginzburg or Anna Magnani, or insidiously flattering, as with
Hitchcock, or with mocking mimicry, as with the vapid Duchess
of Alba, or in outright provocation, as with the poet Salvatore
Quasimodo ("Ed è subito Nobel"), Jotti, and Fellini. Sometimes
the interviewee's idiolect resembles parody: Natalia Ginzburg
speaks in short rapid bursts, with the most elementary syntax
strung together with a series of "poi" or "perché", while "ecco"
is used as a sort of punctuation mark, sometimes following every
clause, and the unusual expression "E poi, poi niente" is her
regular end-stopper. When the interview is interrupted by a
telephone call, Fallaci transcribes Ginzburg's side of the brief
exchange, in which she advises her daughter to bath with the
window open in order to avoid a build-up of carbon dioxide
(Fallaci, 1963: 348). If Fallaci the interviewer here controls the
interviewee's discourse, it is by caricature and exaggeration
rather than by homogenizing it to her own.

This prompts a reflection on Fallaci's writing style outside *Gli
antipatici*, which had always been close and moved ever closer to
a speaking style, to a point which many critics have found
excessive. Yet the distinctively Fallacian style turns out to be
fairly representative of the speaking voice of many of her
interviewees, and we may find a characteristically Fallacian
delivery in a quite unexpected source, Sammy Davis Junior. This
interview, "The Luck to be Ugly", appears in *The Egotists* and was
selected for inclusion in *The Penguin Book of Interviews* (Silvester
1993: 474–83). Listen, at almost any point, to the rhetoric of the

speaking voice in Sammy Davis Junior's insistent verbal emphasis and patterned syntax, his "stile ternario":

> I never open a door, I never let anyone open a door to me, unless I'm sure, confident, that the door will stay open for whoever follows me. I never enter a club that won't admit other Negroes. I never enter a restaurant that won't admit other Negroes. I never work in a theater or a movie that doesn't give work to other Negroes, because I can't forget that if I'm admitted, it's because others entered before me, because they opened those doors, one by one, little by little, so that I can open them a little wider . . .

It may appear from this that the rhetoric of the speaking voice, Fallaci's marker for individual and existential presence, is a language universal, an elsewhere in relation to the speaker, freedom of speech wrapped in unfreedom of language.

Interviewing History

If Fallaci in *Gli antipatici* achieved celebrity status by recording celebrities on tape, in *Intervista con la storia* (*Interview with History*) she attains historic stature by interviewing political leaders. The moral picture-gallery of virtues and vices now includes those in power, their individual psychology shown in its repercussions on how they serve their people and the cause of honesty, freedom and justice. The book is dedicated "To my mother Tosca Fallaci and to all those who do not like power". The personal involvement declared in the Preface is keener than ever, and palpably present in the introductions to the individual interviews, yet virtually invisible in the interviews themselves, where Fallaci's technique is to lull and lure a perceived enemy – the Ethiopian Emperor Haile Selassie, or the Shah of Iran – into making admissions of infallibility, omnipotence and visionary experience. In the case of Kissinger, Fallaci was not even aware she had achieved this objective until the publication of the interview provoked a furore. Italian Christian Democrats like Giovanni Leone and Giulio Andreotti, on the other hand, were too wily to give anything away.

The ordering of the interviews shows a design leading to uplift. Fallaci opens with Henry Kissinger, the man closest to the world's greatest centre of power, and ends with strugglers for freedom – two prelates, Camara and Makarios, who habitually risked their lives for their people, and Alexandros Panagoulis, long "a persecuted hero of the Resistance to the Greek colonels" (*Interview with History*, 1976: 14). What is at stake is the affirmation of heroism in a struggle in which an unattainable ideal of freedom is one of the two opposing poles and the uneliminable reality of power is the other. Its symbol (Fallaci says) is the huge "no" to Nazi occupation painted among the trees on a Greek hillside and whitewashed over by the Greek dictatorship, only to reappear (pp. 11; 13).

". . . I do not understand power, the mechanism by which men or women feel themselves invested or become invested with the right to rule over others and punish them if they do not obey", Fallaci's "Preface" reveals: "Whether it comes from a despotic sovereign or an elected president, from a murderous general or a beloved leader, I see power as an inhuman and hateful phenomenon." She admits the tragic necessity of a governing authority and the impossibility of "absolute freedom", though "it is necessary to behave as though it existed and to look for it. Whatever the price" (pp. 10; 12–13).

Fallaci perceives this impossible "absolute freedom" in individual terms, and power likewise, though her "Preface" opens with the question "is history made by everyone or by a few?" In effect, she sees history as the work of individuals, combating the Marxist argument by asking where Marxism would have been without Marx (pp. 8; 10). The interview is intrinsically an individualistic discourse, and Fallaci applies it in the most individualistic spirit possible, focusing her questions on the interviewee's personality and on personal responsibility, but not on impersonal factors regarding social formations, institutional processes, political theory or group interests.

This is fascinating enough, but the results it produces – including many brilliant introductory narratives, scene-settings and characterizations – are not different in kind from those of *Gli antipatici*. One critic indeed complains that Fallaci "rarely compares, reflects, evaluates. She gazes and she rails. She observes the machinery, but does not take it apart." Thus, "politics, for this most impolitic of journalists on this earth, is a nice clean business", which he attributes to "an innocence in her which is not naïve, but is nurtured upon a great dream of thirty years ago", alluding to the Resistance struggle (Listri 1974). Yet, as portraits of individuals in history, the interviews retain their interest – what Fallaci called "their symbolic meaning and alignment in a symbolic sequence" (pp. 11; 13) – twenty years after the volume appeared, despite critics who felt their value was more ephemeral and journalistic (cf. Manciotti 1974).

7

To the Moon and Back: "Se il sole muore" (1965) and "Quel giorno sulla luna" (1970)

Between Reportage and Novel

*I*n a letter of 1969, the year of her reportage volume on Vietnam, *Niente e cosí sia*, Fallaci rejected as out-of-date the "tired old argument that divides writing into journalism and literature", and continued: "Journalism, nowadays, is often literature, and literature, journalism: there is no longer any boundary". She elaborated:

> The reader, for me, is someone to be seduced without being known. I don't write for "educated" people, as people put it, much less for intellectuals . . . I inform them, in all possible humility, striving to capture their interest so that they won't drop me at the first encounter or along the way . . . I guard against hypocritical claims to objectivity. There is never any such thing because there can't be any such thing. So the only honest solution is to relate the truth as I see it. From what I see as the right angle. Or perhaps I should say meaning.
>
> (quoted in Milani 1971: 24–5; my translation)

The West Indian novelist V. S. Naipaul twenty-five years later largely concurs. He makes the distinction between the "literary novel" and the "blockbuster", and expresses the view that: "The novel form has done its work. The true novelists today are people like Edwina Currie, Jeffrey Archer, John le Carré, Ken Follett . . . I feel that the blockbuster – with its element of the joke, and personal display, not unsophisticated – shows how the form has developed, and it has changed the attitude to fiction." By the 1990s, Naipaul says, the literary novel had changed: "The idea of pinning down reality isn't really there. It's migrated perhaps to other forms. Perhaps something like the essay will give people reality about our confused, mixed world." He stresses the "need to identify who the writer was, who was doing his travelling in the world, who was doing his observation of London or wherever", and regrets his own "suppression of the narrator" in his very first book, *Mr Stone and the Knights Companion*: "To write a book as though you were this third-person omniscient narrator who didn't identify himself was in a way to be fraudulent to the material . . ." (Hussein 1994).

Coming from an accredited "literary" novelist, this reads like a perfect vindication of Fallaci's volumes of reportage on the US space programme and the war in Vietnam, except for that reference to the "true novelists today" as being the writers of "blockbusters", and the explicit contrast with the "literary novel", which again brings in the distinction between "literature" and "journalism" contested by Fallaci. Though here, as by Italo Svevo a century ago, the word "literary" is made by Naipaul to signal a limitation or a disability rather than a superiority.

This is part of a fundamental debate in the Western tradition. Aristotle had compared "history" and "poetry" (which we can read as "fiction" or "creative writing", whether lyric, epic or dramatic), and judged the latter more "philosophical" than the former. The novel had always had strong documentary roots, and not only when it purported to be documentary, as in Defoe's *Journal of the Plague Year*. It has often returned to these roots, as in the post-war season of Italian neorealism. Carlo Levi's testimonial essay–narrative on the south Italian peasants under Fascism, *Cristo si è fermato a Eboli* (*Christ Stopped at Eboli*, 1945), shares many structural features with Fallaci's reportage narratives.

The latest self-renewal of narrative writing from its documentary roots coincided with Fallaci's own literary elaboration of reportage. *Se il sole muore*, on the US space programme, appeared in the year in which Truman Capote's *In Cold Blood* re-inaugurated the "novel of fact". A few years later, the New Journalism and Tom Wolfe's crusade for a new social realism in the US novel further closed the gap between reportage and the novel. Italy in the 1970s also saw a return of the documentary or historically based novel, and this has grown stronger in the 1980s and 1990s both in Italy and internationally, with Tom Wolfe ever in the front line (see Chapter 1 above, "Manufacturing Best-sellers?" and cf. Wolfe 1989; Bradbury 1992).

Reviewers of *Se il sole muore* both in Italy and in the USA remarked on the novelty of Fallaci's enterprise. Domenico Porzio described the work as a *romanzo-saggio* (essay–novel), and said that the "metamorphosis" from reportage (*inchiesta*) to novel "does not spring simply from the use of narrative conventions (the people encountered turning into characters, questions and answers resolved as dialogue, plot etc.) but from the underlying moral enquiry which binds together and gives sinew to the fast-moving account" (Porzio 1965). In the USA, Maurice Dolbier pronounced it "Not a novel, not an essay, but a new kind of writing" (Dolbier 1966), while David Snell likened it to Hemingway's "non-fiction" work, *The Green Hills of Africa* (Snell 1966).

In her typical colloquial rhetoric, Fallaci stresses its factual nature, playing on the words *veri* and *veramente* (as well as the structuring dialogue with her father, which I discuss in due course):

> ... I shall often turn to you in this book. Read it and think about it, Father, whether it amuses you or irritates you: everything in it, from the first page to the last, is what truly happened to me, or is what I truly saw or [truly] felt or [truly] thought. The names of the people [are real] and [the names of] the places are real. The dates [are real] and the conversations I report are real. My doubts and my enthusiasms and my cowardice are real: I have invented nothing [in this book] and have kept very little out of it. This book, Father, is [a diary,] the diary of a year in my life: and I offer it to you by way of continuing the conversation that started on account of that spark of light.

> [Bracketed words show how much of the colloquial rhetoric – the systematic redundancy of speech – has been pruned in translation: pp. 15; 8][1]

While stressing the factual basis of the text, this passage slyly implies its artefactual texture. Hints of this sort recur from time

---

1. *Se il sole muore* was first published in Milan by Rizzoli in 1965. I refer here to the 1981 Rizzoli BUR edition, followed by the English translation by Pamela Swinglehurst, *If the Sun Dies*, published in 1966 in London and New York by Athenaeum. Where relevant to my discussion, my quotations in English show up the colloquial redundancies pruned away in Swinglehurst's translation.

to time. For example, describing "Deke" Slayton, Fallaci (rather overstraining the "fact is stranger than fiction" *topos*) again apostrophizes her father to remark: "If this were a novel instead of the story [*diario*] of a journey, I'd have some fun writing about a type like this, don't you think, Father? I'd make him into a really improbable character. Even when I tell you this or that bit of conversation, I sometimes stop and wonder: did he really talk like this or was I dreaming? He really talked like this: I didn't dream a thing" (pp. 102; 81). The key rhetorical effect here is that Fallaci, in addressing "Father", posits herself and her father as being outside and beyond the text, incontrovertibly "real", though, as textual constructs, Oriana the character and Fallaci the narrator (as well as Fallaci the postulated Author), and Father as interlocutor, are clearly distinct from their "real-life" counterparts. This strengthens the "reality-effect" whereby everyone and everything in the book is simultaneously credited with "real-life" documentary authenticity and the rather different kind of authenticity deriving from the book's authorial discourse, the two kinds of authenticity being passed off as identical by literary or "rhetorical" sleight of hand. Some US reviewers (e.g., Justice 1966; Ley 1967) complain of some factual inaccuracies in Fallaci's account, but this is trivial in relation to the major point that eyewitness authenticity is used as a major means of suasion, while being subsumed into a textual structure which goes beyond passive "reporting".

One of the modern sources of the drive to propel narrative writing in the direction of reportage was the Prague-born Egon Erwin Kisch, who in 1928 claimed that the Great War of 1914–18 had rendered fiction trivial and ushered in the age of "pure reportage", a concept which, in 1935, Kisch pitted against the bourgeois notion of "high culture" as a revolutionary antithesis. Monteath refers to "Kisch's notion of the compatibility of extreme subjectivity and objectivity in reportage" and his argument for a convergence between the modes of fiction and those of reportage: "Kisch . . . whilst demanding objectivity in reportage, also permits and even recommends the insertion into the account of the passionately biassed reporter. The observer of action is also a participant in the action." Monteath quotes the renowned war photographer, Robert Capa: "If a picture is bad, you were not close enough" (Monteath 1989: 72–8).

Kisch was in contention with his fellow-Marxist, Gyorgy

Lukács, who in 1932 had dismissed the "reportage novel" on the grounds that "it conceives a social product as ready-made and final, and precisely describes it as such ('objectively' and 'scientifically')." The reportage novel thus employs a deceptive empiricism to present an "empirical reality" which is "illusory", "inauthentic", a "surrogate", in contradistinction to the true novel, which seeks the "typical" in the "overall process" of a historical situation (Lukács 1980 [1932]: 51–4). Lukács is looking to narrative literature for a "critical realism", for an analysis and a critique of capitalist society, in artistic rather than scientific form, which corresponds to the Marxist analysis and critique, even if the author happens to be Balzac or Thomas Mann. The "typical", for him and for the whole Hegelian literary tradition, is not a statistical or static concept, but an analytical or diagnostic and dynamic one, capturing the essential conflict of the historical moment: classically, the "world-historical individual", who need not be at all outstanding (a Napoleon), but may be a perfectly ordinary human being caught at the divide between two historic orders. Serious reportage, Lukács argues, also represents the "typical", but in a scientific or conceptual rather than artistic form, appealing to the intellect rather than to the emotions (cf. Monteath 1989: 71–2). Since Lukács is the main intellectual authority for the opposition between journalism and literature of which Fallaci has been made a victim, it will be interesting to see how far her reportage "novels" meet his criterion of the "typical", both as scientific meaning and as artistic embodiment, Marxian or not.

Oriana as "Everyman"

Monteath focuses on a landmark reportage narrative and a predecessor of Fallaci's – George Orwell's *Homage to Catalonia*. The subjective element stressed by Kisch is foregrounded in that work in the quasi-fictional "character" of George Orwell (itself a literary pseudonym), which both Williams and Kubal see as being deliberately "created". This "Orwell" acts as the "shock-absorber of the bourgeoisie", and Kubal attributes the success of this work to "the fact that there is a distance between the author and the first-person narrator" (cf. Monteath 1989: 84, fn. 52). Williams (1974 [1971]: 47–8) insists: "Instead of direct realization of what was observed, he created the intermediary figure who goes around and to whom things happen. This figure, in the novels, is not himself, and this is important." The "character" of the narrator in fact undergoes development – a human, moral, and political education: this justifies labelling *Homage to Catalonia* a work of *Bildungsreportage* (parallel to the fictional sub-genre of *Bildungsroman*) (Monteath 1989: 79, quoting Williams 1974 [1971]: 108). Monteath also refers to Orwell's "strategies . . . to establish his reliability as a guarantor of verisimilitude", one of which is to stress the elusiveness of truth, whether subjective or objective (Monteath 1989: 80).

Orwell's *Homage to Catalonia* thus represents a valuable starting-point for comparison with Fallaci's major works of reportage, especially *Niente e cosí sia*, given the similarity of subject-matter. A more immediate, but less repeatable, model of the participant observer was her friend of the 1950s (whom she had probably already met at the liberation of Florence, when she was fourteen), Curzio Malaparte, world-famous for his war-reportages *Kaputt* (1944), on the Eastern front, and *La pelle* (1949: *The Skin*) on the Italian front (cf. Grana 1973: 76–7), and much more prone to the *protagonismo* (self-dramatization) of which Fallaci is ritually accused. The figure of "Oriana" as participant observer engaged in an exploratory quest was an important element of narrative suasion in *I sette peccati di Hollywood*. Tom Wolfe elaborates on this theme: "Any time a non-fiction writer uses an autobiographical approach, he is turning himself into a character in a story. This has a better chance of working if the writer was, in fact, a leading character in the events he is describing." Wolfe compares Norman Mailer's highly effective use of this autobiographical technique in *The Armies of the Night* with its much less effective use in Mailer's *Of a Fire in the Moon*, on the first moon shot – a topic close to Fallaci's *Se il sole muore* (and identical to that of her *Quel giorno sulla luna*). Wolfe asks the question why Mailer's second attempt at autobiographical narration failed so badly, and gives the reply: "Because this time he was not, in fact, a leading character in the event, and his use of an autobiographical point of view merely set up a clumsy and tedious distraction in the foreground, viz, himself" (Wolfe in Wolfe and Johnson, eds, 1973: 188).

Fallaci does not altogether evade this risk in her reportage volumes in which the autobiographically based figure of

"Oriana" is a structuring element. Her texts sometimes fail to maintain the distance between Fallaci the narrator and Oriana the participant that George Orwell maintained between his two textual selves in *Homage to Catalonia*. Moreover, Oriana cannot claim to be an active participant in the sense that George Orwell in *Homage to Catalonia* and Norman Mailer in *The Armies of the Night* were involved in the events they were describing.

Fallaci labours strenuously to remove this disability, engaging Oriana, as in her earlier reportages, in a quest to find out where truth lies, and where her own values lie. Like Orwell, Oriana is engaged in *Bildungsreportage*. She approaches the space programme as a challenge posing the choice between the values of tradition and those of modernity, between nature as something already domesticated and nature (the cosmos) as something yet to be conquered, between attachment to home and the spirit of adventure; while the Vietnam war poses the question of who are the liberators and who are the oppressors: is the war a crusade against neocolonialism and US imperialism, or against communist dictatorship and Soviet imperialism? But, beyond that, given the recurrent human carnage of wars in general, what is the meaning of human life on this planet? Is it possible to retain any faith in humanity, or is the entire species fundamentally vicious? How and where can ethical boundaries be drawn?

These questions are so vast that they risk remaining purely rhetorical, in the sense of vacuous; so serious that they require the utmost seriousness of treatment – a seriousness which need not mean solemnity and which need not exclude comedy or farce (these being in fact powerful elements in much of the most radical anti-war literature from Hašek's *The Good Soldier Švejk* to Heller's *Catch 22* and Saro-Wiwa's *Sozaboy*). Such a quest constitutes the real narrative "action" of Fallaci's reportages: in this important sense, the character "Oriana" is indeed an actor, the central actor, within whose conscience the issues are waged. She is presented, in her individual specificity, with her own personal history and geography, as an "Everyman" figure, standing in for us, the readers, framing our own interrogatives and undergoing the catalytic experiences on our behalf, much like Orwell's "shock-absorber of the bourgeoisie", and consequently undergoing change and development along an oscillating path between two opposed views, two worlds, two value-systems.

The Oriana figure in Fallaci's works thus approximates closely to Lukács's concept of "typicality" involving a "world-historical individual", as identified, for instance, in his study on *The Historical Novel* (1969 [1947]: 29–69), in the "wavering" eponymous hero of Sir Walter Scott's *Waverley*. The essential action, and the essential narrative, of Fallaci's books is not at the level of interpersonal drama, of personal relations, nor at the level of dramatic events, such as those of war, but at a transpersonal level of historical consciousness.

Fallaci spells this out particularly in *Se il sole muore*: "this book (*diario*) must often be an obsessive swing between yesterday and tomorrow" (pp. 15; 8); she describes herself as "a pendulum that never hangs straight but always swings, from one doubt to another" (pp. 31: 15). The whole book is structured, even to excess, on this principle of alternating affirmation and negation and reaffirmation, anticipating by ten years the systematic indeterminacy of *Lettera a un bambino mai nato*. For the Marxist Lukács, the historic issue is essentially one of class hegemony and mode of production. Fallaci in both her major reportage volumes mystifies these issues. In *Se il sole muore*, she presents many of the faceless faces and denaturing and dehumanizing operations of what she calls "the System". But she implicitly also presents the System as essentially creative in making the cosmonauts' quest possible, and counterposes to it no alternative model of ownership and decision-making, nor any radical resistance, but the residual spirit of human individuality and adventure and personal heroism, which somehow survives in spite of all the homogenizing pressures.

Related to the figure of Oriana as questing world-historical waverer is the other major strategy by which Fallaci labours to overcome the problem posed by her continuous presence in these two works. This is to conduct her enquiry (diary, travelogue) as a dialogue with her father. He is represented as categorically opposed to the quest for new worlds, and to the denaturing and dehumanizing new technologies. *Se il sole muore* is the first of the four major works which apostrophize an interlocutor as "tu" and the only case in which the interlocutor (Oriana's father) is also an actor who impinges on the text through having considerable extratextual autonomy. The text dramatizes a radical break between Oriana and her father, the end of their dialogue, when she finally opts for the position antithetical to his. This is signalled at the close of the penultimate chapter, where "Oriana" apostrophizes her father no longer in the second person, no longer as "tu", but in the third person. She has just received a letter from him saying that he has bought her a familiar oak-tree on a neighbour's land to save it from being felled: "I shook my head as I read it. I thought how crazy he is, my father. Buying me a tree. Saving the life of a tree. How crazy he is, my father: I don't understand him any more" (pp. 476; 382).

However, the diary-narrative is conducted systematically as a dialogue with the father and shows all the linguistic markers of a dialogue as discussed in the preceding chapters – primarily the second-person address, with accompanying vocatives and related deictics, and the stylization of the speaking voice, with its informal tone and simplified, redundantly and emphatically iterative syntax. Milani (1971: 30–2) complains of Fallaci's affected and tiresome Tuscan colloquialisms and conversation-markers – present also in *Se il sole muore* – which she finds out of place in the war reportage of *Niente e così sia*: uses like "come" ("kind of"), "ovvio" ("obviously"), "ecco" ("you see?"), "mica" ("not at all"), and shortened verb-forms like "fo", "vo", "esser", "son", "schizzan", etc. Such a dialogic structure risks becoming claustrophobic and is hard to sustain interestingly through a volume four or five hundred pages long, though relieved and varied by the great variety of other hypotexts, voices and speech-situations – particularly the numerous one-to-one interviews. Fallaci's richly developed interview technique is powerfully integrated into both volumes, each chapter comprising scene and interview in varying kind, number, and combination.

Fallaci's Pendulum

The controlling structure of *Se il sole muore* is that denoted in Fallaci's metaphor of the "pendola" and the "altalena" ("see-saw"), Oriana's oscillation between modernity and tradition acting as a carefully measured rhetorical suasion in favour of the see-saw's final resting-place – firmly on the side of the space-quest and of the future. This structure is emphasized in the succession of alternating chapters, the appeal of tradition being succeeded by the pull towards the future. Before examining this localized system of oppositions, I propose to comment first on the same opposition as it operates across the text as a whole.

"In my end is my beginning": Eliot's phrase defines structured discourse, where the conclusion determines everything in the text that comes before. The "end" of the text logically precedes its opening. The title provides the suture between the two. Fallaci's text, which ends by embracing the future, logically starts by recoiling from the present manifestations of that future. Neither that ending nor that beginning, however, are simplistically managed. The costs of "progress" are never lost from sight. And, conversely, the past is seen both with its limitations and as containing the seed of the future, being indeed a future with respect to its own past.

Fallaci's opening is as striking as that of any of her books. Oriana stumbles on a stone and falls flat on her face on the grass verge of one of the Los Angeles freeways, deserted by pedestrians and frequented only by automobiles gliding indifferently by, to find that the grass is not grass and that the earth is not earth but that everything is synthetic, made of seemingly indestructible plastic. Artificial flowers and cacti in her motel room, a fully automatized sterilized kitchen, vol-au-vents ready to use for up to thirty years develop a motif that is to run through the book in innumerable and startling variations. The narrative artifice is highlighted by that stone – the very first word of the text ("Il sasso non si vedeva . . .") – which could not possibly have been there to stumble over in that perfectly synthetic environment. The narrative (and ideological) suasion is effective despite its lack of verisimilitude, so powerful is the shock of that image of modernity, the crisp poetry of the "huge shroud of plastic, of grass that never grows or dies, a mockery", or of the "cold frost" of the shattered glass rose.

In the second and third chapters a sequence of vulgarly gnome-like apostles of the new era of technical progress towards the stars gives way to the high-priest of Fallaci's book, Ray Bradbury, the science fiction writer. He provides the overdramatic title (since the Sun still has a continued life and lifegiving expectancy of five billion years) of Fallaci's book, is invoked from time to time, and reappears in New York for the book's final scene of the burying of the Time Capsule. He does not drive a car (the book's key image of dehumanized modernity), but rides a bicycle (one of the book's talismanic images, associated with Oriana's childhood and her father and

Resistance against the Nazis). He is a paternal figure surrounded by high-spirited family life. He intones the creed of the future, sounding to Oriana "like a priest who recites the Pater Noster and believes in it". The passage, and the second chapter, ends: "the taste of that prayer always remained with me. I have it still" (pp. 31; 15), confirming the suture between two Orianas, subject and object of narration.

Bradbury's "prayer" not only subtends the whole text, but inaugurates its liturgical discourse, in which man supersedes God, and whose ritual – prayer, incantation, litany – is transposed from the field of Catholicism to that of rocketry. References to religious ritual recur at discreet intervals before becoming prominent in the descriptions of rocket launches towards the book's close. Thus, the huge Vertical Assembly Building on Merritt Island, where the rockets are constructed, the tallest building in the world, dwarfing the skyscrapers of Manhattan, is likened to the Pyramids, and linked to mankind's unwitting, childlike search for God (pp. 193–5; 162–3). This acquires sinister connotations in the interview with the ex-Nazi rocket scientist, Von Braun, who claims to read God's will in his own handiwork, naming God in every sentence for two pages (pp. 296–7; 231–2). Von Braun's religiosity is cross-cut with Oriana's flashbacks to the capture of two Yugoslav partisans by the Germans in occupied Italy, and is sucked into the text's insistent movement away from a transcendent, God-centred religion.

Thus Chapter 29 (Chapter 27 in the US edition) describes "a dawn out of Genesis" in the desert where the test launch of "Little Joe" ("he's a living thing, he breathes . . .") is to take place, and in the next chapter blast-off becomes "A burst of flame out of the Apocalypse. A bellow out of Genesis" (pp. 433; 346). These unashamedly trite biblical parallels are a prelude to the hyperbole of the Saturn launch; Little Joe is a rhetorically understated counterpart to the climax which is still to come. Nevertheless, it is already sufficient to release Fallaci's hymn to mankind, and the narrating Oriana, in dialogue with her father, links up again with the Oriana within the narrative in a passage where, as always, the English translation systematically excises the excited, incantatory, iterative rhetoric of the speaking voice:

I wasn't able to say it, Father. I wasn't able to say that for [one minute,] one stupendous minute I had made my peace with men, I had realized that men are truly great, Father. They're still great when they substitute plastic grass for grass, and [they're still great when they] change urine into drinking water, and [they're still great when they] use wheels instead of legs, and [they're still great when they] forget the green and the blue, they're still great when they turn Paradise into Hell, [they're still great] when they kill the creatures they've given life to. And I was proud to have been born among men instead of among trees or fishes: I was proud because . . .
". . . because, Jack, you see, for one minute [, one stupendous minute,) it seemed as if I saw men gambling with God."

(omitted words in brackets: pp. 434; 347)

The explicit moral ambiguity of this passage befits the post-Auschwitz and the post-Hiroshima world in which human achievement has particularly distinguished itself in acts of evil and destruction. The project of colonizing the heavens, even if it can be pursued, seems to share with projects for reaching a spiritual heaven the renunciation of any serious attempt at putting earthly matters to rights. By this criterion, it belongs to the post-modern rather than to modernity. Arrogating divinity to mankind equates mankind with the amoral nature of the universe as pure energy. It is in this sense that Oriana's "religious" experience is confirmed by an external observer, her travel guide, Jeanette: "You've had the Revelation, haven't you? You've been touched by Grace. . . " (pp. 436; 349).

The launch of the great Saturn rocket is announced in terms of prayer by Theodore Freeman, one of Oriana's astronaut heroes and "brothers": "You must see it as a prayer because when we launch that thing it's like praying" (pp. 471; 379). This sets the liturgical scene for the launch, with God mockingly stirring the wind to prevent the blasphemous human challenge: "Never mind if God was amusing Himself humiliating us, making fun of us. Sooner or later He would let us celebrate this rite greater than any Mass, than any sacrifice to a Holy Ghost, than hymns sung inside churches. The church was these three square miles, with the sky for a roof. The altar was the blockhouse, where stood the high priest with his priests, Von Braun with the astronauts and technicians. The hassocks . . ." etc. ". . . and over there stands the Saturn, an enormous candle waiting to be lighted to the glory of ourselves, not of God". When the countdown begins, Fallaci interpolates the Latin rogations, "Te rogamus, Deus, audi nos . . ." and ends with a "Hallelujah!" as "The white volcano opened . . . and even its roar was glorious, it was no longer a roar but Easter bells, the Easter when we are happy and free and good, the Easter we spent together when the war was over, Father, and you were alive, I was alive, Mother was alive, everyone around us was alive . . . " and the sentence zooms on like the rocket (pp. 471–3; 379–81).

At its climactic point, as throughout, Fallaci's book is thus crafted in terms of a literary aesthetic which is not that of the institutionalized literary canon. Its effects are bold, even crude and ugly, but unlike kitsch, which exploits canonical effects (classical or avant-garde) for their prestige value (cf. Eco 1984 [1964]: 65–129, and 1978: 60–8). *Se il sole muore* appears closer to some modern form of folk literature, relying on literacy but stressing the declamatory rhetoric of the speaking voice in its rhythms and intonations. Its effects have often been likened to those of the cinema. This in itself is not particularly illuminating: the conventions of cinema have always been strongly bound up with those of the novel (as well as opera), and much in a venerable classic of Italian narrative literature as unlike *Se il sole muore* as Manzoni's *I promessi sposi* (*The Betrothed*) lends itself to analysis in cinematic terms. But certainly, for Fallaci, the cinema presents a suggestive analogue, and in some ways her work appears systematically cinematic, first and foremost her orchestrated language, which parallels a film's musical score. Close-up and slow-motion, zoom and panning shots, cross-cutting and flashback, set-pieces and fish-eye lens – all these effects are verbally simulated in this work (starting with its opening sequence). Opera also serves as analogue, particularly in the frequently mannered patterning of dialogue, banter and repartee, as also of course in the cadencing of the text as a whole, though radically different from the more experimentally "estranging" use of roughly similar devices in Vittorini's quasi-operatic *Conversazione in Sicilia*. Such pillaging of neighbouring art-forms is not in itself either to be praised or blamed, and is subordinated to a literary design (using "literary" in a value-free sense), but it helps to define Fallaci's individuality as a writer, who, if she writes "blockbusters", does so to no discernible pre-established blueprint, and certainly to no one's but her own.

The blueprint of this book is governed by its "waverings". The small-scale alternations between the traditionalism of Oriana's father and its opposite hinge in large part on her father's role in the Florentine Resistance twenty years earlier. That heroic struggle for freedom and justice stands in Oriana's discourse here (as in all Fallaci's writings) for ethical standards in human behaviour. It also stands for the past as meaningful. Florence, as the foremost embodiment of the Italian Renaissance and a target for airborne destruction during the Second World War, acts as a touchstone of the values of the past and of those who would wipe it out, a touchstone of powerful emotional significance to the two main interlocutors within the text – Oriana and her father – who are passionately attached to their native city. Florence and the events of 1943–5 keep entering the text to delineate the ethical physiognomy of the people whom Oriana encounters. Florence and the Resistance are thus macro-signifiers derived from quasi-folk history, in the sense of lived history preserved in living memory, recalled primarily through the oral medium. Florence and the Resistance contribute to the quasi-folk character of *Se il sole muore*, but also constitute a tacit claim to ethical and cultural authority on the part of Oriana Fallaci in her triple capacity as textual character, narrator and author systematically equivocating between her textual and extratextual status, strenuously labouring to make the boundary between the two disappear.

Let two sets of contrasts suffice to illustrate Fallaci's use of war-time Florence as a litmus test. First come two long interviews in succession with two of the leading US astronauts – Deke Slayton (subsequently appointed to command the moon mission) and John Glenn (Chapters 8 and 10). Slayton's voice has the same timbre as that of Oriana's father, but his discourse is diametrically opposed, being oriented towards the future. Oriana discovers that he had flown bombing raids over Nazi-held Florence, and had quite possibly even been responsible for blasting her off her bicycle as she was carrying soup to her father in prison. Yet she accepts that he was fighting on the same side as they were. In Slayton, the destruction inflicted by the US on Italy is confronted without antagonism, and this acts as a rhetorical move to disarm ultra-nationalist or leftist Italians.

Critique of things and people American abounds in *Se il sole muore*, and the interview with Slayton is followed by one with Alan Shepard, of whom Fallaci paints a full-brush portrait as a "carnivorous plant". But the next interview, with John Glenn, interestingly exploits the symbolic valence of war-time Florence. His face – snub nose, unexplained blushes, and gurgling laughter – reminds her of a tiresome US sergeant nicknamed Ohio whom her father had befriended during the war and to whom he had presented her grandfather's turnip-sized pocket watch. Oriana tackles Glenn on religion and culture, strenuously resisting his charm, and notes incredulously that he speaks passionately while checking his watch. The chapter closes with a nightmare in which Oriana lands with Glenn on another planet identical with present-day earth, at Houston, Texas, where an FBI man is writing "guilty, guilty, guilty" against her name. Oriana turns to Glenn, but: "Glenn went on laughing, laughing, with his beautiful white happy teeth, then he mockingly dangled Grandfather's turnip" (pp. 133–43; 99–106). Ohio and Glenn say and do nothing worse than express American self-assurance, rather engagingly. Yet Oriana's mental associations consign them to the contemptible limbo of the ethically and humanly null. This may or may not be unfair to the individuals involved: the point is that they have been encoded within the moral economy, the symbolic value-system, of Fallaci's book. Yet, within the overall rhetoric of the book, this is another pre-emptive strike. The negative sum in the moral and human balance-sheet of the US astronauts – their insensitivity towards the values of old Italy, their readiness to wipe out past civilization in favour of an apparently uncivilized future – has been deducted in advance, leaving the way clear for a positive accounting of the heroic qualities of other astronauts – Theodore Freeman, Wally Schirra, and Oriana's "brother" Charles, known as "Pete", Conrad.

As Oriana approaches the epiphany of the Saturn launch, another two chapters similarly set up a contrast, involving the symbolic valence of war-time Florence, but this time tilting the suasive balance in favour of the space programme. Chapter 21 (20 in the US edition) is devoted to the interview with the ex-Nazi rocket scientist, Werner Von Braun, and opens with the elusively reminiscent lemon fragrance which he exudes. The chapter's structure is explicit: segments of the interview with Von Braun are systematically cross-cut with the listening Oriana's mental search for the original association of that lemon fragrance, which leads her back to war-time memories of German soldiers who exuded the same fragrance of lemon-scented soap while hunting for her father and capturing two Yugoslav partisans in the Tuscan countryside.

These emotional associations suasively highlight Von Braun's complicity with Nazism (signally in his role as Hitler's leading V-1 and V-2 rocket engineer) and thus undercut his theological justification of the space venture. But this powerful effect of rhetorical suasion turns out to be another case of rhetorical pre-emption. The following chapter describes the meeting with the spacecraft constructor, Ernst Stuhlinger. This opens in the key just established in the Von Braun interview: "in a hearty way he had shot a: 'Goot mornink, Zignorina' at the back of my neck. In a hearty way, but I had shuddered and jerked my head, my arms, the sudden shrinking movement of men when they're shot in the back and seem to get shorter, you know what I mean . . . " (pp. 299; 233). Stuhlinger's German-ness puts him, to start with, in the same sinister category as Von Braun, yet the chapter works to reverse this prejudicial judgement, operating his human and moral rehabilitation, and that of the space enterprise.

Stuhlinger's disarming and unassuming friendliness and tact, in sharp opposition to Von Braun's pompousness, his cordial hospitality and the festive informality of his family life (echoing Bradbury's), his poetic perception of science and of the moon, his parting gift to Oriana of his favourite seashell out of his collection – all these exemplify the participant observer–narrator's avowedly subjective novelistic construction of character sub-ordinated to a highly visible value-system which reduces to a minimum the distance between the narrated and narrating "Oriana" and the authoritatively authorial Fallaci. The reader is led by the nose and left little autonomy in the face of the categorical imperative delivered ready-made by the tight narrative contract established between the various Fallacis. Other voices – even that of Oriana's father – are drowned out. The book's discursive hierarchy privileges the composite Oriana Fallaci voice and prejudices genuine dialogism – the open-ended rendering of conflicting and problematical discourses. The postulated Author delivers a single truth from on high, fore-closing alternatives, amendments, nuances, dictating the very terms of the debate towards a predetermined outcome. The rhetoric of freedom in *Se il sole muore* has an authoritarian bent.

That this problem is so marked in Fallaci's works is a tribute to the seriousness of her endeavour and a mark of its difficulty. Her books embody the converse of Harpham's analysis of Conrad's self-defeating attempt at ethically annihilating anarchism in *The Secret Agent*. Fiction itself turns out to be uncontrollably anarchistic, or at least subversive of the order which the author of (outside) the text purports to be defending (Harpham 1992). Fallaci champions individualistic freedom against repressive or authoritarian systems but uses a somewhat authoritarian system to do so. This in turn leads to the reflection that her book does after all tacitly subscribe to "the System" – a capitalist order that justifies itself (in rivalry with a Soviet order) by its achievements in space. To propose positive values – whether of order or freedom, ethics or aesthetics – in fiction (or even "faction") is to put them at risk, to admit their supplements. To explore the internal problematic of such values – as certain of Fallaci's works do – is more productive. Fiction writers have been more successful in implying a positive by displaying a negative: the individual's responsibility in history emerges strongly from Lampedusa's study of cowardice and betrayal in *Il gattopardo* (*The Leopard*) and from Pavese's in *La casa in collina* (*The house on the hill*); truth to oneself and self-knowledge emerge most clearly from a study in equivocation and self-deception such as Svevo's *La coscienza di Zeno* (*Confessions of Zeno*). Significantly, these are all virtual first-person essays in self-accusation or self-examination predicated on the essential irony of narrative fiction – that the protagonist–narrator–author is really a character only as reliable as the reader judges her or him to be. In *Se il sole muore* such total denuding of the self does not occur. Fiction's central irony is not mobilized.

What People?

Se il sole muore has some naïveties (particularly its title), but it is not a naïve text (except perhaps in the sense of "naïve" art, bordering on folk art). At the end of Chapter 6, describing the huge automated Garrett complex, the character Oriana expresses her awareness of the elusiveness of freedom, the difficulty of not joining the herd of automata into which industrial civilization tends to turn people, and feels she is rapidly turning into one of them. "The System" is invoked repeatedly in the course of the book as something faceless, impersonal, and is represented in the tentacular organization of NASA itself and in the gigantism of its products. Modern corporatism is indeed one of the principal players in this book, and a witty US review commends Fallaci (not quite justly) for her presentation of Oriana as a "Model 1966 Alice" probing through layer after layer of labyrinthine bureaucracy only to find that there is nothing at the centre of it all (Hamilton-Heaton 1966).

Fallaci does not present this corporate character, the System, in terms of ownership of the means of production or power-relationships – though the talismanic character Sally Gates, in Chapter 26 (Chapter 25 of the US version), reveals to a dumb-founded Oriana that the Moon programme is a huge industrial and commercial enterprise (pp. 338, 350; 267, 276) – but in terms of its products: the wonders of modern technology and the debasement of taste, the faceless individuals and the faceless masses who represent it. The latter appear in Chapters 18 and 27 of the Italian edition respectively as the "elephants" – meaning ordinary Americans – who throng the New York Trade Fair, and as the unspeakable American *mamme* whose hostile disapproval confronts Oriana and her soul-sister Sally Gates on Mother's Day. These two chapters have disappeared from the English-language edition. In the original Italian they embody the unspoken para-dox of Fallaci's anti-popular populism, which is contemptuous of the mass of people.

Fallaci's text counterposes against the faceless System and the faceless bureaucrats and the faceless masses who sustain it the miraculous survival of individual heroism, using the unstated parallelism with anti-Fascist fighters like her father, who resisted the oppression of an earlier System: "you used to risk your life for the great illusion you call freedom" (pp. 181; 138). The Resistance is the era of Oriana's childhood heroes, the subject of a book it proved impossible to write, because, when she saw them again seventeen years after that heroic moment, she found them aged and dejected, their heroism absorbed and neutralized by a new system, just as she now finds that the confident astronauts she had met a year before had already turned into greying bureaucrats of the space programme: she therefore turns to her "brand-new heroes" (pp. 342–3; 270–1).

By this logic, "brand-new heroes" are doomed to become age-ing ex-heroes in less than a year. And there is another problem with heroic individualism. Talking to the science columnist Willy

Ley in New York, Oriana had protested that his view of the future would abolish "I" for "we" and the individual in favour of the group. Ley concurs that future achievement can only be collective (pp. 244; 189). Later in the book, after interviewing her new astronaut heroes and brothers and defining them and a few other kindred spirits, the "Turtles", as among the elect, in contradistinction to "the System", Oriana hears a television lecture on heroism in the contemporary world. This defines the solitary, individual hero as a rebel, no longer appropriate to a world where only collective heroism is possible. And indeed, Oriana's heroic individualism is transmuted into group heroism: she herself is admitted to the Turtles as "Oriano", and "we" rather than "I" becomes the dominant pronoun (Chapter 26; Chapter 25). Brotherhood, under the symbolic new paternity of the familial Bradbury and Stuhlinger, is the hard-won prize of "Oriano"'s quest. This privileged company – a sort of anti-System within the System – engages in astral whimsy about drive-ins in space selling rootbeer, their flippant counter-ethos anticipating the hilariously hair-raising fantasies of *The Hitch Hiker's Guide to the Galaxy*. From the ruins of the myth of a lonely heroic individualism (historically inapplicable even to the organized group struggle of the Resistance, and perhaps also to the epic Bronze Age warfare of the *Iliad*), Fallaci conjures up a new heroic aristocracy of space explorers. The heroic chrysm, applied in the inordinately suspenseful final chapter, is the collective braving of death (as Theodore Freeman does in order to avoiding crash-landing amid dwelling-houses).

Milani's remarks on the style of *Niente e così sia* are relevant to a consideration of the value-system of *Se il sole muore*: "It is an attempt at modernizing the language which, however, involves, not a stylistic heightening, as might perhaps have been intended, but a slumping down to the level of advertising language . . .". Milani sees in Fallaci "a journalistic technique typical of the pulp magazine writer but often also to be found in contemporary novels and essayistic writing . . . for instance the 'mysterious' opening . . . Just the opposite, in fact, to the five-point rule of journalistic reporting – who? where? when? how? why?" As well as the slow-motion technique of action-movies, she remarks on the paratactic syntax, with accompanying punctuation and rhythm (Milani 1971). These comments imply a standard of literariness which excludes Fallaci's writing as belonging neither to traditional nor to avant-garde modes of the "literary". This ignores Fallaci's rejection of fixed borders of literariness. Milani demonstrates systematic stylistic differences between Fallaci's reports from Vietnam as published in *L'Europeo* and the accounts of the same episodes as published in the book and shows that they amount to a literary stylization on Fallaci's part, but condemns this stylization as literary kitsch. Much of Milani's analysis, however, demonstrates not kitschiness (defined by Eco as the exploitation for mass consumption of stylemes derived from classical or avant-garde "high" literature (1984 [1964]: 65–129, and 1978: 60–8)), but what I have suggested above is a deliberately demotic stylization – that is, attempts at a "low" folk or popular mode of expression which discriminates between certain folk and others.

The vague kinship of *Se il sole muore* with *The Hitch Hiker's Guide to the Galaxy* points up its claims to belonging to the folk-literature of a literate age. If such a thing existed, or could be properly defined (Hašek's *Good Soldier Švejk*, Silone's *Fontamara* and Guareschi's *Don Camillo* might mark areas of its domain), strong effects, bold lines and structures, marked and often repetitive patterning, elements of the farcical, the caricature, the preposterous, overtones of epic that carry historic happenings beyond the calendar of mere chronicle and lend a timeless quality to the fleeting moment, and traces of the demotic speaking voice – all discernible in Fallaci's book – might characterize it and link it to the oral folk-literature of the past. Most English translations of Fallaci's texts, as of the others mentioned (until Cecil Parrott's wonderful translation of *The Good Soldier Švejk*), have consistently understated their quasi-oral, populist character.

These characteristics which I have mentioned mark out Fallaci's book from less populist treatments of the theme. Mailer's *Of a Fire on the Moon* (1970), a reportage on the first moon landing, has striking similarities with *Se il sole muore*. Mailer casts himself as the third-person narrator Aquarius, in a flimsy effort to establish a distance between his writing and his observing selves, but attributes to Aquarius the same doubts that beset Oriana: "he hardly knew whether the Space Program was the noblest expression of the Twentieth Century or the quintessential statement of our fundamental insanity" (Mailer 1970: 15). Having set himself up as moral and aesthetic investigator, he ends with a tentative affirmation not far removed from Oriana's own drift: "Yes, we might have to go out into space until the mystery of new discovery would force us to regard the world once again as poets, behold it as savages who knew that if the universe was a lock, its key was metaphor rather than measure" (1970: 471). *En route*, he emits judgements against the System that are politically more pointed and ethically more categorical, but less novelistically articulated, than Fallaci's: "the corporate son of the old capitalist . . . speaks of a society of reason and tells lies every time he opens his mouth. The more simple and ubiquitous is his commodity, the greater are his lies" (pp. 183–5). But the "high" literariness of this idiom in contrast with the "low" literariness of Oriana's domestic dialogue with her father is immediately evident, and the dialogic element, with the attendant drama of its encounters, is almost completely absent, as is the quest. Mailer's literary reportage is here generally remote from the novelistic, and even more remote from the elements of modern folk-epic which are (perhaps dimly) discernible in Fallaci's work. His *non*-description and *non*-characterization of "Deke" Slayton (p. 325), in contrast to Fallaci's bold, surprising, and effective dramatization, is illustration enough.

Tom Wolfe's documentary novel of the earlier years of the space programme, *The Right Stuff* (1979), indicates in its title the heroism and *esprit de corps* that largely animates Fallaci's text, the "right stuff" being, in fact, the quiet courage, comradeship and determination needed to bring the astral enterprise to fruition. In Wolfe's book, however, literary integrity is assured. The novelistic metamorphosis is complete. Everything is reduced to "omniscient" third-person narrative: on the one hand the personal lives and relationships of the astronauts as cosmic and utterly mundane soap opera punctuated by ghastly death; on the other hand the race between the United States and its Soviet rivals. The values and ethos of the United States and its space effort are very fully captured, but it is arguable whether Wolfe achieves greater penetration and comprehensiveness than Fallaci in his own domain, which is only a part of her considerably different and broader discursive universe. Alan Shepard and Deke Slayton's *Moon Shot* (1994) is a long retrospective of material similar to Wolfe's centred on the story of how NASA and its men worked up over the years to their successful moon landing.

Fallaci wrote a straightforward international reportage on that event which was republished in book form as *Quel giorno sulla luna* (1970; "That Day on the Moon", not translated into English) in a school edition with copious explanatory notes. The information is highly professional and largely scientific in content and presentation. The voice is that of the well-known journalist Oriana Fallaci cordially addressing her familiar readership via the high-circulation weekly, *L'Europeo*. It is a critical voice, mercilessly castigating the lacklustre personalities of the astronauts, playing down the element of heroism, exposing the unsolved scientific problems and risks of the enterprise, and questioning the values at stake in it. Its literary stance is remote from that of *Se il sole muore* – perhaps at zero. As much as a rejection of the Apollo moon mission, *Quel giorno sulla luna* reads like a rejection of *Se il sole muore*. In between had come Vietnam.

8

To Vietnam and Back: "Niente e così sia" (1969)

Framing Atrocities

... Elisabetta huddles up to me in bed, tiny, defenseless, happy. "The moon, look at the moon!" A spaceship with three men on board is orbiting the moon, and others will soon land there to extend the frontiers of our treachery and our pain: look at it, there on the television screen. I used to love the moon, and envy those who would go there. But now that I look at it, so gray and empty and with nothing good or evil alive upon it, already exploited to make us forget the sorrow and the shame we have here, to distract us from ourselves, I remember what you said, François: "The moon is a dream for those who have no dreams." (pp. 354; 319)[1]

So, ending her account of her experience of Vietnam, Oriana bids farewell to her "dream" of a fellowship of adventurers which had been so hard earned by the quest of *Se il sole muore*. Her new work is the negation and the converse of the one before.

This time, the second-person address does not structure the book's entire discourse but frames it within an interrogation. Oriana's small sister Elisabetta, not yet five, asks her at the outset: "Life, what is it?", providing the cue for Oriana to record and then write up her war diary in an attempt to resolve the "incoherence" of human life (pp. 7, 9; 1, 3). But, as the above opening quotation shows, Oriana's real dialogue is with François Pelou, then Saigon head of Agence France Presse, to whom the book is dedicated. François is a recurring presence and a major actor throughout the narrative, and the privileged voice – as here

---

1. O. Fallaci, *Niente e così sia*, Milan, Rizzoli, 1969. English translation by Isabel Quigly, London, Michael Joseph, 1972, under the title *Nothing and Amen*, and New York, Doubleday, 1972, under the title *Nothing and So Be It*. Quotations in English are from this translation. Page references are to the original and to the London edition.

– that articulates its concepts. Dated diary entries govern the text's structure, but are pitched in the speaking voice (and Milani's critique of the stylization of the narrative demonstrates this (Milani 1971)). Fallaci's diary is, characteristically, again hospitable to other voices, while imperiously subordinating them to its own discursive hierarchy and conceptual universe.

This discursive hierarchy is the result of a particular elaboration. Each chapter opens with retrospective scene-setting and reflection, using the past tense, and then follows with the present-tense dated diary entries. But these are not the original annotations: they are worked up from the neatly written little black notebooks referred to at the start of Chapter 6 (and available for inspection in the Mugar Library of Boston University). The diaristic basis of the text is authentic. Its diaristic immediacy is not: it is the essential literary fiction of the book, the product of the Fallaci who has come out of the Vietnam experience and given it a literary shape, not the unrehearsed impressions of the Oriana who was living that experience moment by moment, and whom the author can no longer reach. The discursive transmission becomes highly nuanced and extended: from the participant observer Oriana to the Oriana taking notes in her little black notebooks, to the Oriana Fallaci filling out those diary entries within a narrative which includes retrospectively and prospectively connective and reflective passages. Talking of Oriana's loss of nerve in refusing to take the plane to beleaguered Khe San, the reflecting Fallaci writes: "Today I congratulate myself on my wisdom. But then I didn't call it wisdom, I called it cowardice. And I despised myself. I was mad" (pp. 172–3; 151–2). The raw diary is conscripted into the service of a novelistic argument, a narrative progress.

The most evident instance of this comes at the cardinal point of the book, the seventh chapter. Its opening changes radically in the English version as compared to the Italian. The Italian volume opens with a preface presenting the massacre by US troops of the occupants of My Lai – exclusively women, children and old folks (cf. Bilton and Sim 1992). This preface mirrors the account of another massacre which closes the book – that of protesting students by the Mexican military in Mexico City just before the opening there of the Olympic Games. In the Italian version, the two massacres thus frame the entire book, producing a powerful rhetorical effect of suasion towards the text (commanding attention) and towards the argument (inducing reflection).

In the English version, this framing effect is lost. The My Lai account, abbreviated and carefully integrated into the book's argument, is shifted to the opening of Chapter 7. This produces an instructively different articulation of Fallaci's discursive strategy. In the Italian, these pages (pp. 212–13) give an explanation of Fallaci's initial diaristic intentions and of Vietnam as, initially, representative of war in general. Against this, she pits the destabilizing effect of François Pelou's *indipendenza ideologica* amounting to paradox, and his insistence that the generally reviled General Loan and Marshal Ky spoke and acted much more honestly and representatively for Vietnam than they were given credit for. Fallaci then announces her forthcoming interviews with the two leaders, and, in a more far-reaching prolepsis, defines them as: "a foretaste of what I was to understand later on, on my third tour of duty, when François made me read Pascal and what he has to say about men" (p. 213, my translation). Fallaci thus underscores Oriana's tardy learning process just when she is suspended between her two monumental acts of "cowardice". She has flunked a visit to the death-trap at Khe San, and now is interested only in choosing an orphaned child for adoption. She is captivated by a three-year-old girl, and especially by the girl's eyes. On returning to the orphanage to institute adoption procedures, she discovers that the girl has been moved elsewhere, and that she is totally blind. Oriana, to her own profound shame, flunks again. She confesses: "Yes, war does something good: it reveals us to ourselves" (pp. 234; 205).

In the English version, the proleptic account of how Pelou and Pascal were to transform her outlook is omitted. My Lai intervenes instead, in its exact chronological location, linking Oriana's two acts of pusillanimity. Both versions stress that by no means all US citizens share in complicity with the guilt for My Lai and other US atrocities (cf. Bilton and Sim 1992; Gatt-Rutter and Prenzler, forthcoming), and that there is no US monopoly in atrocity. The English version recruits the reader into sharing in Fallaci's self-discovery and retrospective learning no longer as an isolated personal experience but as one shared by humanity in general.

Interview with Vietnam

Fallaci interviews the Vietnam war through a multiplicity of encounters, ranging from formal full-length interviews – sometimes in two instalments – as with the interrogator, Captain Pham Quant Tan, his Vietcong captive, Nguyen Van Sam, the Chief of Police, General Loan, and Vice-President Cao Ky – to ongoing situations of all sorts: the Saigon journalist milieu, including Vietnamese service staff; Buddhist temples; orphanages; American embassy officialdom (with another recurrent presence in the person of Barry Zorthian); and numerous air or ground battlefront experiences (including a dive-bombing raid) involving acquaintance with combat personnel and Catholic priests: a typically Fallacian "chorus" of other people's voices (cf. Frangipane 1970).

Aricò (1990a) has demonstrated Fallaci's use once again of Tom Wolfe's New Journalism categories of novelistic techniques in *Niente e cosí sia*: scene-by-scene construction; dialogue (which focuses on psychological characterization); another person's viewpoint (Pelou being the privileged eyewitness, and the diaries of a Vietcong and of a North Vietnamese soldier providing the most clear-cut shifts in perspective); and "social autopsy" – selectively diagnostic physical descriptions of persons and personal effects, properties or milieux. This analysis, however, omits the dominant of Oriana's diary, and another of Wolfe's categories – her own dual role as character and narrator, as participant observer, as Orwellian "shock-absorber of the bourgeoisie", or as the magnetic tape on which the experience of Vietnam is imprinted (Guiducci 1970). What dominates the discourse, once again, is Fallaci's voice, which filters, adjudicates, and ranks according to her moral hierarchy all the other voices which are co-opted into the text – including Oriana's.

Milani defines the style of the volume, as compared with the journalistic dispatches published in *L'Europeo*, as oratorical dialogue marked by an "omnipresent *tu* (thou, you)" which is really "I" (Milani 1971: 49). This needs some refinement. Many linguistic markers of the dialogue form are indeed present: iterative patterning, syntactic simplification, colloquial touches in lexis and phonology, direct forms of address like the rhetorical question, the use of the first person and related deictics. This amounts, once again, to the tone and rhetoric of the speaking voice. But the second-person address is hardly ever used (other than in dialogues embedded within the narrative), and almost exclusively at the start and end of the narrative, to address Elisabetta or François, and in one or two other striking instances. The narration is addressed to an implied thou, and eschews impersonality, but this implied thou is not identified, and in this respect *Niente e cosí sia* differs sharply from *Se il sole muore*, *Lettera a un bambino mai nato* and *Un uomo*. As an open diary, *Niente e cosí sia* is addressed by the author–narrator in the first place to herself – and in this sense the implied "thou" can only be "I" – and secondly to her readership, who are tacitly invited to eavesdrop on her self-communings like a theatre audience, which is supposedly "not there", listening from the auditorium to a soliloquy on stage. *Niente e cosí sia* is Fallaci's most confessional text.

The diary-confession is a quest: a quest to resolve that incoherence opened up by Elisabetta's question; but also another adventurous quest, this time into the experience of war, another search for brothers – whether among Vietcong or GIs or fellow-journalists or Buddhists – akin to that which had led her to the astronauts. It is conducted with the same narrative dynamic as Fallaci's other reportage quests: the bewildering incoherence of reality is encountered in a sequence of experiences which elude interpretation and have little logical connection between them, in a progression towards all-embracing negativity, as one delusion after another evaporates, until at last a painful new wisdom emerges out of this disillusioned negativity.

There is thus what Aricò (1986a) calls a "discovery of truth". Oriana does arrive at some sort of understanding of the nightmare of Vietnam. These truth-claims, as Aricò points out, include the discovery that the Vietcong are not the spotlessly noble fighters for *giustizia e libertà*, a reincarnation of an idealized Italian Resistance (pp. 31–2, 261; 24, 232), but that they also massacre civilians and shoot journalists; that the Americans and their Vietnamese allies, even the apparently abominable Loan, are as human as their enemies and as capable of heroism and nobility; and that Pascal, the seventeenth-century apologist for Christianity against the arguments of sceptics and humanists, was right in affirming that true and false are always inextricably confused in human discourse, just as human beings are an inextricable confusion of angel and beast.

But it is not merely a case of Fallaci's becoming less "anti-American" and "more mature". Certainly, the book displays an abstract pre-Rawlsian moralism and a delusion of political agnosticism or impartiality. Oriana's sympathies go to a poverty-stricken peasant people in their struggle against the powerful foreigners on their soil, but she does not emerge here as a Lukácsian world-historical waverer, caught in a clear-cut opposition between old and new – peasant society and capitalism, or capitalism and socialist new order. This book's emotional and experiential resolution is not the same as mental clarity. Craig and Egan point out what we may call the "eyewitness fallacy" which belies the truism "I know because I was there": ". . . it is exactly the power of the finest artist to be the most wholly embroiled. It is not a simple matter of who was there and who was not" (1979: 260). Seriousness of personal involvement, more than firsthand reportage, is what counts, though the two reinforce one another.

Despite the overwhelming impact of the documentary reportage, it is the confessional element in *Niente e cosí sia* that is paradigmatic, and that makes Oriana truly the book's protagonist. She confesses her infatuation with war as "the natural habitat of heroism" (pp. 71–2; 61–2), an infatuation which has been widespread and widely commented on – for instance, with regard to the Great War – and displayed in literature. Philip Toynbee, remarking on "the experience of rejoicing in the sublime terror of risking and inflicting death" and on "war's terrible fascination" and "overpowering seduction", observes that "it is not only non-combatants who are seduced by war". "How are men", he asks, "to rid themselves of this repulsive attraction?" (Toynbee 1980 on Wohl 1980). Fallaci's book represents an exorcism of this "sickly glamour" in the person of Oriana.

Chapter 4 opens with Oriana back in New York, having learned from her first Vietnam assignment "to love the miracle of having been born". But she quickly rebuts the implication of Graham Greene's remark that war consists mostly of passive waiting. Her frenetically busy but predictable life in New York is incomparably more tedious than any amount of waiting in Saigon, where the unexpected may happen at any time, where you are not merely among a detached audience, but part of the show, part of the heroic atmosphere. As always with Fallaci,

Oriana's reflections and moods have intense narrative mobility. They are more a matter of "showing" rather than "telling". And in this instance they are overtaken by the astounding news of the Vietcong's massive Tet offensive. The war drags her like a magnet away from the humdrum business of normal living.

But Oriana's narrative pendulum quickly swings back to knock out the escape from boredom as a justification for this voyeuristic attraction of war, questioning her professional stake as a journalist in purveying the voyeuristic experience to a safely remote public. Early in Chapter 6, Oriana rejects this justification as *squallido*, and she subsequently admits that the war dead are "the goods I sell" (pp. 193; 170). Malcolm Lowry through one of his characters in *Under the Volcano* had foreshadowed this development: "In the war to come correspondents would assume unheard of importance, plunging through flame to feed the public its little gobbets of dehydrated excrement" (Lowry 1963 [1947]: 157; quoted in Craig and Egan 1979: 249). The Vietnam War brought this issue to a head. Phillip Knightley, in his anthology of war reportage, entitled *The First Casualty*, declares: "Vietnam stands out, for it was there that correspondents began seriously to question the ethics of their business." He entitles one section of his anthology "War is fun", and quotes Nora Ephron: ". . . the awful truth is that for correspondents war is not hell. It is fun" (1975: 408).

Oriana's self-criticism progresses through the book towards dissociation from the war. On her third assignment in Vietnam, she speculates with regard to a new correspondent in Saigon that he may be after what she had once been after - "the fascination of war, the satisfaction of curiosity" (pp. 245; 217). And she returns with revulsion later to the metaphor of war as theatrical spectacle with the Westerners (*i bianchi*) in Saigon gathering in the evenings at the Hotel Caravelle for a grandstand view of dive-bombing raids on the poor quarters of Saigon as they sip their whiskies or hot chocolate, like rich Romans watching gladiators in the Colosseum: so that Oriana ends by reciting her parody of the Lord's Prayer ("give us this day our daily massacre"), which provides a leitmotiv of the book, as well as its title and closing line, and by cabling her paper that she won't send any more stories from Vietnam (pp. 268–9, 275; 239–40, 245–6). Again, the narrative articulation is strong: the swing of the emotional pendulum against humanity's inhumanity precipitates her departure from Vietnam and brings her tale to within one last major step from its close.

Vietnam Truths

Despite the massive media exposure which the US involvement in Vietnam received, truth was still a casualty of that war. Martha Gellhorn was refused permission to return to Vietnam as a result of her embarrassing reports on the US role there (Knightley 1975: 390; cf. Gellhorn 1993). This did not happen to Fallaci, though threateningly hinted at by Barry Zorthian; but she refers to the notoriously prolonged suppression of news of the My Lai massacre.

Nevertheless, Vietnam war journalism played a key truth-telling role. Nayar commends the British novelist Graham Greene's presentation of Alden Pyle, the "quiet American" of his 1956 Vietnam novel's title, as suggesting that "setting out to kill people for political motives in a foreign country, without much knowledge of what is going on there, is not innocent: belief in your own innocence is not the thing itself". Nayar further observes that US literary treatments of Vietnam, responding to the immediacy of personal experience, have been strikingly unselfcritical, in the mode of Alden Pyle, while "The best American journalism of the Vietnam war is famous for its sharp probing of US *Realpolitik*, and its willingness to present the Vietnam side of the story"; this is in sharp distinction from "the view we get from fiction and memoirs about the war by American combatants", for whom "the unique horror of the war lay in Vietnam itself, not in the American project there". Nayar sums up: "Pyle returns as Kurtz [of Conrad's *Heart of Darkness*], a way of evading blame while apparently accepting it" (Nayar 1993).

Fallaci, too, errs on the side of the novelistic or the memorialistic (that is, on the side of the experiential), looking away from the political to the personal immediacy of the situation, attempting to define a human essence, the meaning of life, through the lived moment. Despite her generic "anti-Americanism", she presents nothing as sharply critical of callous US "high technology" brutality towards the Vietnamese (with little distinction between friends, enemies, or neutrals,

combatants and civilians) and accompanying cynical hypocrisy
as appears in American anthologies by Wolfe and Johnson (1973)
and Mills (1974), and she fails to notice characteristics such as
those observed by Jason (1990) in his "Sexism and Racism in
Vietnam War Fiction".

Oriana admits her confusion about Vietnam. Chapter 6 ends:
"God, what a madhouse. War is a madhouse." And Chapter 7
begins, addressing a mysterious, absolute "thou" (who can
hardly be the four-year-old Elisabetta, but who may be an absent
God, the reader) – "Tu sai" – in two successive sentences, omitted
in the English: ". . . this diary is only an attempt to document a
single experience, it doesn't want to explain the bloodthirsty
madness of the war in Vietnam", Vietnam having been chosen as
a representative "tragedy", a war like any other war. Her interviews with reviled personalities like Loan and Ky teach her that
good and evil are never unmixed in any individual (pp. 211–13;
187, 190, 197). In the English version, this avowal is sand-
wiched in between a discussion of the My Lai massacre and
the agonizing issues which it raises, yet responsibility is
systematically personalized rather than politicized. Virtually
every chapter ends with an admission of confusion and
uncertainty. The confusion and uncertainty of the human mind is
the central message of the book's privileged intertextual authority, Pascal's *Pensées*. Fallaci's self-critical presentation of
Oriana's journalistic experience in Vietnam corresponds to the
devastating analysis of the journalistic "culture" of war correspondents in El Salvador by Pedelty (1995).

Oriana's political agnosticism about Vietnam was clearly
deliberate avoidance. The nakedness of US power politics was
evident to many US and other journalists (Tomalin 1966 in Wolfe
and Johnson 1973, and Halberstam, Schell, Breslin, and Duncan
in Mills 1974). Patriotic Americans fighting in Vietnam and
believing in their own cause, such as Sheehan (*A Bright Shining
Lie* 1988) found themselves constrained to turn against it, and
scholarly histories, from as early as Frances Fitzgerald's *Fire in the
Lake* (1972) to Joseph Amter's *Vietnam Verdict: A Citizen's History*
(1982) and Stanley Karnow's *Vietnam: A History* (1983), produced
an indictment of US war policy which its defenders could not
convincingly counter.

Oriana plausibly pleads being lost in the political labyrinth,
but she sows contrary evidence in her text. She reports in

Chapter 2 discovering that François Pelou – her mentor in the ways of men, war and Vietnam – is the François Perrin mentioned in Han Suyin's *A Many-Splendoured Thing*. Oriana searches the book for a mention, and finds it in one of Mark Elliott's letters from the Korean War (pp. 48; 39; cf. Han 1952: 358–74), where Perrin/Pelou remarks to Elliott on the soldiers on the Western side wanting to know what they are fighting and dying for. Oriana has thus re-read Elliott's letters and knows that they are an indictment of US involvement and behaviour in Korea (including indiscriminate, and implicitly racist, aerial bombardment) that in many respects matches the US involvement in Vietnam fifteen or twenty years later. Fallaci therefore consciously abstracts ethical judgement from political analysis. Here lie the difficulties, but also the achievement, of her book.

Much of the narrative and inserted discourse – interviews, diaries of captured Vietcong and North Vietnamese, eyewitness accounts of Buddhist monks burning themselves to death, battlefront encounters and conversations – is directed towards Oriana's judgements on individuals in the face of death, judgements expressed in the calculus of heroism. One case, crisply narrated mainly through dialogue (pp. 181–5; 161–3), is particularly interesting: the soldier Sanford Collins feigns blindness after the battle for Hué and tells Oriana a tear-jerker tale of family tragedy. The discovery of Sanford's deception, the supposed war hero's fall from grace, shakes the "religion of man" which Oriana is painfully trying to build out of the horrors of war: "Now I'm trying to get back to Hué, alone. I feel so much alone, because Sanford Collins has reminded me that men are ugly."

That absolute-sounding judgement is in fact self-characterization by Oriana, strictly articulated in terms of her essential and ever-on-the-move narrative business of trying to come to terms with life, death, and humanity. The judgement itself is at odds with much that has already been presented regarding the widespread incomprehension among the US forces about the meaning of the war, their unwillingness to be a part of it, and their sense that it is the less privileged that are compelled to risk their lives. The judgement is also at odds with the book's final rejection of war and killing as obscene in themselves, though an unavoidable part of mankind's bestial component, and – as we shall see – equally at odds with the book's final rejection of the US intervention in Vietnam. The book's overall logic invites a re-reading of Sanford's cowardice as being a perfectly justifiable attempt at self-preservation and a morally coherent response to the obscenity of war, like that of Joseph Heller's Yossarian in *Catch 22* or Jaroslav Hašek's Švejk: abstention, escape.

Oriana's obsession with heroism reaches its culmination and reversal on the 25th of May, after she has been exposed once more to the horrors of front-line combat at Dak To, and to Pascal's corrosive critique of humanism and the modernist project, and after she has learned from Pelou about one of the most heinous products of human ingenuity, the M16 bullet, which she develops as an emblem of human murderousness, the poetry of evil, in a long passage (pp. 322–5; 289–91), and which figures again prominently in *Un uomo* and *Insciallah*.

Yet, after her faith in humanity has been so systematically demolished, that same evening, Pelou reopens the argument about heroism: "'This little country has given us too much, it's given us the awareness of being men . . . what we say against war is all very well, but we shouldn't spit too much on something called "heroism".'" Recapitulating the most striking aspects of the crazy-seeming courage of "'this little country that has fought and is still fighting against the strongest army in the world'" and that "'almost makes you accept war. Because it's the only people in the world that are fighting for their freedom today,'" he concludes: "'Of course I shall miss Vietnam: it's the most heroic battlefield of all time and you can't live without heroism.'"

Oriana resists this: "For a long period of my life I was sick [i.e., infected] with heroism, and here in Vietnam I was stricken with a new attack of it; but now I've sworn to myself that I'll give it up. Because if you admit heroism you've got to admit war. And I mustn't, I can't, I won't admit war" (pp. 328; 294). Heroism and war are indeed all too closely and falsely linked, and Oriana's attempt at exorcism is understandable. But Pelou insinuates that Vietnam is the wrong place to attempt such an exorcism, which is tantamount to abandoning the Vietnamese to their fate. The political question implicitly keeps coming back in. Is evil to be resisted? If it is, then it must first be identified, and ethics becomes political and polemical. Chapter 10 ends with Oriana departing from Vietnam as confused and uncertain as she has been every time her pendulum has reached the end of its arc and lingered motionless for one instant before swinging back the other way. Mental confusion and uncertainty are as programmatic and as radical in *Niente e così sia* as they were in *Se il sole muore* and as they are to be again in *Lettera a un bambino mai nato*.

But the pendulum makes one final swing, no longer in Vietnam, but in the five-hour massacre of protesting students and other citizens in Mexico City on 2 October 1968, in which hundreds are gunned down, and in which Oriana herself gets three bullets in the back and thigh.

Those bullets inscribe the rhetoric of freedom on the body of Oriana Fallaci, the unanswerable rhetoric which she had so far resisted: "this isn't war and they put bits of metal into you just the same ... the Vietcong are right – you've got to fight even if you make mistakes, even if you have to sacrifice innocent people ... it's the price of the dream ... the point is to look for what's right ... and then what's important isn't dying but dying on the right side, and I'm dying on the right side ..." (pp. 344–5; 310). In "the well of truth" (pp. 343; 309) Oriana Fallaci has lost her fear and has regained certainty, love for her fellow human beings, and an absurd love of life, which will illuminate, despite all her errors and contradictions, her following works, and, retrospectively, her preceding ones. She has gone through the door that leads from ethics into politics. She has taken sides.

This does not mean that any problems have been solved, but that the way of stating them has changed. The political gain is slight. Oriana goes no further than dividing the world in two – those who are for Power and those who are against it. Power is not analysed or understood. Thus, of the authors of the Mexico City massacre, as of all those engaged in the manufacture of the M16 bullet, she points out that they included working-class people ("figli del popolo"), who were thus complicit in the slaughter of other working-class people: "Those who killed these sons of the people on the evening of October 18, 1968, weren't they sons of the people themselves?" (pp. 342; 308).[2] Fallaci's

2. Fallaci's Italian text consistently gives the date of the massacre in the Plaza de las Tres Culturas as Wednesday, 2 October (pp. 334, 342). This is confirmed by her original report in *L'Europeo* of 17 October (O. Fallaci 1968a). It is unclear why the English translation of the book consistently gives the date as Tuesday, 18 October (pp. 300, 308). The *New Encyclopaedia Britannica* (15th edition, 1974–92) does not mention the massacre in its sanitized summary of Mexican history.

simplistic anti-Marxism and anti-Leftism takes Marxism and Leftism to be equally simplistic, mistaking class as an essence rather than a structure.

The decisive but inarticulate rhetoric of those bullets cutting their message through Oriana's flesh gets translated into a textual rhetoric and acquires a shape. The extratextual authority of Oriana's wounds is converted into text, in which her reflections on "figli del popolo" slaughtering their own kind are balanced by the image of the white-gloved and white-shirted élite "Olympia" police battalion who pin down the crowd to be machine-gunned by the army gunships. Fallaci's syntax, in the dozen pages covering the episode, produces crescendos worthy of a symphonic finale, forging a Manichaean opposition of heroes and anti-heroes as the hideous epiphany of an eternal struggle between good and evil to which there is no conceivable alternative, except reportage, the rhetoric of freedom, suasion towards the witnessed scenario and its projected values. This may not be enough for you or me, but the meticulous account of the horrendous slaughter itself and of its aftermath of torture and heroic endurance or limp betrayal shatters the precious and fragile diaphragm of literariness and braves the aesthetic hazards of what Craig and Egan (1979) have called "extreme situations".

The essential rhetoric reveals itself in ending a book on Vietnam with a culminating passage set in Mexico City. But the charge of "protagonismo" so often levelled against Fallaci is misplaced. The real subject of the book, the real text, was always Fallaci's prior self, called Oriana, and her heroic longings. She was always bound to come, sooner or later, between those bullets and the reader. That she did so when she least expected it makes their rhetoric, and hers, all the more powerful.

Part V

Mediterranean

9

Alekos – A Greek Tragedy: "Un uomo" (1979)

J'accuse

Those bullets in the Plaza de las Tres Culturas, and their textual effects, enshrined Fallaci as one of the people of the heady year, 1968, the year of the worldwide outbreak of people power that was to achieve ever more numerous successes over the next quarter of a century, from Iran and the Philippines to Moscow, Prague and Berlin, challenging the tyrannical logic of the Cold War. *Un uomo (A Man)*[1] carries Fallaci's protest against that logic into Mediterranean Europe and into individual existence, and opens with a colossal image of the People as an octopus with a million arms, a huge river of fleece made of millions of sheeplike humans from all over the Greek mainland and islands.

Un uomo, in its most concrete and immediate guise, is the meticulous reconstruction of an apparent political murder which was never subjected to satisfactory judicial process, and was thereby tacitly sanctioned by the State and its foreign friends and allies (cf. Andrews 1980). Fallaci's book thus indicts the political system as such, both Greek and international. This accusation has never been seriously addressed in literary analyses of the text (even in Pattavina's lengthy "saggio politico-letterario" on *Un uomo* (1984)), though it subtends the work's literary rhetoric.

The critical silence on the matter does not make Fallaci's indictment either fanciful or trivial. Events in Italy and worldwide since, as before, 1968 suggest that the political forces of

---

1. Oriana Fallaci, *Un uomo*, Milan, Rizzoli, 1979; *A Man* (translated by William Weaver), New York, Simon and Schuster, 1980, and London–Sydney–Toronto, The Bodley Head, 1981. Page references are to the Italian original and to the London edition.

the kind indicted in her book have been a persistent threat. Right-wing conspiracy, terrorism and assassination erupted in Italy from 1969 (after earlier attempted *coups d'état* and political conspiracies), and the State was slow to pursue them. Strong suspicions, and ever more disturbing evidence, of political conspiracy still surround the murders of Pasolini in 1975 and of Christian Democrat leader Aldo Moro in 1978, as well as that, in 1981, of the investigative journalist Mino Pecorelli – and one could go as far back as the death of Italy's energy chief, Enrico Mattei, in 1962.

The subject-matter of *Un uomo* is therefore very close to home for Italians, and much of the action takes place in Italy, including surveillance of Panagoulis (and an apparent murder attempt off Ischia) by undercover agents, some of whom are identified as being associated with Otto Skorzeny's neo-Nazi *Die Spinne* ("The Spider") organization (cf. Part III, esp. Chapter 3). The charge of Manichaeism is one often levelled against Fallaci, and particularly in connection with this book; but a categorical division between good and evil may be difficult or impossible to avoid when confronted by a Hitler or a Stalin or their latter-day imitators. Political analysis cannot be my primary aim, but to exclude it from literary analysis – and particularly of *Un uomo* – would be politically devious in itself.

Yet, if the book purports to document a perversion of justice and the machinations of those in power, why does the author label it *Romanzo* ("A Novel")? And why is the judicial accumulation of evidence swamped by literary rhetoric?

The main answer to these questions is axiomatic to the logic of the work: if the judicial process is deemed to have failed and to have been subordinated to the interests of those in power, the appeal must be directed to a higher or wider tribunal, a notional humanity accessible through the printed word and identified with the widest possible reading public (an unprecedented 1,800,000 copies being sold in Italy within two years (Rosa 1982: 79)). The appeal is broadened, even universalized: the particular instance of the death of Panagoulis is taken as paradigmatic of the machinations of oppressive power. Fallaci has therefore opted for the rhetoric of "high mimetic" or even "romance", of heroic and tragic myth, of folk literature linked by the rhythms of the speaking voice to its origins in oral tradition (cf. Frye 1957), though Fallaci herself stressed Propp's paradigm rather than

Frye's as her main guide (cf. Erbani 1979), and rejected Lajolo's (1979) parallel with Céline. Disconcertingly, she fuses this "romance" with the "low mimetic" of the comic novel in a literary project which has few parallels (the Italian medieval and Renaissance popular epics from *I Reali di Francia* to Boiardo and the Florentines Pulci and Berni, and, in the twentieth century, Silone's works being partial precedents).

Genre Overturnings

Rosa (1982: 58) incisively demonstrates Fallaci's systematic *ribaltamento* ("overturning") of the traditional modes of popular fiction, springing from the key structure of the writer's direct address to her dead companion as "tu" ("thou"). The effect of apostrophe is even more dramatic here than in *Lettera a un bambino mai nato*, from the very first sentence, where the huge crowd attending Panagoulis's funeral roars out "the great lie. Zi, zi, zi! He lives, he lives, he lives! A roar that had nothing human about it." This, twenty-five lines of Cyclopean prose before the second-person pronoun is introduced with dramatic casualness.

As in *Lettera*, Rosa argues, Oriana's fictive address to her Alekos is doubled by Fallaci's address to her readership. And, as in *Se il sole muore* and *Niente e cosí sia*, her "I" is doubled as, to use Genette's terms (Genette 1980), the extradiegetic author–narrator Fallaci and the intradiegetic narrated "I" of the largely uncomprehending Oriana, who distances herself from Alekos on two key occasions, including that leading to his death. The narrating Fallaci not only points out blank spaces in Alekos's recollections and in Oriana's past perceptions of his self-sacrificial mission, but orchestrates the "musicality" of the prose (Sabelli Fioretti 1979: 219–20), guides the reader with forward and backward narrative pointers, weaves in leitmotivs of images and verbal repetitions of phrases, sentences and whole paragraphs, and conducts reflections on politics, passion, destiny, and on the Proppian paradigm of the hero.

Rosa emphasizes the simultaneous exploitation and "overturning" of the tropes of popular culture: the lone hero, armed only with his extraordinary moral courage, taking on an unethical system against all the odds – but failing; the linear narrative of failed exploits, hideous tortures, years of confinement in a tomb-like cell, then release, the cat-and-mouse game with mysterious pursuers, the car chases – all subverted, drained of their narrative suspense by the "Prologue" which presents the hero as already dead; the romantic coupling of love and death, in which death proves the more reliable lover and sado-masochistic ambiguities pervade Alekos's relationship both with his torturers and with Oriana; the emotional and rhetorical barrage of the prose combined with filmic narrative; physical coarseness combined with cultural name-dropping. Alekos emerges as the symmetrical inversion of the James Bond type.

All this, for Rosa (following Spinazzola), amounts to a market strategy calculated to maximize readership and, by yet another overturning, establish Oriana (or Fallaci) herself by her literary credentials as "the mythically supreme image of the totally female" (Spinazzola 1979, quoted in Rosa 1982: 77, 80), as the unnamed and invisible, but vocal, protagonist, over the corpse of the presumed protagonist, Alekos: the triumph of the female over the male and of the literary over the political. Panagoulis's biography becomes a chapter in Fallaci's autobiography.

Spinazzola's and Rosa's disjuncture of male and female, of political and literary, of thou and I, itself has its political correlative. Panagoulis's political project, powerfully underwritten (and not subsumed) by Fallaci's text, was to torpedo the post-1974 Defence Minister, Averoff, as the architect of "transition" from the bankrupt dictatorship of the colonels to a sham democracy masking the continuity of an arbitrary Power. Panagoulis held Averoff guilty of collusion with the Italian Fascist government after the Italian invasion of Greece, and thereafter with the various right-wing Greek regimes and with their security organization the KYP, the CIA, and their neo-Nazi helpers. When *Un uomo* appeared in 1979, the Italian Communists had long pursued a not dissimilar strategy of "historic compromise" with the tainted Christian Democrats, who were the main party of government uninterruptedly from 1948 until their ignominious obliteration in the elections of 1994. The massive readership success of Fallaci's book represented a stumbling-block to such political compromise.

Panagoulis's political forecast proved wrong. The 1977 Greek elections weakened, and those of 1981 threw out, the centre-right government of Karamanlis and Averoff (thanks partly to the publication in *Vradyní* of the incriminating letter sent by Averoff to President Gizikis on 20 January 1974, also included in *Un uomo* (cf. Andrews 1980: Appendix C; and *Un uomo* pp. 396–400; 402–6)); and the Papandreou government, whatever its faults, did effect changes in the articulation of power and the spread of social justice and freedom in Greece, whereas Alekos in *Un uomo* attaches scant importance to the abolition of the monarchy by referendum (pp. 300; 306), or to his own election to Parliament in 1974. It was the 1974 elections that really brought to an end the Greek Civil War of the 1940s (cf. Fifis 1994: 45). The Greek electorate, those octopus-like masses contemptuously portrayed at the beginning and ending of *Un uomo*, showed their political shrewdness in voting in the centre-right Karamanlis as a transition from dictatorship to democracy: "It is Karamanlis or the tanks", the composer Theodorakis had pronounced (Diamandouros 1991: 22). The million-and-a-half mourners at Panagoulis's funeral in 1976 were signalling their commitment to the liberties for which he had died.

Un uomo presents a categorical imperative of political ethics – freedom, truth and justice in all the purity of their perfection – as against the meliorist and progressive perspectives of practical politics. This must partly explain the book's popularity in an Italy in which the ethics of the political managers already roused grave disquiet. It also supports the mythic structure of the work, with an abstract, eternal, unchanging, invincible Power temporarily personified in the "dragon", Averoff (Part IV, Chapter 2), challenged by the exceptional "individual" Panagoulis, to the exclusion, as Rosa points out, of other recognizable characters except Panagoulis's gaolers and, of course, Oriana.

The timeless mythic structure is thus not merely superimposed on the documentary account (cf. Marchionne Picchione 1979): Fallaci holds the two discourses in tension with her characteristic excess of explicitness and emphasis. *Un uomo* – unlike Fallaci's works prior to *Lettera a un bambino mai nato* – flaunts intertextual and metanarrative discourse so as to develop the heroic paradigm of which Alekos is not the triumphant mythic fulfilment but the all too real and anguished historic "overturning" in defeat. Heroes from the Hindu warrior Muchukunda to the god Dionysus and, particularly, Don Quixote, provide the author with points of comparison, but Fallaci maintains strict silence on the more striking analogies with Christ and Prometheus – though her introduction to Panagoulis in *Intervista con la storia* insistently describes him in terms of Christ crucified (pp. 612–15; 332–6).

As Ishmael to Panagoulis's Ahab, fulfilling her hero's injunction to record his struggle with his Moby Dick, that is with Power as locally embodied by Averoff (pp. 315, 385; 321–2, 391), Fallaci closely follows the narrative outlined by Panagoulis himself (pp. 441–2; 448) – starting with the assassination attempt and ending with the documents incriminating Averoff – which she frames between the Prologue and final chapter, respectively covering the funeral and death of Alekos. The prophetic dream-imagery, mythic fabric and thinking about politics, existence and destiny, and nearly all the reported speech in the book are attributed to Alekos, while Oriana is cast in the role of Sancho Panza to his Don Quixote. If Fallaci has appropriated Panagoulis, she has done so self-effacingly. She ends *Un uomo* with the death and funeral of Alekos, making no mention of her own campaign for a serious investigation into his death and her indictment of Averoff's authoritarian machinations (cf. Andrews 1980: 280, 304–13).

Many who knew Panagoulis angrily rejected Fallaci's portrait of him as a travesty (cf. Cederna 1990), shaming the dead man, his family and his cause. Yet what motive could Fallaci have for misrepresenting Panagoulis? Publicity-seeking scandal-mongering or revenge are quite out of keeping with the discursive stance of *Un uomo*. To some facts – the kick in the belly that caused the miscarriage of their child, his sexual libido, his urinating on the cars of the rich in Florence – Oriana is the best, if not the only, witness, and her loyalty and judgement are more at issue than her reliability. To other points – his drunken riotousness and debauchery in Athens – no doubt plenty of others could testify. Fallaci has avoided censoring and sanitizing his image. Within the narrative of *Un uomo*, Alekos's behaviour follows the logic of his persecuted existence as a man obsessed by the drive to lay bare the murderous machinations of a power equally bent on quelling real freedom, truth or justice. At times, he publicly tries to provoke the authorities to throw him back into prison; at others, he is prey to despair and frustration; always, he is devising schemes to discomfit those in power, outfacing their death-threats and their schemes to simulate his accidental death. How far is he his own, before becoming Fallaci's, paradoxical hero, lusting powerfully, and simultaneously, for life and for death? It would take a detailed biographical study of the man to illuminate this literary crux of Fallaci's novel.

The title *Un uomo* takes up the finale of Fallaci's interview with Panagoulis upon his release from prison, which closes *Intervista con la storia* (pp. 653; 376). Here he denies being a hero, a symbol, or a leader, and expresses his fear of disappointing those who see him as a hero and not simply a man. He defines a man in fairly heroic terms: "It means to have courage, to have dignity. It means to believe in humanity. It means to love without allowing love to become an anchor. It means to struggle. And to win." To which Fallaci replies: "I'd say that a man is what you are, Alekos."

The flesh-and-blood, unsublimated hero of *Un uomo* constitutes one of the book's central "overturnings", the overturning of the trope, common to both "high" and "low" culture, of the heroic sublime. Fallaci's Alekos is a challenge to the dubious proprieties of politics and other proprieties. His carnality is as subversive and anarchic as the "physicality" (*fiziologichnost*) of Hašek's good soldier Švejk (cf. Skachkov 1928: 117), and has a genealogy which includes Rabelais. Alekos insists that human liberty must involve not only the brain, but heart, intestines and sphincter as well (pp. 246; 252). This is no controlled desublimation or consumer mystification, yet, like Švejk, proves highly marketable outside a censorious literary readership, and highly problematical. It is what civilization, or its dominant interests, must repress.

". . . Dostoevsky furnishes us with a pair of literary characters who function as mythic constructs in the imaginative mind of early twentieth-century European culture", writes John Hoyles. "Who can doubt that the Grand Inquisitor and the Underground Man are symbiotically related?" (1991: 12). Hoyles attributes to Dostoevsky's creations a representative function in literature about totalitarianism, culminating in the works of Kafka. *Un uomo*, as reportage novel, provides a documentary link between the literary imagination and political history. Alekos in his tomb-like cell, wedded to his gaolers in his defiance and to death as a liberating gesture, problematizing the Grand Inquisitor's inverse ratio between freedom and happiness, is an Underground Man in late-twentieth-century guise, insistently projected by Fallaci as representative of countless others imprisoned, tortured and killed in our contemporary world, and through the ages, for resisting the omnipresent Inquisitor's false equation of happiness with unfreedom.

And what of Fallaci's style? Do we write it off as middlebrow kitsch? As the "journalistic sublime" (Rosa 1982)? As the out-pourings of a Liala – the prolific and popular Italian Barbara Cartland – (Guarini 1979)? "Prose as massage" and "exalted log-orrhea" (Duchêne 1981) or histrionics (Arato 1979)? Or do we slyly concur with the eminent Carlo Bo (1979) that "l'accademia della letteratura qui non c'entra" ("we are not in the groves of literary academe here"), corralling off the sacred precinct of "the literary" and assigning *Un uomo* to a non-aesthetic function of writing?

Fallaci's denial of a dividing line between reportage and lit-erature and her frank interest in maximizing her readership amount to one of the perennial maverick attempts by populist writers to annul the aura of the literary as a secular version of the sacral and overcome the distinction between high and low culture, to democratize the word by making the furthest reaches of its power accessible to all without mystification and without condescension (cf. the opening, as well as the general argument, of Chapter 7 above). How far she is successful in this, and how suitable an instrument is her declamatory second-person add-ress, are matters open to debate.

I have suggested that Fallaci is no more fallible or subject to falsification than her critics and detractors. Seriousness (artistic and ethical or human) transcends fixed aesthetic criteria. The oft-quoted Liala-like segment held against *Un uomo* (including the duplicated: "You were running. You were crossing the beach and you ran with the broad strides of a happy colt, your trousers clung to your strong thighs, the T-shirt stretched over your strong shoulders, and your hair flowed light in black waves of silk. The night before we had loved each other for the first time in a bed, marrying our two solitudes, and in the afternoon we had gone to the sea where the summer blazed in a glory of sun, of blue. Flooded with sun, with blue, you yelled happily: 'I zoi, i zoi! Life, life!' (pp. 156, 443; 161, 455)) is one brief dreamlike moment that stands out by its difference against the harsh unsentimentality which characterizes the overall treatment of a physically and soc-ially unprepossessing Alekos and his relationship with Oriana, and against the description of his shattered corpse.

What do we make of this? A naïve lapse into sentimental kitsch? Or an only slightly less naïve, though deliberate, stylistic clash, one of the book's "effettucci e effettacci" (Guarini 1979)? Is this sub-literary or para-literary entrapment in the prefabricated forms of mass culture and conventional ideology? Or is it a more self-consciously postmodernist "quotation" and "overturning" of those prefabricated forms through which reality is perceived and experienced (or which are experienced as reality), and thus an exposure of entrapment?

In view of the overwhelmingly explicit nature of Fallaci's literary aesthetic, any non-explicit implication must be regarded as unintentional or subconscious. The bold, even coarse, effect is primary, as is the filmic effect of the several car- and boat-chases in the book, which more than once explicitly foregrounds both the filmic (pp. 265; 271) and the automobile as protagonist, or rather, antagonist (pp. 353–4; 360). James Dean and John Wayne provide points of reference. The tyrant's black Lincoln on the way to Glyfada and the grim black Cadillac that tails Alekos and Oriana in Athens; the white police car that follows them in Crete and the blue car that tries to force them off the road between Chania and Heraklion; the red BMW and the silver-grey Peugeot seen racing Alekos's green Fiat before it crashed; the green Fiat itself, Alekos's steed, dubbed "Primavera", and purchased for Alekos by Oriana in her Proppian function as donor or helper; Alekos's urinating on the cars parked on the Piazzale Michelangelo – the paradigm of the automobile is as central to the idiom of contemporary Western narrative, and thus to Fallaci's metathriller, as it is to the semiosis of contemporary Western living. Cinema likewise. Celluloid has become the prime carrier and an inevitable diaphragm of our images of the world, factual or fictive and always axiomatically factitious, a material of creation, production and consumption. The thriller genre mimics the mayhem of living reality, which returns the compliment. None of this is new, or necessarily kitschy. Before heroes and villains drove cars, the world of chivalry depended on the horse. Before we had cinema, the theatre was a pervasive paradigm of existence.

10

Plotting Chaos – Italians and Shiites in Beirut: "InsciAllah" (1990)

Plotting Chaos

*T*he English version of *InshAllah*[1] is presented as a "Translation by Oriana Fallaci from a translation by James Marcus". The following page declares: "The characters in this novel are imaginary. Their stories are imaginary, the plot is imaginary. The events from which the plot departs are real. The landscape is real, the war in which the story unfolds is real." The novel is dedicated to the four hundred US and French soldiers slaughtered in the twin Beirut bomb blasts of Sunday 23 October 1983 and to the victims of all massacres of "the eternal massacre called war", as "an act of love for them and for Life".

Already we have here many huge issues. Readers (if they have not read Fallaci's account in *Niente e cosí sia* of the 1968 massacre in Mexico City) might suspect that love for the real victims of a real massacre in a real war might be not unconnected with the sales potential of a work of fiction. "To talk 'of' war in order to talk 'against' war is a slippery business", remarks one hostile reviewer (Giorgi 1990). We may recall the voyeurism of the horrific exorcized in *Niente e cosí sia*. The seriousness with which Fallaci relates the "imaginary" to the "real" therefore needs examining.

---

1. Oriana Fallaci, *InsciAllah*, Milan: Rizzoli, 1990; English translation, *InshAllah*, New York: Doubleday, and London: Chatto and Windus, 1992. References to the Milan and London editions (in that order) are given in the text either by Act, Chapter, Section or by page numbers.

Language is crucial in transmitting both the real and the imaginary. But to think of language as singular is a common philosophical delusion. The plurality of languages involves both "standard" languages and an infinity of dialects, sociolects, idiolects. Semioticians, structuralists, post-structuralists, postmodernists and deconstructionists have extended our sense of the infinitely and infinitesimally varied warping and shifting of the ways in which meanings are inscribed, transmitted and received. Language (to revert now to a panoramic, collective singular) is thus an aspect of chaos – or, more precisely, of indeterminacy.

This is strongly foregrounded in *InsciAllah*, even in the title itself. And we may wonder about that word "departs" (somewhat misleadingly translating "prende l'avvio") in the dedication: does the novel "depart" from real events as one departs from the truth? And what of that always problematical translation of *vero* by "real"? We shall see. I cite these microscopic examples not trivially, questioning Fallaci's adequacy as her own translator, but because *InsciAllah* is largely composed of translation.

Translation indeterminacy (cf. Quine 1960) and linguistic indeterminacy are uniquely relevant to *InsciAllah*. Joyce, Gadda, Queneau play with the opacity of language, the unpredictability of its ludic or semantic outcomes, and the untranslatability between different language codes, foregrounding language as chaos or indeterminacy or irreducible mental object. *InsciAllah* is different. Its characters, in the Babel which is the Beirut of 1983, with its peace-keeping force of US, Italian, French and British troops, speak their native tongues among the Arabic-speaking inhabitants. Their speech is reported bilingually, in snatches first of their own language, then in Italian translation. *InsciAllah* has it both ways: by presenting utterances in their native tongues, it proclaims the autonomy of each tongue, its uniqueness and untranslatability, language difference as an existential dimension; whereas, by presenting translations of those utterances in Italian, it proclaims a translingual human communality, the possibility of communicating across language differences. Take the chant of the heroic dwarf-like street-sweeper Bilal, a leader of the Shiite Amal militia, who, against all the odds, has stormed a tower held by the Christian-led Lebanese Army: "beasnani-saudàfeh-haza-al-bourji-beasnani, beasnani-saudàfeh-haza-al-quariatna-beasnani"/ "with-my-teeth-I-will-defend-this-tower-with-my-teeth, with-my-teeth-I-will-defend-this-quarter-with-my-teeth" (pp. 476; 354).

This reflects the translator's enterprise as such – a transaction between the uniqueness of cultures and their common human basis. One novelistic peak of this translingual motif comes when the mysterious Ninette, who has been pursuing the Italian Angelo, writes him a parting letter, not in her native Arabic, nor in her cultured French, but in English. He has to have it translated, supposedly word-for-word (pp. 375–80; 276–80). Ninette cites this as an example of chaos and of Boltzmann's theory of entropy, which is Angelo's private obsession:

> Darling, somebody will translate this for you, and of course I don't like to think that you'll know its content through an interpreter. That is, a witness or rather a judge of our story. If I could, I would write it in French: a language I know more than perfectly. But I cannot. I must not. And it's not my fault if Mister Boltzmann's chaos includes the babel of languages, the disorder which better than any disorder expresses the accuracy of his $S = K \ln W$.

Translingual communication within *InsciAllah* has, indeed, all too visible limits, precisely where it matters most. In novels which Manichaeistically project opposed poles of good and evil, evil cannot be subject, it cannot be accredited with the existential inner voice of what Husserl called "silent speech", or it might be transformed into a positive by the anarchic ironies of the fictive process (cf. Gatt-Rutter 1989; Harpham 1992). In *InsciAllah*, the unspeakable and the speechless Other is not so much embodied in the poor ignorant fighters for Islam. These are given a voice in the novel in the person of Bilal, who is internally focalized and brought well within the pale of human or novelistic sympathy. So is his antagonist, the Maronite Christian Lebanese Army Captain, Gassàn, who is bent on killing Bilal so as to avenge the assassination of his own father. Ninette, also a Christian, is the only other Lebanese to be so privileged.

But the pivotal champions of Islam in the novel, the Imam Zandra Sadr and his sons, and the Amal commander Rashid and his lover, the fourteen-year-old boy Khalid, nicknamed Passepartout, are not so privileged. They constitute a key silence within the text. *InsciAllah* is an instance of what Edward Said (1978) has called "orientalism" – a negative representation within Western culture of non-Western culture as irredeemably other and implicitly inferior, as an irrationality irrelevant to the project of rationality. Translatability breaks down, or rather, is not envisaged. The gap between cultures remains unbridgeable.

This contrasts with various kinds of transcultural and translingual bridge-building in the novel. One major sequence involves the tender relationship between five French nuns and five Italian officers quartered in their mansion. The nuns too represent the sacred, and are not internally focalized. But they also represent the human, and the linguistic exchanges between them and the Italians develop from an initial cloistering and erection of physical barriers to banqueting together and a progressive warmth of sympathetic understanding. The humane mission of the nuns and of the peace-keepers leads to fellowship between them. After the peace-keepers have left, the nuns will be horribly martyred by the devotees of the rival religion.

The Italian peace-keeping contingent is collective subject, accounting for the majority – all male – of the novel's 103 characters, focalized either by exterior or interior monologue or both, mostly in dialect, from Sicilian and Neapolitan to Genoese and Venetian (as is much of the dialogue), followed by Italian translation. The same is true of dialogue in French, English or Arabic. So the translator's transaction between sociocultural and sociolinguistic differences and human communality is at work here too. Only, here it is in the service of Italian unity: that is, the construction of Italy as a heterogeneity expressed as *plurilinguismo*, linguistic diversity. Italian, the novel's privileged language, mediates between the subaltern dialects as the nation-state mediates between the regions. Chaos is plotted novelistically as harmony. This effect cannot be transported into another language universe. The English version simply omits the dialects and loses a whole dimension of signification.

The novel opens with a crescendo of irrational chaos – from the feral dogs haunting Beirut and the demented roosters crowing at any hour of day or night to the horrific scene of the destruction of the US Marine headquarters by a lorry-load of high explosive. It closes with a rationalization of chaos – Rashid's speedboat, also laden with high explosive, following the course mathematically plotted by Angelo to blow up the Italian troop-carrying ship. The opening is closely based on documented fact. The close fulfils long-suspended conjecture – a possible ending, not a factual one. Narrative propulsion throughout is provided by the Italians' fear of a third suicide-bomb attack.

This eventuality is plotted by the mathematically-minded

Angelo in terms of Boltzmann's formula for entropy – that is, the running down of energy – which he calls the Formula of Death, and which he desperately tries to disprove. That Boltzmann himself committed suicide, and that his mathematics is notorious for inducing suicide, enters the novel's calculus. Yet the very existence of a formula for chaos or indeterminacy, their reduction to the simple and apparently absolute language of mathematics – $S = K \ln W$, a mere six symbols – belies chaos and indeterminacy. As with Fallaci's tendency (within Eurocentric limits) to plot the chaos of language within a novelistic masterplan of harmony, so too in other respects her novel mimes the leap from modernity to the postmodern, but remains rooted in the project of modernity, a self-defining reason.

Several motifs in the novel signal indeterminacy, often using verbal cues. One motif is that of the inventory and its dissolution: the former linked to military organization, the latter to its withdrawal. The inventory is defined by the related yet opposed words *museo* and *babele*, with regard to the secret store room of the weapons expert, nicknamed Zucchero (Sugar): "On the floor near the entry, a jumble (*babele*) of hand grenades and sardine tins, helmets and cans of tuna in oil, M12 guns and sausages, cartridges and *panettoni*, nightscopes and chocolates, flak jackets and wine bottles, walkie-talkies, medicines. In short, the necessary provisions for the autonomy of a separate republic" (pp. 79; 57). Two parallel lists of military and non-military supplies show chaos under rational control: a military control, posited as the basis of republican autonomy.

Italian generosity in medical supplies, including blood plasma, and facilities, is instrumental in maintaining a truce with the Shiites, while gifts of food and bonds of affection come from many individual Arabs to various of the Italian personnel. Towards the end of the novel, the motif of Italian largesse becomes dominant. Their entire field hospital is left as a gift to the people of West Beirut, as well as their entire quartermaster's stores.[2] The inventory of these items is recited – and priced – from memory by an Italian staff officer in a scene whose comic tone enhances this prodigy of order (3.6.3). The same supplies, in

---

2. A paper co-authored by the commander of the Italian contingent in Beirut, General Angioni, corroborates the perspective which emerges from *InsciAllah* (Angioni and Cremasco 1991).

the Epilogue, are reduced by looting and vandalism, under Shiite authority, to litter and quagmire.

Insciallah makes explicit an implicit function of narrative fiction: plotting chaos – indeterminacy – and revealing its coherence. Incoherence, equated with the unknowable, the irrational, is rejected: this is marked by the perfectly orderly withdrawal of the Italian peace-keeping force from its finally untenable position in a disorderly Beirut. Disorder in Italy itself, or in the Western-dominated world as a whole, is kept outside the novel's vision. The disorder of Beirut is plotted with all the precision of military cartography. The Italians know their section of the city not as the inhabitants do, from personal acquaintance, but from their maps and vehicles. But the privilege of narration sets up a precise topography which transcends the knowledge of any of the participant characters, just as the same privilege of narration sets up a knowledge of each character that is not available to that or other characters, and a linguistic standard again shared by novelist and reader, but denied to many of the characters. We have here the traditional model of science, called omniscience, and the novel as an expression of a culture-bound cognitive empire (cf. Said 1993: xii–xiii).

Plot is the novelistic rhetoric for mapping as destiny the chance concatenations by which things happen. Metanarrative pointers are planted all along *InsciAllah* showing how things could have happened any number of ways but actually fell out in one particular way, fastidiously advertising the tiny coincidences that lead to Passepartout's murdering Ninette, Angelo's killing Passepartout in turn, and Rashid's blowing up the Italian troopship. Indeterminacy before the event becomes determinism after the event (often preannounced). This asymmetrical irreversibility of time is what narrative is largely about. The novel's fatalistic title – *insciAllah*, which means "as God wills" – is revealed in Ninette's letter as the answer to Boltzmann's Formula of Death: acceptance of dissolution as the Formula of Life.

Lukács (1980 [1932]: 58–9) had argued that Tolstoy's *Resurrection* "portrays the living and dialectical combination and inextricable coalescence of accident and necessity" and that "with Tolstoy each particular feature both 'has a cause' and 'has no cause', and is therefore alive . . .". Coincidence justifies itself as necessity, and vice versa. *InsciAllah*'s trans-historical metanarrative argument posits war as a perennial human condition of all-determining indeterminacy. Catastrophe is destined to occur by chance.

This is another quest narrative. The answer to Angelo's tormenting problem comes in his interior monologue in the Epilogue, just prior to his being blown up, and affirms chaos not as dissolution but as the renewal of life through death. But the final words of the shadowy narrator within the text, the Italian second-in-command, known as the Professor, invoke a redefinition of Good and Evil as the only conceivable hope for any human betterment (3.6.9). This is rationality at the end of its tether, and it comes to this admission of impotence by precipitating into a *mise en abîme*, when the narrator declares his non-existence and admits that he and the book have been written by the woman journalist from Saigon – that is, "Fallaci".

InsciAllah carries on a metanarrative argument, and is accordingly divided into three Acts and an Epilogue. Characters and incidents are labelled or highlighted in terms of their importance to the plot, the tone intended, the role of coincidence. At the end of each Act, the narrator soliloquizes in the form of a letter addressed to an imaginary wife (Fallaci's irreducible "thou"), in which he muses about the *piccola Iliade* which he is writing; about himself as *mise en abîme*; about the indissolubility of *fantasia* and *realtà*, fact and fiction; and about the morality or immorality of writing and of writers. The reader is continually reminded of a plot in the making, of characters as creations, of writing as invention, and of discourse as subjective.

Fallaci's text thus flaunts self-reflexivity, yet looks like a restoration of traditional narrative: characters are distinct and determinate, space is distinctly mapped out, time is consecutive and linear though within its continuum memory is recursive, the narrative language is transparent, the narration ends with closure. The self-reflexive metanarrative level thus seems to be superimposed on a conventional narrative, rather than transforming it from within. The narrator keeps returning to a timeless, eternal history (*storia*, translated as "story"), echoing the Pascalian trope of *Niente e cosí sia*:

> ... the story doesn't change. The eternal story, the eternal novel of Man who at war manifests himself in all his truth. Because nothing, unfortunately, reveals us as much as war. Nothing exacerbates with the same strength our beauty and our ugliness, our intelligence and

our stupidity, our bestiality and our humanity, our courage and our cowardice: our enigma. In fact the danger lies in narrating a story already narrated, a novel already written.

(pp. 207; 150)

When Fallaci was writing her book, Chaos Theory was just entering the popular domain with James Gleick's book, *Chaos – Making a New Science* (1988 [1987]). One of Gleick's subheadings reads: "Order masquerading as randomness". That is to say, not chaos at all, but something different – non-linearity, fractals. Linear plotting gives way to stochastic calculation – that is, statistically driven probabilistic prediction. So-called chaos theory is in fact a denial of chaos.

Angelo appears as a victim of historical irony – dying a moment before the solution to his agonizing conundrum was revealed, since "chaos theory" is indeed the "science of life", as the narrating Professor had long hinted. Yet we could speak of convergence. Not scientifically, but emotionally, Angelo has come to accept chaos and death as part of the equation of renewal and life, independently of the scientific and mathematical break-through. His own and other deaths are part of the pattern, of the fractal to which a shake of the kaleidoscope will give a completely new configuration (though the narrative does not transcend its deathly closure with any concrete expectation of renewal or rebirth). But chaos appears in Fallaci's book primarily as a metaphor for moral disorder in the human world, and in particular for war – a moral disorder driven by ideological imperatives of religion or nationalism, of capitalism or revolution – and Fallaci has declared that Angelo's obsession with Boltzmann's equation, which seems so inextricably integrated into her text, was an afterthought (Ostellino 1990).

Where, then, does that leave us? Fallaci's text constructs Italy as humanly accessible across its dialectal chaos, and a wider humanity – French and Arabic, Christian and Muslim, Shiite and Maronite, Lebanese and Palestinian – as also potentially accessible across boundaries of ethnicity, language and religion. But an absolute, insurmountable difference intervenes, a religious power, or power masquerading as religion, in the face of which the rational community represented by the Italians can only withdraw, defeated.

This seems to repeat in pessimistic vein the Enlightenment

rejection of intolerance and absolutism. But it does so by wilfully isolating and simplifying the Lebanese chaos within the wider Middle East chaos, which is itself part of a world chaos – an absolutism or intolerance of a different order, another irrational power masquerading as reason, which was expressed in President Reagan's pronouncement in the wake of the horrendous Beirut bomb blasts that what was at stake was Western access to the Middle East's oil.[3]

The text's message is defined as much by what it does not say as by what it says. Fallaci's novel falls foul of the political questions which it begs. It takes on either too little (despite its length) or too much, contrasting in this respect with the ending of Malraux's *La Condition humaine* (cf. Craig and Egan 1979: 205–7). It refuses to translate the absolute, abominable language of the lorry-bombs. It deploys the rhetoric of chaos, but fails to confront the heart of darkness as Conrad did in metonymically linking the Congo to the Thames.

Fallaci's Orientalism

Borges's brief tale "Averroës' Search" (1970 [1949]) is a gem-like illustration of the Whorf–Sapir hypothesis about mental conditioning by language and culture, about the difficulty of thinking outside our native language and culture, or those of which we have an intimate knowledge. Abulgualid Muhammad Ibn-Ahmad ibn-Muhammad ibn-Rushd – known to the West as Averroës – is working in Cordoba, one of the great centres of learning of twelfth-century Muslim Spain, on his commentaries on Aristotle, which are to become one of the essential bridges between Europe's classical antiquity and modernity. Working from an Arabic translation of a Syriac translation, he gets stuck on the terms *tragedy* and *comedy*, for which Islamic Arabic culture possesses no objective correlative. He is distracted from this puzzle by the chatter of the traveller Abulcasim Al-Ashari about spectacles in China at which masked people represented a story

3. On 24 October 1983, the day after the double bomb blast, US President Ronald Reagan spoke of "a tyranny of forces hostile to the West" threatening "the vast resources of the Arabian peninsula". Secretary of State George Schultz spoke in similar vein. (*Keesing's Contemporary Archive*, XXX, 1984, 32647). Pier Paolo Pasolini thematized oil as a central reality radiating in all directions, in Italy or elsewhere, in his massive unfinished novel, *Petrolio* (1992).

upon a terrace within a great hall. Averroës cannot make the connection between Chinese and ancient Greek drama, being unable to conceptualize either.

Borges gives his story a surprise ending. He deconstructs both the story itself and his own authorial authority, concluding that his own attempt to portray Averroës is as futile as Averroës' search for the meaning of the words *tragedy* and *comedy*, and cites as his all too inadequate sources some of the famous European orientalists who are the subjects of Edward Said's work, *Orientalism* (1978). Borges's short tale works across cultures "contrapuntally" (to use Said's term in *Culture and Imperialism* (1993)), implying that such transculturalism is at once indispensable and unrealizable. In "Averroës' Search", cultural imperialism and hegemonic thinking are twice disavowed. Borges narrates the impossibility of both quests, *by* and *for* Averroës, indicated by the Spanish title, "La busca de Averroës." There is no privileged site of knowledge between or above or beyond cultures, no universal rationality. Borges's characterization of Averroës is undone before our eyes.

Borges's short tale and Fallaci's huge novel have nothing in common except that they both engage the interface between the Islamic world and the Occident. But Borges points up the difference in Fallaci's engagement with Islam, putting at issue precisely the presumption of rationality as residing in the West and the presumption that what in the Other does not conform to that rationality marks that Other – in this case, Islam, or one version of Islam – as irrational (cf. Parekh 1992, 1994). Given that *InsciAllah* displays both literary and best-selling ambitions, this issue directly involves the Europe of today, where Islam in diverse guises is an important presence, both around the peripheries to Europe's south and east, and within the European heartlands (cf. *Religioni e Società* 1991; Gellner 1992a, 1992b; Allievi and Dassetto 1993). The same presumptions of rationality and irrationality apply to the world as a whole, where a new confrontation may be developing between the dominant West and the Islamic universe (Wright 1992; Huntington 1993). Fallaci's book seems calculated to reinforce this confrontation and the rationalization of Western power. It produces this effect by the deployment of remarkably traditional novelistic strategies.

InsciAllah opens with soldiers from the Italian contingent arriving at the scene of devastation caused by the truck-load of high explosive at the headquarters of the US contingent of the peace-keeping force in Beirut. They fail to save a Marine impaled on a girder. One Italian, Fabio, picks up the head of his Italo-American friend John. Another unearths a toilet into which the doorkeeper's little daughter Fawzia, everybody's darling, has been compressed headfirst like a sausage. Angelo, the novel's central character, mentally compares the gleeful suicide-bomber to the legendary Italian hero Pietro Micca, who in 1706 blew himself up together with the invading French grenadiers who were tunnelling their way under the defences of Turin. He dismisses the comparison: Micca sacrificed himself to save his city from an aggressor; the Lebanese terrorist had despicably taken the lives of hundreds of members of a peace-keeping force (pp. 29; 19). The horror of the carnage and the image of the little Arab girl catapulted into the lavatory bowl prepare the reader for this judgement of Angelo's. This is an instance of the classic rhetoric of fiction, guiding the reader's evaluation through the perceptions of an apparently neutral or innocent observer within the fictive action itself. The "delegated" character, Angelo, "lives" the experience for the reader.

If this involvement of the reader in the reactions of a character within the fiction is one key rhetorical effect in the novel, referentiality is another. The text deals largely with documented fact, converting it into truth through the conversion of the journalistic eyewitness account into the "imaginary" novelistic experiential re-enactment. The truth thus generated retains the status of fact thanks to its always visible documentary and referential basis. The relationship between fact and value, between events in the real world and people's judgements of those events – a relationship which is as familiar and as problematical to the historian as to the philosopher or the literary theorist – tends to be short-circuited in *InsciAllah*, imposing a Rawlsian kind of ethical judgement upon acts taken in isolation.

But judgement, Angelo realizes, is not that easy. He reflects that for the suicide-bomber his act was justified by what he saw as a war situation. The second chapter opens with a brief and "omniscient"-sounding account of conditions in Beirut and Lebanon. This tallies in substance with the lapidary summation of the respected Fouad Ajami: "The most profound truth about Lebanon is as old as the land: the primacy of the religious sect and the clan, and the will of the 'big man' leading a particular sect" (1985: 791; quoted in Pelcovits 1991: 57), but falls well short of Ajami's own earlier and fuller political analysis that "a populist strand of Islam offered people a way of attacking inequality without being branded with the stigma of communism or ateism" and that this expressed Muslim and Arab *hiqd*, or resentment against all-pervasive Western hegemony (1981: 146–62; 182–7). It ignores Gilmour's socio-economic analysis (1987: 8–11). In particular, *InsciAllah* does not mention that masses of Shiite peasants were driven out of South Lebanon into an already over-crowded Beirut by the scorched-earth strategy employed by the Israelis during their 1982 invasion, directly supported by the Lebanese Christians and indirectly by the US (Gilmour 1987: 10–11; Chomsky 1988: 123).

In the ensuing dialogue between the Italian intelligence officer, nicknamed Charlie, and the Italian commander (pp. 61; 43), the two soldiers recognize that the Shiites are engaged in a power-struggle with the Christian-dominated Lebanese government and its Western allies (as appears in McDermott and Skjelsbaek 1991, particularly the papers by Pelcovits and Thakur). These Western allies implicitly include the Italians themselves, who are concerned that a third suicide bomb may be aimed at them. The narrative structure of the novel – that is, its fundamental rhetorical structure – hinges on this threat.

However, this awareness that the Italians are perceived as being complicit with Islam's enemies is swamped by the novel's emphasis on the Muslims' apparent fanatical hatred. Fabio, the Italian who has just picked up the severed head of his American friend John, returns to his post at Chatila to find a crowd of Shiites exulting over the carnage, jeering at the Italians and taunting them that it will be their turn next. One old mullah, however, quietly and insistently offers the indignant Italians his coffee to drink, his eyes flashing with hatred, until one of them empties the coffee cup over the mullah's head. Fabio, panicking at the evident fury of the mullah and the surrounding crowd, rushes forward and drinks up the contents of his coffee-pot, making obsequious compliments and earning himself a kiss on both cheeks from the mullah and the contempt of his fellow-Italians (pp. 42–6; 29–32).

From this incident, several motifs trail through the novel. One is Fabio's struggle to redeem himself from his ignominy. This he succeeds in doing, in Chapters 2–4 of Act 2, by rescuing Jasmine from "la viltà piú vile che esista" ("the most disgusting vileness that exists" – pp. 314; 229: but *viltà* and *vile* in Italian indicate cowardice) – brutalization and prostitution by her terrifying husband Ahmed. This earns him the title of Mister Coraggio, suggesting that Fabio is defying not simply Ahmed himself, but the murderous power of the Shiites in Beirut. This sequence intertwines contrastively with the hashish-smoking of Fabio's comrade-in-arms, Matteo. The hashish is Matteo's refuge from his loss of purpose. Many Italians resort to it, and the hashish-growers' song closes the book's second chapter, following the havoc of the two bomb blasts. It becomes a dominant note, expressing the Italians' sense of futility over their mission. The same chant is repeated three times in Chapter 7 of Act 3, which is a prose-poem on the unheroic, on demoralization, on surrender. The sickly, sweetly pungent stench of the weed is the "stench of weakness, of feebleness, of cowardice" (pp. 743; 558). It becomes the symbol of all that is negative in the novel, summed up in the key word *viltà*, and is strongly associated with the Lebanese Arabs who produce it. The Italians, it is implied, have been sucked into the moral quagmire of Beirut, in a war that is not a war and a peace that is not a peace.

Ingestion – of hashish, coffee, other drinks and food, and, most signally, of blood plasma – is one of the book's most important semiotic sub-systems. A major contrast is built up between Europe and Asia on the basis of food. Much of Act 2 revolves around the tender feelings that spring up between Italian officers and French nuns, feelings expressed largely in delicate feats of cuisine. This contrasts brusquely with the two pages of descriptive rage in the Epilogue where the Shiite religious leaders are depicted presiding over the laying waste of the pork products and alcoholic beverages which the departing Italians have left behind for the non-Muslims of Beirut. As if that contrast were not emphatic enough, the final section of Act 3 has three of those same French nuns butchered by a detachment of Izbollah (Sons of God) Shiites led by a mullah.

The theme of ingestion has other strands which set up other connections. Tea as sickly sweet as the old mullah's coffee is routinely associated with the Imam Zandra Sadr, the religious and political leader of the Beirut Shiites. Espresso coffee Italian-style, brewed in a Neapolitan coffee-pot, on the other hand, is an identity-marker of an Italian officer known as Aquila Uno

(Eagle), a Neapolitan Jew. In the thick of the shelling between Maronites and Shiites, Aquila Uno witnesses the shriek of a Palestinian mother, whose child, Mahomet, with her the only other survivor of a numerous family from the infamous massacre of Chatila, has been killed. Mahomet had braved the inferno of battle in order to carry a pot of *hummus* and *shawarma* (roast lamb) freshly cooked by his mother to his surrogate father, the Italian Ferruccio: he is blown into the air, the upturned food emptying over his head. That anguished shriek makes Eagle renounce in shame his Jewish hatred and contempt for Arabs and Muslims. He reflects that the enemies of his people, in their viciousness or in their degradation, are themselves pawns of their religious leaders.

This compassion towards Muslims as victims of Islam is one of many points in the novel where that religion is made to bear guilt for atrocity. True, this is part of a larger argument in which the religion of Christ is also implicated, and with it all creeds, secular as well as theistic, all the political and other doctrines for which human beings tear each other apart. But Shiite Islam is presented here as the evil heart of darkness. Christianity is most visibly present in the French nuns, cheerfully and selflessly devoting themselves to the care of others. The secular Western world enters the novel in the guise of the peace-keeping force, with little colour given to the Muslims' perception that it is the agent of the powers working for their subordination. The dominant discursive strategy in the presentation of the Italians is that they are a multifarious medley, speaking their mutually unintelligible dialects, driven by their different, non-communicating geographies and histories, and yet subsuming their differences within their broader Italian identity. They represent rationality in contrast to the murderous divisions between the Arabs.

Whereas many Italian characters are focalized in interior monologue, and so also the Christian Maronites Natalie Narakat Al Sharif (Ninette) and Captain Gassàn, only the diminutive street-sweeper Bilal among the Shiites is similarly privileged. Here authorial omnipotence or textual authority are at their most precarious. Borges backed away from representing Averroës, and Fallaci's attempt at representing the subjectivity of Bilal is the most daring feat in her novel, the furthest she ventures towards Islam as Other. Bilal is the hero of the Shiites, and one of the novel's heroes, defender of his home and his people, devoted to his wife and his numerous progeny. But his novelistic stature is based on anything but his Islamic beliefs. He is a simple man, who owns half a book, which he has found in a dustbin, and which he devours laboriously and eagerly. He fits into the overall discourse of the novel as one of the many whom the mosque keeps in poverty and ignorance. His heroism, far from accruing to the glory of Islam, is a mark of the extremity of his oppression by a religious power which divides human beings and gives rise to warfare and its atrocities. This is stated by the narrator, but cannot be narrated, since the novel's cultural closure imposes silence. One may wonder if the book could be read in translation by a Lebanese Shiite, or by any Muslim.

Manhood in the Feminine

The Shiite Amal commander in Beirut, Rashid, is given an unsavoury colouring in Charlie's interior monologue by his homosexual association with the vile fourteen-year-old Khalid, nicknamed Passepartout. Homosexuality is, apart from Islam, this novel's other Other, and much of the narrative is dedicated to sublimating it, in the Italian Martino, who feels the formidable weight of military machismo pitted against him. In one of the boldest moves of the work's narrative rhetoric, Martino attempts to come out of the closet and reveal his secret to Angelo just when the latter is totally absorbed in his discovery of Ninette's identity (pp. 753–9; 566–71). So Martino's condition dares at last to speak its name, yet remains unheard. The confessional seal remains unbroken within the narrative secrecy shared between narrator and reader, the voice of sublimated homophilia not silenced but drowned beneath that of sublimated heterophilia.

Martino's sublimated homosexuality does not appear more unnatural or evil than any other sort of sexuality. Yet the arbitrary association of homosexuality with the Amal leadership (whether it has any documentary basis or not) is made to suggest a compound of one anti-human irrationality with another. This strongly implied closure, arrogating rationality and humanity to one side in a murky political conflict, suggests grave limitations in the models of rationality and humanity that are being tacitly invoked.

As the narrating "Professor", the author Fallaci appropriates male narrativity, while delegating a residual femaleness to the Professor's imaginary wife as narratee and to "the Saigon journalist" as extratextual narrator or author. Male power is not problematized in *InsciAllah* any more than in Fallaci's other works except *Penelope alla guerra* and *Lettera a un bambino mai nato*. It is simply taken for granted that armies are male organizations. And nothing is made of the fact that all the pernicious factions in the Lebanese cauldron consist of males: what the text foregrounds is that they are Shiites or Maronites or Druses, all responsible for the carnage, and all equally despicable. The alternative presented is not that of the Catholic nuns. We see them engaged not in their humanitarian work, but in their sentimental relationships with Italian officers. It is the peace-keeping forces – exclusively male – who stand in contrast, with all their lovable faults and problems and virtues, against the warring Arabs. It is "virtù contro a furore" all over again (the Latin *virtus* boldly invoking maleness), centuries after Petrarch and the Crusades.

Gender power in society, then, is not at issue: it seems irrelevant to the novel that the Lebanese warlords and warriors are male. As long before in *Penelope*, sexual politics in *InsciAllah* is limited to sex, and it is in this area that novelistic invention "departs" furthest from documentary reportage. One of the most systematic contrasts in the novel is that, occupying much of Act 2, between the almost incorporeal and spiritual group *innamoramento* between Italian officers and French nuns, and the wholly material group *innamoramento* involving Lady Godiva, a life-size inflatable doll which hardly needs to be described.[4] "She" is a passionately contested possession of a group of Italian soldiers, who, hilariously, all fail to prove their manhood with her, and, in frustration and shame, go as far as bayoneting her. The virility test passes to the closet homosexual Martino, who is totally at odds with the army's cult of the phallus. Wrestling with his difference, he concludes that what matters is not to be a male, but to be a man – *uomo* again. Serene in this conviction, he feels able to accomplish the act imposed on him, only to find that during his musings the lovely lady has deflated. Martino still

4. Sharon Wood has drawn my attention to this motif in Brancati's *Don Giovanni in Sicilia*. What in Brancati's novel is an incidental and allusive motif becomes central in Fallaci's and a far-reaching emblem of female reification.

saves the situation. He points out to Stefano, the most serious and heartbroken of Lady Godiva's suitors, that *Amor vincit omnia*, that if he really cares for her, all else will follow. Stefano takes this lesson to heart and discovers true and tender love with the dummy.

Lady Godiva carries *InsciAllah* from realism to surrealism or the absurd, and towards its liveliest cognitive and critical reach. The literal deflation of the sexual fantasies of the male ego throws into contrastive relief the tragic story of Ninette, in whom the female subject, externally focalized and grandiose in its isolation, re-enters the narrative world which Oriana in her female persona seemed to have deserted. Ninette occasions the narrator's reflections on courage – especially in love – as the mainspring of life (pp. 537; 398–9) and an Italian trooper's remark: "For Christsake! ["Cazzo!"] Does that woman have balls!" (pp. 581; 431). Ninette is the pivot around which *InsciAllah* is made to revolve, womanly love in its fullness destroyed by the hideous male machinery of war, yet thereby negating that male madness. She stands out against the havoc of the bomb blast in Act 1 and the murderous Christmas battle in Act 3, and against the group *innamoramenti* and other tender relationships in Act 2, as the high point of the novelistic rhetoric. As the mystery that the narrative must reveal, her figure carries the novel's main burden of meaning: her identity, her inexplicable passion for Angelo, her acceptance of death (*insciAllah*) as the "formula of life". The figuration of Ninette flaunts its descent from the adventurous world of Dumas *père*, using the rhetoric of popular fiction, in a manner roughly analogous to that of Graham Greene's theological thrillers. But *InsciAllah* applies this narrative address to a constrictive value-system of polar opposites and peremptory totalizations – "life : death", "order : chaos", "love : war", "coraggio : viltà". The first two of these are merely asserted to be reversible. Only the antinomial couple "chance : necessity" (or "casuality : causality") is concretely articulated through the narrative as being reversible, or as an illusory opposition.

Prestigious reviewers (Gorlier, Turoldo, Vigorelli), while admiring the narrative energy of *InsciAllah*, have praised its ethical urgency in terms that interpret the death-of-God theology of the Professor's voice-over as a thirst for religious certainty. They suggest that the novel's moral seriousness demands a level of judgement that goes beyond the aesthetic or literary: "No, one cannot remain satisfied by a purely aesthetic and literary reading of the book" (Turoldo 1990); and "[*InsciAllah*] could and should ... be put at the centre of a global discussion on literature and culture which can no longer be deferred, for the least we can say about *InsciAllah* is that it carries a moral charge which brooks no evasion and which is perhaps without precedent in our country" (Vigorelli 1990). Certainly, *InsciAllah* presents the carnage of war as anything but seductive, even when it is the theatre of courage. Certainly, that carnage is contrasted with heart-warming instances of interethnic and transcultural amity. Certainly, the reader is confronted, if not with the human capacity for evil (except perhaps in Passepartout and the mullah who leads the massacre of the nuns), at least with the external manifestations of that capacity. And certainly again, moral seriousness and urgency transcend conventional literary judgement. The question is, how far is the moral concern conveyed through the Professor's voice-over realized in the narrative? And here ethical seriousness and aesthetic seriousness are not distinct criteria, but indivisible aspects of a single textual endeavour. The closures which I see in *InsciAllah* exist at all levels and in all dimensions – aesthetic, literary, cognitive, cultural, political and ethical as well. The novel proclaims its engagement with evil but fails to locate that evil, assigning it elliptically to areas of silence. Rashid, Khalid–Passepartout, the Shiite mullahs and the Imam Zandra Sadr are cast by the narrative as sources of that evil, but remain unknown, are not given a voice except obliquely, ambiguously, via Bilal, who is credited with having read half a book, but not with the Koranic literacy that enables him to do so.

The global awareness of the narrative is no greater than that which it ascribes to its *dramatis personae*, and Washington and Tel Aviv, Rome and Paris and London are more invisible within it than the Arabs' *hiqd* which is their shadow. Yet the two invented atrocities – the blowing up of the Italian troop-carrier and the massacre of the nuns – enter the narrative rhetoric as indictments of Shiite inhumanity. *InsciAllah* here takes to extremes the equivocation between two orders of truth – the documentary and the imaginative – which had led Manzoni, a century and a half before, to dismiss the historical novel as an illegitimate hybrid, and Lukács subsequently, and for cognate reasons, to do the same for the reportage novel. *InsciAllah* attempts to have it both ways, combining the rhetorical authority and mode of signification of documented fact with those of fiction. The Professor's equation of his own *fantasia* with *realtà* amounts to an arrogation of more than God-like power, since the one thing which is beyond the power of the deity as destiny (*insciAllah*) is to undo itself, to reverse time, to make things happen otherwise than they did, or to make events unhappen. *InsciAllah* presents itself as a cry against the eternal massacre called war, yet compounds the cause of war by positing evil in the Other, thus falling prey to the very charge of intolerance and irrationality which is imputed to that Other. Moreover, *InsciAllah* tends to compound the cause of war that is presently most globally prevalent – the West's identification of Islamic radicalism as evil Other. Now that conflict across the world most frequently involves confrontation with versions of Islamic radicalism – from Algeria to the Sudan, from Bosnia and Chechnya to the Philippines – Fallaci's book lends itself to one-sided appropriation, fuelling a sense of moral and civic superiority on one side, *hiqd* on the other. The fact that Algeria's Armed Islamic Group, ten or twelve years after the events on which *InsciAllah* is based, are committing actions similar to those invented by Fallaci – suicide bombings, slaughter of Catholic clergy, the attempted blowing up of an airliner over Paris – gives her book some of the status and the responsibility of self-fulfilling prophecy, which mistakes symptoms for causes.

There is thus a massive incoherence – aesthetic, cognitive, political, and ethical – at the heart of this massive novel, for all its good intentions and narrative energy. Saleability is no consolation. Yet *InsciAllah* is in many ways a courageous and impressive achievement. It deploys the aesthetic and rhetorical resources of popular fiction with considerably more far-reaching seriousness of effect than catastrophe novels such as Katz's *Black Death* or epics such as Leon Uris's *Exodus*. Saliency, explicitness, boldness of effect, rather than literary preciosity, subtle suggestion, tacit irony or *sottinteso* that is sensed between the lines, are its characteristics. Despite its surface complexity, *InsciAllah* lacks the genuine paradox and the self-questioning of Fallaci's previous works. Though conceptually couched in terms of dilemma (dissolution or renewal), it presents, much more than they did, many of the features of "authoritarian fiction" (Suleiman 1983). Fallaci's voice is never so loud as in its ventriloquism. There is the Professor's "authoritative" voice-over explicitly conceptualizing the narrative business. There is demonstrative symbolism: the feral dogs; the white mare that becomes the target for demented shooting from all quarters. There is a questing disciple character (Angelo) and a teacher and priestess of wisdom (Ninette). There is a didactic reiteration of analogous episodes: the numerous instances of warm relationships between Italians and Lebanese (not to mention the French nuns, and others, even including Lady Godiva), which are blotted out by death in the horrific Christmas battle and the Italian withdrawal. Giorgi (1990) sardonically compares Fallaci's "male versions of grieving motherhood" to the figure of the dead Cecilia's mother in the plague-stricken Milan of Manzoni's *I promessi sposi* [*The Betrothed*]. These aspects – however traditional or unfashionable – do not of themselves disqualify Fallaci's novel any more than Manzoni's (cf. Gatt-Rutter 1990), and indeed, to the extent that any narrative is bound to be a *roman à thèse*, embodying a given perspective, their prominence is a matter of degree, or of the poetic governing the specific work. In *InsciAllah* they serve the demonstrative purpose of de-glamourizing war, of illustrating its destruction of bonds of affection across socio-cultural boundaries. As such, it is a noble experiment in the narrative of extreme situations.

Part VI
Overview

11

The Fallaci Project: Freedom as an Absolute

*F*allaci's starting-point is the existentialist one: death as the individual's return to non-existence, nothingness; life as projected against non-being. Self-realization in the space between the nothing before and the nothing after is therefore her primary project. Freedom is the absolute and axiomatic condition of such self-realization, and an imperative for the entire human species.

This starting-point, and this imperative, can be read forwards, backwards and sideways in all Fallaci's published volumes. The author has consistently stated that she was formed by the experience of the Resistance, in which the imminent eventuality of death was the condition of the struggle for freedom. First-person exposure – in factual or fictive guise, explicitly or, as in *Penelope alla guerra*, virtually – is paramount in all her work, receding only in *InsciAllah*, where it is novelistically displaced to a multiplicity of Others faced by the imminent eventuality of death, and where the figure of the author–narrator is reduced by *mise-en-abîme* to a simulacrum.

Even in her less intimate travelogues on Hollywood and on women in other worlds, Fallaci drives straight towards the existential core of her "characters" – interlocutors, interviewees, companions – usually finding there a hollow, an evasion, a terror, in the case of the screen idols; and, in a more confused and undefined way, in the case of "the useless sex", a corresponding alienation, an entrammelment at best in subordinate competition or power manoeuvres in male-dominated worlds. In the more intimate explorations – *Lettera a un bambino mai nato*, *Un uomo*, *InsciAllah* – self-accusation figures centrally, not always prominently, but perceptibly, in connection with the death of the protagonist or protagonists. These accusations are serious, involving a failure of love, of relationship, of faith in the Other. For this reason, they reach towards the tragic, unrelieved by catharsis.

Penelope enacts a sort of death, a death-in-life. Its protagonist, Gio, having rebelled against the authority of the Mother, is faced by the power of father-surrogates. Abandoning the loved one on discovering possession to be impossible, and herself abandoned according to the same convention, she projects a loveless, relationless challenge to the male world. In *Il sesso inutile*, it seems (though obscurely, and though not illuminated by a death) to be sisterhood that is repudiated. *Se il sole muore* (portentously envisaging planetary death and consecrated by the death of Theodore Freeman) explicitly confirms the break with the father and momentarily acclaims newfound brothers, while *Lettera a un bambino mai nato* nakedly wrestles with the protagonist's own motherhood role and her rejection of the Child. *Un uomo* is partly confession and atonement for less than total faith in the Companion, while the earlier *Niente e cosí sia* analogously makes amends for a breach of faith with a people seeking freedom – *giustizia e libertà* – in a re-run of the Resistance. Vietnam and Greece are the hard schools where brother- and sisterhood with worldwide liberation struggles is painfully negotiated. Small wonder that all this transgression, all this crisis of the primary loyalties of the self, has attracted readers in millions and dumbfounded literary critics and intellectuals.

The reaction of these latter against Fallaci has been to dismiss her books as "journalistic", "paraliterary", or " bestsellers". This literary ostracism of Fallaci fits John Carey's argument (1992) regarding "pride and prejudice among the literary intelligentsia" in Britain against the "clerks", the lower-middle-class reading public, and the development of the literary avant-garde as a defence of cultural aristocracy against the vulgar. The sociology of the aesthetic domain has been theorized by Bourdieu as "the market of symbolic goods", peremptorily characterized by "the opposition between the field of restricted production as a system producing cultural goods . . . objectively destined for a public of producers of cultural goods, and the field of large-scale pro-duction of cultural goods destined for non-producers of cultural goods, 'the public at large'" (1993: 115).

"Literariness" is often implicitly or explicitly invoked as an essence distinguishing the literary from the non-literary (journalism or bestsellers, as in Fallaci's case), but Bourdieu (p. 190) views this as a variable sociological construct of the field, as does Corsini (1974: 20–4). Jakobson and other proponents of the concept have never succeeded in establishing reliable formal or aesthetic criteria for the distinction, and several critics have shown the unreliability of the criteria proposed. Werth (1976) finds that Jakobson's linguistic and formal markers of the literary do not discriminate between Shakespeare's Sonnet 129 and McGonagall's doggerel or a newspaper article on chemical products for use against fleas, and Jakobson himself admitted that the "marks disclosing the implementation of the aesthetic function [as "dominant"] are not unchangeable or always uniform" and that entire genres might in certain periods be classed as extra-literary and at others as literary (1987: 42, 45). Genette makes it a simple axiom that poetry and fiction are constitutionally literary modes ("genres"), and that to deny literariness to a novel is really to say that it is a bad novel. He finds no clear-cut formal distinction between fictional and factual narrative, but rather a gradation between the two. Moreover, even writing that is not "constitutionally" literary may be "conditionally" literary – that is, its literary quality may be prominent or dominant (1991: 91, 95–151, esp. 148–9; cf. 35).

Italian theorists in effect have come to agree that what is at issue is not literariness as such (as opposed to the paraliterary, "kitsch", journalism, bestsellers etc.) but judgements about the literary level of specific works (Ferretti 1988: 42, 68, 81), and that a Gramscian "national–popular" extension of the reading public to sectors previously excluded is a serious issue where aesthetic and socio-political considerations intersect (Ferretti 1990). Ferretti (1988: 73–91) also discusses Franco Moretti's linkage of the "impure" reader's "aesthetic pleasure" with the text's "formal conciliation" of conflict and its *funzione inquietante* ("destabilizing function"): an approach which devalues experimentalism for its own sake (*sperimentalismo tautologico*), and even Joycian irony and ambiguity – aesthetic intransitivity, in a word – in favour of a more traditional (i.e., realist) mode of narrative literature, including "hybrid" or "impure" genres such as reportage and essay – that is, the very ground occupied by Fallaci. Ceserani (1986: 165) outlines a simple taxonomy or hierarchy of texts that dismisses the dichotomy between traditionalism (realism) and avant-garde (anti-realism): first, texts that capture

a rich complex of meanings through far-reaching formal elaboration, and thus reach extremely varied audiences; then less
far-reaching texts that nevertheless offer something new to a
socially and historically more restricted audience; and finally a
great mass of superficially and ephemerally entertaining writing.
I have discussed Fallaci's works in some detail in this book with
a view to making possible a serious consideration of her status
as a writer, and Ceserani's broad criteria are useful in assessing
the complexity and originality of both the web of meanings and
the means used. How sharp a challenge do her works present to
the established way of looking at things? How great and
manifold are the conflicts negotiated, and with what outcomes?
How effective and original are the literary means deployed?

Before further addressing these questions, I propose to
consider briefly Eco's analysis of kitsch and Spinazzola's criteria
by which Fallaci is all too often summarily found wanting. In
Apocalittici e integrati, Eco considers Dwight Macdonald's
categories of "midcult" and "masscult", "highbrow", "middle-
brow", and "lowbrow", and dismisses their implications of both
social and aesthetic hierarchy. Eco's argument against social hierarchy is the less convincing of the two, since an intellectual might
indeed well enjoy a lowbrow artform, but a non-intellectual is
unlikely to access a highbrow art-form. On the other hand, lowbrow art might have an aesthetic originality, integrity, meaning
and beauty of its own (and we may think of various forms of
folk-art, from Umbrian ceramics to a Marx Brothers film) (cf.
Eco 1984 [1964]: 53–4). It may thus be asked of Fallaci's works
whether they attain such integrity, and whether or where they
can be placed along the non-evaluative continuum from "high"
to "low".

Eco (ibid. 65–129) argues for a structural (and therefore basic)
difference between art and kitsch. He defines the artwork as a
message that generates messages through the active participation
of the beholder, while kitsch is a formal fake, using prefabricated
stylemes to produce prefabricated effects under the pretence of
art, which is thus fetishized and commodified. Kitsch therefore
tends towards "redundancy" or repetitiveness of effect, reiter-
ating an unambiguous message instead of opening out a diverse
array of messages. Eco picks out Ray Bradbury, the tutelary
sage of Fallaci's *Se il sole muore*, as a practitioner of artistically
pretentious kitsch (cf. ibid.: 123–6). In *Il superuomo di massa*,

Eco reinforced his definition of kitsch (including the pseudo-democratic popular fiction of Eugène Sue) as the signposting of pre-established literary effects, the creation of would-be archetypal figures which are really clichés, and the overuse of a documentary-type slow-motion technique to magnify the desired dramatic effect (1978: 58–60). The fundamental falsehood of what Eco damningly labels the "popular" novel lies in its simplistic, ready-made notion of good and evil, which the narrative does nothing to problematize or develop, but simply and soothingly reiterates, whether the hero triumphs or dies in the service of the supposed good (1978: 13).

Spinazzola has bracketed Fallaci and other writers in a piece whose title translates as "Zero value success: entertainment literature since the war" (1990 [1985]: 225–62). He takes Fallaci to task for her "hybridly magmatic" style, at once declamatory and racily plebeian (p. 250), and includes her among those for whom "the new signal of mutual recognition between writers and younger readers is best defined precisely by the drastic lowering of the standards of expressive decorum" (pp. 252–3). He implicitly associates her with "unbridled vitalism" and a "neo-traditionalism of narrative structures" combined with "the anti-literary ostentation of an insolent and coarse style bordering on vulgarity" (p. 252). Her heroes are ravingly emotional supermen, and mental and social normality is systematically outraged (p. 240). She is one of those for whom what really matters is "the virtues and vices of the individual I" (p. 244), whose central character is presented in the round, in the physical, emotional and instinctual immediacy of his vitalistic energy, without psychological complexities or contradictions (pp. 238–9). Though he grants that the heroes of writers such as he takes Fallaci to be do not necessarily achieve a reassuring relationship with the world, Spinazzola claims that narrative closure by these writers generally consigns the reader to behavioural norms and a horizon of certainty presumed to be universally valid, all the more effectively for the preceding defiance of legality and of social taboos and prohibitions (pp. 240–1).

This indiscriminate essay casually refers to Fallaci's "protagonists" and "books" in the plural, but its remarks appear relevant only to *Un uomo*, of which they present a travesty by no means comparable to the seriousness of Rosa's criticism. Moreover, Spinazzola repeatedly bundles together several authors including Fallaci in a kind of cluster-bombing, so that it is impossible to extricate what is specifically relevant to her. He thus falls short of his own earlier perception, in *La democrazia letteraria*, of the bestseller as a phenomenon that cuts across the distinction between art and non-art (for which he resorts to the Crocean formulation "poesia e non poesia"), just as he forgets his own proposal to extend literary critical enquiry beyond the field of *belle lettere* on the ground that: "It would . . . be quite wrong to regard the present upheavals with the usual supercilious disbelief and arrogance" (1984: 164–5). This failure on Spinazzola's part is itself a symptom of the "climate of total confusion of values" (ibid.), which we can attribute to the aftermath of 1968–9 in Italy. He castigates the "paraliterary" as a relatively unmediated appeal to the unconscious, and defines its readership as the politically ambiguous and volatile petty bourgeoisie, dismissing the perception, from Todorov (1970) onwards, of the "fantastic" in literature as a challenge to established order (and even correcting himself as to its genuinely experimental and democratizing potential). He persuasively stresses its aspect of what we may call controlled desublimation, which permits the return of the repressed in nightmarish guise all the better to reaffirm civilized norms of Good and Evil through narrative closure. Yet he himself falls back on neo-classical aesthetic norms of *elegante convenienza armoniosa* ("harmoniously elegant aptness": pp. 151–8). Spinazzola's self-contradictory argument strengthens the claims of Fallaci's *Penelope alla guerra*, which certainly offers no edifying closure; and it suggests a vindication in similar terms of *Un uomo*, which has drawn most fire from the critics as being Fallaci's most prominent literary and political target. My own discussion of that work in Part V above offers, I hope, considerable material for a defence against such charges.

What is so wide of the mark as to appear gratuitously and maliciously demeaning is the frequent coupling of Fallaci's name with that of Liala, pseudonym of Liana Cambiasi Negretti, author of countless vapidly romantic novels of upward social mobility whose heroines' horizons are limited to stylish domesticity or courtesanship (cf. Eco 1979b; Pozzato 1979). To cite against Fallaci the few Liala-like passages that stand out against the harsh grain of *Un uomo* is to misrepresent her and possibly to miss the function and effect of those passages. The one point of similarity between Fallaci and Liala is in the rhetoric of the speaking voice: this is put to quite different use from Liala, and, as I have suggested, most effectively in *Lettera a un bambino mai nato*, with its complex of stylistic systems and self-deletions, and its existential projection of the bodily voice between being and non-being. It is at once one of Fallaci's areas of strength and originality, and a weakness – when it unjustifiably swamps other elements of discourse, a tendency which is endemic in the writer.

The declamatory voice is closely linked with another tendential weakness in Fallaci: the rhetorical "redundancy" of emphasis and reiteration is used to enforce a conceptual closure, impose a rigid set of oppositions, over-simplified positive and negative values that leave the reader little mental autonomy. The simplistic conceptualization is not necessarily greatly enriched by the swing of the pendulum – the indecision of the participant observer, Oriana, or of the focalized protagonist (the Mother in *Lettera*, Angelo in *InsciAllah*) between two poles along a predetermined axis. The simplistic tendency is often more effectively counterbalanced and corrected by the dialogic mode, the "interview" (as, for instance, in much of *Niente e cosí sia*), or by the phenomenological variety of reportage material. But, to the extent that it does prevail, this tendency results in an excess of "readability", limiting the text's capacity for "generating messages". This factor explains both Fallaci's ease of access to a wider public and the resistance to her work by a more intellectual readership. Yet there is no gainsaying the uncompromisingly problematical challenge presented by her works. Even politically, the categorical principle of the ethical autonomy of the individual – though it does not lend itself to the articulation of social action in the complex organization of modern life – often highlights a confused reality: in *Niente e cosí sia*, the contradictions of the US position in Vietnam; the paucity of options open to the Mother in *Lettera*; the inadequacy of party politics in the Centre Union's dealings with Panagoulis in *Un uomo*.

Rather than Liala, another pseudonymous writer, significantly male, Fallaci's fellow-Tuscan, Curzio Malaparte (alias Kurt Suckert), is more appropriately referred to, usually with disparaging intent, as a term of comparison for Fallaci. More appropriately, not only because Malaparte was actually a friend and mentor as fellow-journalist and -writer of Fallaci's, but because, like her, he had a predilection for extreme situations and overwhelming effects and a talent for readership success. Like her, he is the participant observer, and perhaps a more immediate model than George Orwell; but he is, much more than Fallaci, his own protagonist and unimpeachable fount of ethics. By comparison, Oriana is self-effacing, self-doubting, self-accusing.

Nevertheless, the charge of *protagonismo* – self-dramatization – is one that is ritually levelled at Fallaci. It applies probably more to her public persona than to her simulacrum as textual author, narrator, diarist or "character", but, as regards her literary "character", that charge testifies to a barely dissimulated auto-biographical compulsion which is not hard to locate within the changing gender landscape of the Western world since the 1950s. Each of Fallaci's works – reportage or fiction or both combined – is in part a piece of Oriana's own history. John Sturrock has defined canonical autobiography as a genre in which deviancy (extraordinary individuality) is sanctioned as literary (1993: 291), and which "wills the unity of its subject" (ibid., p. 5), in effect reintegrating the self into society (which, in the process, she helps to redefine). Fallaci, however, has written no autobiography (the third-person fiction of *Penelope alla guerra* being her nearest analogue), but has only injected auto-biographical material into other textual tissues. In this, she more closely approaches the model proposed by Sidonie Smith, for whom "the excluded and colourful [a formulation which corrals together gender, race and other specificities] use autobiography to challenge the historically constructed subject" (1993: 20–1). The fragmented Oriana-figure (who may also call herself Giovanna–Penelope or Ninette or mother) stands as an overt challenge to the male-gendered projects of procreation, society, progress, power and war. As noted in Part I above, Fallaci evidences her own "immasculation" into "the historically constructed subject" of occidental modernity as impersonal and universal, but implicitly male and hegemonic. But, by doing so, as female "person", she invades the gendered space, helping to force its self-redefinition to include virgin, lover, career-woman and expectant mother. In this, she can be seen as a not insignificant actor in a broad social process which has seen a diversification not only of women's motherhood options (cf. Neiger 1993: 12) but of their total social role.

Following Smith, I would argue that Fallaci also points forward to the imminent end of the "unified I" and hence to the "generic extinction" of autobiography at the same time as excluded groups evince a drive towards autobiography (ibid., pp. 60–1). Taking up Cora Kaplan's cue in "Resisting Autobiography" (1992), Smith sees an outcome in "outlaw genres" (ibid., p. 154). *Fluidità intergenerica* has been widely noted as a characteristic of literature in Italy and elsewhere since the 1968–9 watershed (e.g. Spinazzola 1990: 237), and Fallaci's works may be taken singly as unostentatious exemplars of "outlaw genres" (the reportage novel, Gothic-realist fiction, the diary, imaginative biography). Collectively, they may be seen as jagged splinters of an autobiographical *Bildungsroman*, a spiritual odyssey with no destination. In this respect they suggest an updated counterpart to the "essayism" of Conrad, Musil and Pirandello which Thomas Harrison defines as the analytical discourse which "essays" to construct the self amid the ruin of nineteenth-century certainties (1992: cf. 2–3). In Fallaci's case, this nicely marries the two notions of "essay" as topical discussion and self-construction which are always inseparable components in her work.

The marriage of the subject and object of discourse is central to Fallaci as it is to the New Journalism. It produces unruly-seeming artefacts which are more at home in English-language cultures than in Italy (despite the now canonically established precedents of Carlo Levi, Primo Levi, Leonardo Sciascia and others). Fallaci still remains more Italian, more stylistically measured – restrained or constrained – than her American brothers, but it is pleasurable to end this impersonal dialogue with her by evoking Tom Wolfe's call upon an ever-renewed realism and an ever-renewed social novel to get up and to get out and "stalk the billion-footed beast", a form of fiction apparently chaotic in its pursuit of a chaotic reality, "(more notable for its content than its aesthetic release) … reworking … established, familiar and habitually commercial genres, from realism to fantasy, from Gothic to myth and legend" (Wolfe 1989, quoted in Bradbury 1992). Whether she is in pursuit of a billion-footed humanity busy at slaughter or at the hubristic assault on the heavens, or whether she is in pursuit of a two-legged human Oriana (or someone remarkably like her) or an Alekos grappling with the terms of existence – biosocial or biopolitical – Fallaci brings the literary enterprise right up to the front line between being and non-being, desperately seeking to wrest an affirmation out of defeat or destruction. Despite the existential poverty and rigidity of her intellectual and ethical code, her disconcerting and defiant individualism, she often enacts vital and dramatic dilemmas of our time within narrative and discursive structures of unfashionable originality whose aesthetic impurity has opened up the literary arena to an unprecedented number of readers, thus empowering them to participate in the responsibilities of citizenship in civil society, strengthening it worldwide.

Bibliography

A. Works by Oriana Fallaci

No attempt is made here at an exhaustive catalogue of Fallaci's voluminous journalistic output. Her Italian book publications are listed below, with their English-language translations. Interviews given by Oriana Fallaci are listed in section B below under the interviewer's name and are distinguished by an asterisk. The tapes of interviews conducted by Fallaci are held in the Mugar Library of the University of Boston. None of these are listed here.

1958 *I sette peccati di Hollywood*, Milan: Longanesi.

1961 *Il sesso inutile: viaggio intorno alla donna*, Milan: Rizzoli. *The Useless Sex*, trans. by Pamela Swinglehurst. London: Michael Joseph, 1964.

1962a *Penelope alla guerra*, Milan: Rizzoli. Edition used: Rizzoli, BUR, 1976. *Penelope at the War*, trans. by Pamela Swinglehurst. London: Michael Joseph, 1966.

1962b "Gli Antipatici: 1 – A. Armstrong-Jones – La fiaba di Cenerentolo", *L'Europeo*, 21 Jan. 1962, XVIII.3.848: 30–5.

1962c "Gli Antipatici: 2 – La figlia del successo – A colloquio con Françoise Sagan dopo le sue nozze con Bob Westhoff", *L'Europeo*, 28 Jan. 1962, XVIII. 4. 849: 30–2.

1962d "Gli Antipatici: 3 – L'uomo che sarà presidente – Orson Welles", *L'Europeo*, 4 Feb. 1962, XVIII. 5. 850: 28–34.

1963 *Gli antipatici*, Milan: Rizzoli. Trans. by Pamela Swinglehurst: *Limelighters*, London: Michael Joseph, 1967, and *The Egotists: Sixteen Surprising Interviews*, Chicago: Henry Regnery Co., 1968.

1965 *Se il sole muore*, Milan: Rizzoli. Edition used: Rizzoli, BUR, 1981. *If the Sun Dies*, trans. Pamela Swinglehurst, London and New York: Athenaeum, 1966.

1968a "La notte di sangue in cui sono stata ferita", *L'Europeo*, 17 Oct. 1968, XXIV.42.1197: 24–47.

1968b "Ecco il servizio che avevo perduto", *L'Europeo*, 31 Oct. 1968, XXIV.44.1199: 30–3.

1969 *Niente e cosí sia*, Milan: Rizzoli. Trans. by Isabel Quigly: *Nothing and Amen*, London: Michael Joseph, 1972; *Nothing and So Be It*, New York: Doubleday, 1972.

1970 *Quel giorno sulla luna*, ed. for schools by Alberto Pozzolini, Milan: Rizzoli.

1973 "Perspective – The Press Must Rip off Masks" (excerpts from speech given in Washington, DC, to American Society of Newspaper Editors), *Chicago Tribune*, 15 May.

1974 *Intervista con la storia*, Milan: Rizzoli. Extended and revised in 1977. Edition used: Rizzoli, BUR, 1990. *Interview with History*, trans. John Shepley, London: Michael Joseph, 1976.

1975a *Lettera a un bambino mai nato*, Milan: Rizzoli. Audio recording: "Oriana Fallaci legge *Lettera a un bambino mai nato*", Milan: Rizzoli, 1993. *Letter to a Child Never Born*, trans. by John Shepley, London: Arlington Books, 1975, and New York: Simon and Schuster, 1976. English edition used: London, Hamlyn, 1982 (revised translation).

1975b "*Il richiamo della foresta*, inno alla libertà", introduction to translation of Jack London, *The Call of the Wild*, by Ugo Déttore, Milan: Rizzoli (1953), Rizzoli, BUR, 1975.

1979a *Un uomo*, Milan: Rizzoli. *A Man*, trans. William Weaver, New York: Simon and Schuster, 1980; London, Arrow Books, 1981.

1979b "An Interview with Khomeini", *New York Times Magazine*, 7 Oct.

1988 "Io e Gheddafi. E gli porsi il cappio perché si impiccasse da solo", *Corriere della Sera*, 24 April.

1990a *InsciAllah*, Milan: RCS Rizzoli Libri; *InshAllah*, trans. with James Marcus, New York: Doubleday, 1992; London: Chatto & Windus, 1992.

1990b "Grazie, babbo, della tua inflessibilità" (1988), *Europeo* 33, 18 Aug.: 63–4.

B. Other works consulted

This list includes only the more useful reviews of Fallaci's work, as well as every serious study of the author that I have been able to find. Other items more generally concern literary, political, social and gender issues and histories relevant to Fallaci's various texts. A number of book reviews and journalistic pieces on Fallaci have been listed for which full details have not yet been recovered. Some of these are cuttings held in the Mugar Library of Boston University.

* denotes an interview given by Fallaci.

Mugar – denotes the Fallaci Collection in the Mugar Library of the University of Boston.

ABBATE, Michele 1969 "Dall'inferno con amore", *Gazzetta del Mezzogiorno*, 22 Nov.

AFFINATI, Eraldo 1990 "Che scoperta dell'America", *Europeo*, 14 Dec., 50: 104–9.

AGNELLO-MODICA, Franca 1992 *L'opera narrativa di Oriana Fallaci*, Ph.D. thesis, University of Wisconsin, Madison, 1991. Dissertation Abstracts International. UMI. Ann Arbor.

AJAMI, Fouad 1981 *The Arab Predicament. Arab Political Thought and Practice since 1967*, Cambridge: Cambridge University Press.

—— 1985 "Lebanon and its Inheritors", *Foreign Affairs*, Spring. Quoted in PELCOVITS 1991.

ALLIEVI, S. and F. D'ASSETTO 1993 *Il ritorno dell'Islam: i musulmani in Italia*, Rome: Lavoro ISCOS (Istituto Sindacale per la Cooperazione allo Sviluppo).

AL-SHAYKH, Hanan 1986 *The Story of Zahra*, London: Quartet Books, 1986, 1991.

ALTOMONTE, A. 1974 "Diciotto interviste per la storia", *Il Tempo*, 31 May.

—— 1979 "Ucciso da tutti", *Il Tempo*, 8 July.

AMTER, Joseph A. 1982 *Vietnam Verdict: A Citizen's History*, New York: The Continuum Publishing Company.

ANDREWS, Kevin 1980 "Panagoulis Dead and Alive", pp. 227–81 in *Greece in the Dark*, Amsterdam: Adolf M. Hakkert.

ANGIONI, F. and M. CREMASCO 1991 "Italy's Role in Peace-keeping Operations", pp. 150–8 in McDERMOTT and

SKJELSBAEK (eds) 1991.

APTER, T. E. 1982 "The Uncanny: Freud, E.T.A. Hoffmann, Edgar Allan Poe", pp. 32–48 in *Fantasy Literature: An Approach to Reality*, London: Macmillan.

ARATO, Guido 1979 "Un successo perché – Fallaci a valanga", *Il Secolo XIX*, 22 Dec.

ARDENTI, Piero 1976 "Quando un libro interessa la gente", in *Il Giornale di Calabria*, 24 March.

ARICÒ, Santo L. 1986a "Oriana Fallaci's Discovery of Truth in *Niente e cosí sia*", *European Studies Journal* 3.2: 11–23.

—— 1986b "Breaking the Ice: An In-Depth Look at Oriana Fallaci's Interview Technique", *Journalism Quarterly* 63.3: 587–93.

—— 1990a "Oriana Fallaci's Journalistic Novel: *Niente e cosí sia*", in ARICÒ 1990: 171–82.

—— (ed.) 1990b *Contemporary Women Writers in Italy: A Modern Renaissance*, Amherst: University of Massachussetts Press.

ARSLAN, Antonia 1979 "Un uomo, l'amore: una vita per la libertà", *L'Eco di Parma*, 25 July.

ASPESI, Natalia* 1975 "L'ultimo libro di Oriana Fallaci – Intervista con un figlio che non verrà", *Il Giorno*, 4 Sept.

BAER, Eugen 1991 "The Logic of Autobiography", pp. 395–403 in Myrdene Anderson and Floyd Merrell (eds), *On Semiotic Modeling*, Berlin – New York: Mouton de Gruyter.

BARAŃSKI, Z. G. and L. PERTILE (eds) 1993 *The Italian Novel Today*, Edinburgh: Edinburgh University Press.

BARAŃSKI, Z. G. and S. VINALL (eds) 1991 *Women and Italy: Essays on Gender, Culture and History*, New York: St Martin's Press.

BARTHES, Roland 1953 *Le Degré zéro de l'écriture*, Paris: Seuil. Translation used: *Writing Degree Zero and Elements of Semiology*, by Annette Lavers and Colin Smith, London: Jonathan Cape, 1984.

BEAUVOIR (see de BEAUVOIR)

BELSEY, Catherine 1980 *Critical Practice*, London: Methuen.

BENELLI, Bruno 1970 "Il volume di cui si parla: *Niente e cosí sia* della Fallaci", *Sabato*, 19 Sept.

BERNARDINI, Aldo 1985 *Le dive*, Bari – Rome: Laterza.

BEVILACQUA, A. 1969 "Toscana, Messico o Vietnam: l'inferno è uguale per tutti", *Oggi*, 10 Dec. Also in *Il Commercio del Popolo*, April 1970.

BEVILACQUA, M. G.* 1980 "I miei privilegi: nata povera e donna", source unknown.

BILTON, Michael and Kevin SIM 1992 *Four Hours in My Lai: A War Crime and its Aftermath*, Harmondsworth: Viking.

BIMBI, Franca 1993 "Three Generations of Women: Transformations of Female Identity Models in Italy", in CICIONI and PRUNSTER (eds) 1993: 149–66.

BIONDI, Dino 1961 "Alla ricerca delle donne felici", source unknown. Mugar Box 11/F9.

BLUM, Joanne 1988 *Transcending Gender: The Male/Female Double in Women's Fiction*, Ann Arbor – London: UMI Research Press.

BO, Carlo 1961 "Oriana Fallaci: proficuo viaggio attorno al sesso inutile", *L'Europeo*, precise source unknown.

—— 1975 "Oriana Fallaci: una rivincita della donna", *L'Europeo*, 5 Dec.

—— 1979 "Il grande continente del dolore", *L'Europeo*, 16 Aug.: 6–7.

BONAVIRI, G. 1974 Review of *Intervista con la storia*, *Nuova Antologia*, July.

BONFANTE, Jordan* 1975 "An Interview is a Love Story", *Time*, 20 Oct.

BOOTH, Wayne 1961 *The Rhetoric of Fiction*, Chicago: University of Chicago Press.

BORGES, Jorge Luís 1949 "La busca de Averroës", in *El Aleph*; now in *Prosa Completa*, Vol. 2, Barcelona: Bruguera, 1980 (pp. 69–76). Translation used: "Averroës' Search", by James E. Irley, in *Labyrinths: Selected Stories and Other Writings*, ed. Donald A. Yates, Harmondsworth: Penguin Books, 1970 (pp. 180–8).

BOURDIEU, Pierre 1993 *The Field of Cultural Production*, Cambridge: Polity Press.

br – see *(die) WELTWOCHE*

BRADBURY, M. 1992 "Closer to Chaos: American Fiction in the 1980s", pp. 17–18 in *Times Literary Supplement*, 22 May.

BRESLIN, Jimmy 1974 "How He Saw the War in Vietnam", in MILLS (ed.) 1974: 81–102.

BROOKE-ROSE, C. 1981 *A Rhetoric of the Unreal*, Cambridge: Cambridge University Press.

BUNTING, Josiah 1972 Review of *Nothing and So Be It*, *Washington Post*, 23 Feb. (pp. B1, B7).

BURKE, Kenneth 1968 "Lexicon Rhetoricae", pp. 123–83 in *Counter-statement*, Berkeley and Los Angeles: University of

California Press.

BUTOR, Michel 1962 *Mobile: étude pour une représentation des Etats-Unis*, Paris: Gallimard.

BUTTAFAVA, M.* 1975 "Questo mio bambino nato col dolore", *Oggi Illustrato*, pp. 84–5. Exact source unknown.

CADIOLI, Alberto 1982 "La strategia dei best-seller", in SPINAZZOLA (ed.) 1982: 215–37.

CAESAR, Michael 1991 "Italian Fiction in the Nineteen-Eighties", in SMYTH (ed.) 1991: 74–89.

CANCOGNI, Manlio* 1974 "Oriana Fallaci incontra i potenti – Imbrogliata da uno solo". Source unknown.

CAREY, John 1992 *The Intellectuals and the Masses: Pride and Prejudice among the Literary Intelligentsia, 1880–1939*, London: Faber and Faber.

CARRANO, Patrizia* 1978 "Oriana Fallaci", pp. 69–102 in *Le signore grandi firme*, Rimini – Florence: Guaraldi.

CASES, Cesare 1990 "Il poeta e la figlia del macellaio" (1978), pp. 195–221 in *Il boom di Roscellino: satire e polemiche*, Turin: Einaudi.

CASOLI, Claudio 1970 Review of *Niente e cosí sia*, in *Città Nuova*, 10 Oct.

—— 1975 "L'urlo di una madre mancata", *Città Nuova – Oggi-mondo*, 10 Oct.

CECCHI, Ottavio and E. GHIDETTI (eds) 1986 *Fare storia della letteratura*, Rome: Riuniti.

CECCHI, Umberto 1990 "Una notte, cercando *Insciallah*", in *Europeo* 33, 18 Aug.: 59–62.

CEDERNA, Camilla 1990 "Madame Veleno e i calzini di Panagulis", in *Wimbledon – La gente che legge*, I.5, July–Aug.: 1–3.

CESERANI, R. 1986 "Come insegnare letteratura", in CECCHI and GHIDETTI (eds) 1986: 151–72.

—— et al. 1983 *La narrazione fantastica*, Pisa: Nistri-Lischi.

CHADEAU, Danielle 1962 "A la découverte du 'Sexe inutile'", in *Démocratie*, 18 Jan.: 117.

CHAMBERS, Ross 1984 *Story and Situation: Narrative Seduction and the Power of Fiction*, Manchester: Manchester University Press.

—— 1991 *Room for Maneuver: Reading (the) Oppositional (in) Narrative*, Chicago and London: University of Chicago Press.

CHATMAN, Seymour 1989 "The 'Rhetoric' of 'Fiction'", in James

PHELAN (ed.), *Reading Narrative: Form, Ethics, Ideology*, Columbus: Ohio State University.

CHESTER, Phyllis 1979 *With Child*, New York: Thomas Crowell.

CHIERICI, Maurizio 1961 "Il viaggio 'attraverso la donna' di Oriana Fallaci, pettegola di classe", *Gazzetta di Parma*, precise date unknown (Mugar Box 11/F9.)

CHOMSKY, Noam 1988 "Middle East Terrorism and the American Ideological System", in SAID and HITCHENS (eds) 1988.

CICIONI, Mirna and N. PRUNSTER (eds) 1993 *Visions and Revisions: Women in Italian Culture*, Providence and Oxford: Berg.

COLOMBO, Furio 1990 "Chi ha paura di Oriana?", *Europeo* 33, 18 Aug.: 55–8.

COLUMBIA COLLEGE, CHICAGO 1994 Note from Carol Bryant, College Relations Officer.

CORRIERE DELLA SERA 1991 Report on award to Fallaci of Premio Hemingway, 26 May.

CORSINI, Gianfranco 1974 *L'istituzione letteraria*, Naples: Liguori.

—— (ed.) 1982 *Letteratura e sociologia*, Bologna: Zanichelli.

COSTANTINI, C. 1979 "Lo conosceva poco e male", *Il Messaggero*, 5 July.

COTT, Jonathan* 1976 Interview with Oriana Fallaci, *Rolling Stone*, 17 June.

COWARD, Rosalind 1989 "Are Women's Novels Feminist Novels?" in SHOWALTER (ed.) 1989b: 225–39.

CRAIG, David and Michael EGAN 1979 *Extreme Situations: Literature and Crisis from the Great War to the Atom Bomb*, London: Macmillan.

CRIMI, Bruno 1980 "Oriana Fallaci, in arte Liala", *Panorama*, 19 May: 169.

de BEAUVOIR, S. 1972 *The Second Sex*, Harmondsworth: Penguin. Also used: London: Cape, 1953. First published as *Le Deuxième Sexe*, Paris, 1949.

DEL BUONO, Oreste 1961 "Lungo viaggio intorno alla donna", *Settimana Incom*, precise source unknown.

DERRIDA, Jacques 1973 *Speech and Phenomena and Other Essays on Husserl's Theory of Signs*, Evanston: Northwestern University Press. (1986 edition used.) First published as *La Voix et le phénomène*, Paris: Presses Universitaires de France, 1967.

DEUTSCH, Helene 1944 *The Psychology of Women: A Psychoanalytical Interpretation*, 2 vols, 1944–5, New York: Grune and

Stratton. (Italian translation: *Psicologia della donna*, Turin: Boringhieri, 1977.)

DIAMANDOUROS, N. 1991 "PASOK and State–Society Relations in Post-Authoritarian Greece (1974–1988)", in VRYONIS (ed.) 1991: 15–35.

DI GRAZIA, C. A. 1975 "Viaggio tra il nulla e la vita", *Il Telegrafo*, 4 Oct.

DOLBIER, Maurice 1966 "Not a novel, not an essay, but a new kind of writing", *World Journal Tribune*, 26 Oct.

DOMINIJANNI, I. 1993 "Aborto, dove salta il confine tra laici e cattolici", *Il Manifesto*, 7 Jan.: 11.

DUCHÊNE, Anne 1981 "Massage parlare", *Times Literary Supplement*, 22 May.

DUMAS, Francine Review of *Le Sexe inutile*, in *Esprit*, date unknown.

DUNCAN, Donald 1974 "The Whole Thing Was a Lie!" in MILLS (ed.) 1974: 103–18.

DUNN, Cyril 1966 "Oriana and the Astronauts", *The Observer*, 3 Sept.

du PLESSIX GRAY, F. 1977 "Oriana Fallaci: Italian Soap Opera", *New York Times Book Review*, 13 Feb.: 3.

ECO, Umberto 1978 *Il superuomo di massa*, Milan: Bompiani.

—— 1979a *Lector in fabula: la cooperazione interpretativa nei testi narrativi*, Milan: Bompiani. English trans.: *The Role of the Reader: Explorations in the Semiotics of Texts*, London: Hutchinson, 1981.

—— 1979b "Tre donne intorno al cor. . ." in ECO *et al.* 1979: 5–27.

—— 1984 *Apocalittici e integrati*, Milan: Bompiani. (First edn 1964.)

—— 1989 *The Open Work*, London: Radius. (Trans. of *Opera aperta*, 1962.)

ECO, U. *et al.* 1979 "Carolina Invernizio, Matilde Serao, Liala", *Il Castoro* 145, Florence: La Nuova Italia.

ERBANI, F. 1979 "Polemiche – Il caso Fallaci: un uomo, una donna e numerosi dubbi", *Roma*, 21 July.

FABBRETTI, N. 1975a "Oriana Fallaci: io sto dalla parte della vita", *Gazzetta del Popolo*, 10 Oct.

—— 1975b "Sempre dalla parte della vita", *Alba*, 17 Oct.

—— 1979a "L'ultima lettera di Oriana Fallaci", *Gazzetta del Popolo*, 7 July.

—— 1979b "Lettera a un uomo mai morto", *Alba*, 21 Sept.

FABI, Gianfranco 1975 "Un appassionato inno alla vita in una società senza ideali", *Giornale del Popolo*, 2 Oct.

FALLACI, Paola 1975* "È una lettera alle mamme", *Annabella*, 18 Oct.

—— 1979a* "Una donna chiamata Oriana", *Annabella*, 30 Aug.: 18–25.

—— 1979b* "E spiccò il volo poi venne la tragedia", *Annabella*, 6 Sept.: 16–25.

—— 1991* "Ma il successo può essere fonte di grande infelicità", *Oggi*, 24 Dec.: 24–8.

FARINA MAGGIONI, Mary 1975 "Autointervista di Oriana", *Il Giornale di Vicenza*, 25 Sept.

FELMAN, Shoshana 1994 *What Does a Woman Want? Reading and Sexual Difference*, Baltimore: Johns Hopkins University Press.

FERRETTI, G. C. 1983 *Il best seller all'italiana. Fortune e formule del romanzo "di qualità"*, Rome – Bari: Laterza.

—— 1988 *La fortuna letteraria*, Milan: Transeuropa.

—— 1990 "L'editore mediatore", *Belfagor* 1, 31 Jan.: 23–9.

FERRIERI, Giuliano 1975* "Oriana Fallaci spiega il suo libro", *L'Europeo* 39, 26 Sept.

FETTERLEY, Judith 1978 *The Resisting Reader: A Feminist Approach to American Fiction*, Bloomington: Indiana University Press.

FIFIS, C. N. 1994 "Oral Histories of the Greek Civil War", *Migration Action* XVI, 2/3, Dec.: 43–6.

FIRESTONE, S. 1970 *Dialectic of Sex*, New York: William Morrow.

FISHEL, W. R. (ed.) *Vietnam: Anatomy of a Conflict*, Itasca, Ill.: F. E. Peacock.

FITZGERALD, Frances 1972 *Fire in the Lake: The Vietnamese and the Americans in Vietnam*, Boston: Little, Brown & Co.

FLANNER, Janet 1973 "Oriana", *Vogue*, April.

FORGACS, David 1990 *Italian Culture in the Industrial Era: Cultural Industries, Politics and the Public*, Manchester: Manchester University Press.

FOSSATI, R. and I. MAZZONIS 1976 "La maternità come destino", pp. 67–76 in P. Bruzzichelli and M. L. Algini (eds) *Donna, cultura e tradizione*, Milan: Mazzotta, 1976.

FRANGIPANE, V. 1970 "Un libro di Oriana Fallaci sul Vietnam", *Messaggero Veneto*, 19 Feb.

FRANKS, Lucinda 1981 "Behind the Fallaci Image", *Saturday Review*, Jan.: 18–22.

FREIXAS, Laura 1988 "Mi mama me mima", in *El asesino en la muñeca*, Barcelona: Editorial Anagrama. Trans. L. Charnon-

Deutsch, "My Momma Spoils Me", *Tulsa Studies in Women's Literature*, Spring 1991, 10.1: 13–15.

FRIEDMAN, S. S. 1987 "Creativity and the Childbirth Metaphor: Gender Difference in Literary Discourse", *Feminist Studies* 13.1: 49–82; repr. in WARHOL and HERNDL (eds) 1991: 379–96.

FRYE, Northrop 1957 *Anatomy of Criticism: Four Essays*, Princeton University Press. (Repr. 1973.)

GALLAGHER, C. 1993 "The Networking Muse: Aphra Behn as Heroine of Frankness and Self-Discovery", *Times Literary Supplement*, 10 Sept.: 3–4.

GARDINER, Judith K. 1981 "On Female Identity and Writing by Women", in Elizabeth Abel (ed.), *Writing and Sexual Difference*, special no. of *Critical Inquiry*, Winter 1981, 8.2: 347–61.

GATTA, Bruno 1974 Review of *Intervista con la storia*, *Il Mattino*, 23 May.

GATT-RUTTER, J. 1989 "Revolution and Redemption: Manzoni's *The Betrothed*, Dostoevsky's *The Brothers Karamazov*, and the Birth of the Christian Novel", *Southern Review* 22.3: 275–89.

—— 1990 "When the Killing Had to Stop: Manzoni's Paradigm of Christian Conversion", *The Italianist*, 10: 1–30.

—— 1991 "Macrohistories and Microhistories: Jaroslav Hašek's *Osudy dobrého vojáka Švejka za světové války*", *Journal of European Studies*, 21: 1–17.

GATT-RUTTER, J. and Tim PRENZLER f/c "Tragedy, My Lai, and Media".

GELLHORN, Martha 1993 *The Face of War* (1959), revised edn, London: Granta Books.

GELLNER, Ernest 1992a "From the Ruins of the Great Contest. Civil Society, Nationalism and Islam", *Times Literary Supplement*, 13 March: 9–10.

—— 1992b "La fine del marxismo nell'ex-URSS e l'affermazione del sacro nell'Islam", *Linea d'ombra*, May: 11–12.

GENETTE, Gérard 1980 *Narrative Discourse*, trans. Jane E. Lewin, Oxford: Basil Blackwell. (*Figures III*, Paris: Seuil, 1972.)

—— 1991 *Fiction et diction*, Paris: Seuil.

GEROSA, Guido 1976* "*Playboy* intervista: Oriana Fallaci", *Playboy* (Rome), Jan.: 15–17, 108, 110, 112.

GIACONI, Elettra 1976 "Pietà per un bambino mai nato", *Vita Sociale*, May–June: 196–200.

GIACOTTO, D. 1975 "Caro figlio, non ti voglio", *Stampa Sera*, 7 Oct.

GILMOUR, David 1987 *Lebanon: The Fractured Country* (1983), revised edn, London: Sphere Books.

GIORGI, Stefania 1990 "Parlar di guerra fa bene alla guerra", *Noidonne*, Nov.: 84–5.

Il GIORNALE 1979 "Proteste della famiglia Panagulis" (unsigned), 4 July.

GLEICK, James 1988 *Chaos – Making a New Science* (1987), London: Sphere Books.

GORIA, Giulio 1974 "Intervistati 'senza pietà' diciotto personaggi famosi", *Paese Sera*, 24 May.

GORLIER, Claudio 1990 "*Insciallah*, un romanzo popolare per raccontare il Caos", *La Stampa – Tuttolibri*, 11 Aug.

GRANA, Gianni 1973 "Curzio Malaparte" (1968), *Il Castoro*, Florence: La Nuova Italia.

GRENIER, Richard 1992 "JFK and Vietnam", *Times Literary Supplement*, 20 March.

GRENVILLE, Kenneth 1972 *The Saving of South Vietnam*, Sydney: Alpha Books.

GUARINI, Ruggero 1979 "Come si fabbrica un romanzo di stagione", *Il Messaggero*, 24 June.

GUIDUCCI, Armanda 1970 "Nessun Messico può guarirci del Vietnam", *Avanti!*, 1 Feb.

GUOLO, R. and F. MOROSINI 1993 "Islam e Occidente, la lunga sfida", *Il Ponte* 49.7, July: 810–19.

HALBERSTAM, D. 1974 "The Making of a Quagmire", in MILLS (ed.) 1974: 59–72.

HAN, Suyin 1952 *A Many-Splendoured Thing*, London: Jonathan Cape.

HANNE, Michael 1994 "Salman Rushdie: *The Satanic Verses* (1988)", pp. 189–224 in *The Power of the Story: Fiction and Political Change*, Providence and Oxford: Berghahn Books.

HARPHAM, G. G. 1992 *Getting It Right: Language, Literature and Ethics*, Chicago and London: University of Chicago Press.

HARRISON, T. J. 1992 *Essayism: Conrad, Musil and Pirandello*, Baltimore: Johns Hopkins University Press.

HEILBRUN, C. G. 1982 *Toward a Recognition of Androgyny* (1964, 1974), New York and London: W. W. Norton.

HENNIKER-HEATON, P. J. 1966 Review of *If the Sun Dies*, in *The Christian Science Monitor*, Nov. 17.

HERSH, Seymour M. 1970 *My Lai 4: A Report on the Massacre and its Aftermath*, New York: Random House.

—— 1972 *Cover-up: The Army's Secret Investigation of the Massacre at My Lai 4*, New York: Vintage.

HILL, Barry 1992 "Mailer's Ghost", *The Age*, 4 Jan.

HOYLES, John 1991 *The Literary Underground. Writers and the Totalitarian Experience, 1900–1950*, New York – London: Harvester Wheatsheaf.

HUNTINGTON, S. P. 1993 "The Clash of Civilizations?" *Foreign Affairs*, Summer, 72.3: 22–49.

HUSSEIN, Hamer 1994 "Delivering the Truth – An Interview with V. S. Naipaul", *Times Literary Supplement*, 2 Sept.: 3–4.

IMPERATORI, G. 1979 "La bella fiaba dell'eroe assassinato dal Potere", *Il Mattino di Padova*, 13 July.

l'INVITATO 1965 "Il Nuovo Mondo", *Il Mondo*, 20 July.

IRIGARAY, Luce 1993 *Je, tu, nous* (trans. Alison Martin), New York: Routledge.

JACKSON, Rosemary 1981 *Fantasy: The Literature of Subversion*, London and New York: Methuen.

JAKOBSON, Roman 1987 *Language in Literature*, ed. K. Pomorska and S. Rudy, Cambridge (Mass.) and London: Harvard University Press.

JASON, Philip K. 1990 "Sexism and Racism in Vietnam War Fiction", *Mosaic*, Summer, 23.3: 125–37.

JENTSCH, Ernst 1906 "Sulla psicologia dell'*Unheimliche*" ("Zur Psychologie des Unheimlichen"), in CESERANI *et al.* 1983: 399–410.

JOHNSON, Barbara 1986 "Apostrophe, animation and abortion", *Diacritics* 16.1: 29–39, in WARHOL and HERNDL (eds) 1991: 630–43.

JUSTICE, Blair 1966 "Can NASA Make Man Eternal?" *The Houston Post*, 23 Oct.: 10.

KAPLAN, Cora 1992 "Resisting Autobiography: Outlaw Genres and Transnational Feminist Subjects", in SMITH and WATSON (eds) 1992: 115–38.

KARNOW, Stanley 1983 *Vietnam, A History*, New York: Viking Press.

KATSOUDAS, D. 1991 "New Democracy: In or Out of Social Democracy", in VRYONIS (ed.) 1991: 1–14.

KEESING'S CONTEMPORARY ARCHIVE 1984 VOL. XXX: 32647. Report on Beirut bomb blasts of 23 Oct. 1983 and international reaction.

KLEMESRUD, Judy 1973 "Oriana Fallaci, an Interviewer who

goes for the Jugular in Four Languages", *New York Times*, 25 Jan.

KNIGHTLEY, Phillip 1975 *The First Casualty. The War Correspondent as Hero, Propagandist and Myth Maker from the Crimea to Vietnam*, London: André Deutsch.

KOSOFSKY SEDGWICK, Eve 1985 *Between Men: English Literature and Male Homosocial Desire*, New York: Columbia University Press.

KRACHMALNICOFF, P. 1970 "Il libro di Oriana Fallaci sul conflitto vietnamita", *Gazzetta del Popolo*, 21 Jan.

KUBAL, David 1972 *Outside the Whale: George Orwell's Art and Politics*, Notre Dame, Indiana: University of Notre Dame Press.

LAJOLO, Davide 1979* "Una donna, un uomo", *Gazzetta del Popolo*, 19 July; repr. as "C'è anche la mafia letteraria. Colloquio con Oriana scrittrice e giornalista", *Alto Adige*, 4 Aug.

LANNUTTI, G. 1965 "Emigreremo sui pianeti", *Avanti!*, 3 Aug.

LAURENZI, Carlo 1979 "Un uomo di nome Alekos", *Il Giornale*, 4 July.

LAZZARINI, G. 1980* "E mentre cova la guerra gli immutabili dormono", *Oggi*, 28 May: 47–51.

LEJEUNE, Philippe 1982 "The autobiographical contract", pp. 192–222 in T. Todorov (ed.), *French Literary Theory Today: A Reader*, trans. by R. Carter, Cambridge – New York: Cambridge University Press.

LEPSCHY, Giulio 1991 "Language and Sexism", in BARAŃSKI and VINALL (eds) 1991: 117–40.

LESER, David 1993* "The Fallaci Encounter", *HQ magazine*, Sept.–Oct., No. 30: 90–8.

LETTE, Kathy 1994 *Foetal Attraction*, London: Picador.

LEY, Willy 1967 "Out of Orbit", *New York Times Review of Books*, 5 Feb.: 49.

LISTRI, P. F. 1974 Review of *Intervista con la storia*, *La Nazione*, 30 April.

LODI, Carlo 1977 "La 'lettera' della Fallaci: un urlo senza aggettivi", precise source unknown.

—— 1979 "L'ultima Fallaci: 'Ghía se' (io per te)!", *Gazzetta di Mantova*, 11 July.

LOWRY, Malcolm 1963 *Under the Volcano* (1947), London: Cape.

LUKÁCS, Gyorgy 1969 *The Historical Novel* (1947), trans. H. and S. Mitchell, Harmondsworth: Peregrine Books.

—— 1980 "Reportage or Portrayal?" (1932), pp. 45–75 in *Essays on Realism*, London: Laurence and Wishart.

McDERMOTT, Anthony and Kjell SKJELSBAEK (eds) 1991 *The Multinational Force in Beirut 1982–1984*, Miami: Florida International University Press.

MADEO, Liliana 1990 "Duello tra le regine del giornalismo", *La Stampa*, 23 Dec.: 7.

MAILER, Norman 1970 *Of a Fire on the Moon*, Boston: Little, Brown & Co.

—— 1991 *Harlot's Ghost*, London: Michael Joseph.

MAIORE, Ignazio 1975 "L'utero rifiutato", *Paese Sera*, 30 Sept.

MALDINI, Sergio 1974 "Oriana fra le guerre", *Il Resto del Carlino*, 30 April.

MANCIOTTI, Mauro 1974 "Una giornalista contesta i potenti", *Il Secolo XIX*, 13 June.

MARABINI, Claudio 1979 "Panagulis, amore mio", *La Nazione*, 28 June.

MARCHETTI, G. 1979 "Glorificazione di Panagulis", *Gazzetta di Parma*, 7 July.

MARCHIONNE PICCHIONE, Luciana 1979 Review of *Un uomo*, in *Canadian Journal of Italian Studies*, Spring–Summer, 4.34: 327–8.

MARTINA, G. 1975 Review of *Lettera a un bambino mai nato*, in *La Civiltà Cattolica*, 18 Oct.

MATTEI, Paolo 1990 "Dicono di lei 'Troppo mistero, non è mica Thomas Man", *Wimbledon – La gente che legge*, I.5, July–Aug.: 3–4.

Il MATTINO 1992 3 Dec.: report on Fallaci's breast cancer.

MAURO, Walter 1966 "Fantascienza e letteratura in Italia – Ci insegnano ad esorcizzare i nostri 'mostri' quotidiani", *Gazzetta del Mezzogiorno*, 19 March.

MEDAIL, Cesare 1976 "I perché di un best-seller in libreria", *Corriere della Sera*, 22 March: 3.

MERRY, Bruce 1990 *Women in Modern Italian Literature: Four Studies Based on the Work of Grazia Deledda, Alba De Céspedes, Natalia Ginzburg and Dacia Maraini*, Townsville: Department of Modern Languages, James Cook University.

Il MESSAGGERO 1979 "Quanta immaginazione", unsigned interview with Stathis Panagoulis, 5 July.

MEZZALANA BALDINI, Bruna 1979 "Il 'best-seller' di Oriana Fallaci – Considerazioni su *Un uomo*", *Il Giornale di Vicenza*, 27 Dec.

MILANI, Marisa 1971 "La lingua 'effimera' di Oriana Fallaci", *La*

Battana, VIII.25: 23–49.

MILELLA, Liana and Luciano GALASSI 1993 "Divo bugiardo", Panorama, 3 Oct.: 56–7.

MILLS, Nicolaus (ed.) 1974 The New Journalism. A Historical Anthology, New York: McGraw-Hill.

MONTANELLI, Indro 1961 "Il sesso inutile – Da Oriana si lasciano spennare solo perché è donna anche lei", Corriere d'informazione, 19–20 May.

MONTEATH, Peter 1989 "The Spanish Civil War and the Aesthetics of Reportage", pp. 69–85 in David Bevan (ed.), Literature and War, Amsterdam: Rodopi.

MOSCA, Carla 1965 Review of Se il sole muore, in Roma (Naples), 5 Aug.

MUKAŘOVSKÝ, Jan 1977 "Dialogue and Monologue" (1940), pp. 81–112 in The Word and Verbal Art: Selected Essays, trans. and ed. by John Burbank and Peter Steiner, New Haven and London: Yale University Press.

MURPHY, James E. 1974 The New Journalism: A Critical Perspective, Journalism Monographs 34, May.

NASCIMBENI, Giulio 1962? "Una ragazza nata per scrivere – La fiorentina di Manhattan", source unknown, Mugar Box 11/F9.

NAYAR, Radhakrishnan 1993 "Jungle of Irresponsibility", review of Tobey C. Herzog, Vietnam War Stories: Innocence Lost, in Times Literary Supplement, 6 Aug.

NEHAMAS, Alexander 1981 "The Postulated Author: Critical Monism as a Regulative Ideal", Critical Inquiry, Autumn, 8.1: 133–49.

NEIGER, Ada (ed.) 1993 Maternità trasgressiva e letteratura, Naples: Liguori.

NEWSWEEK 1964 "Oriana's World", 17 Aug.: 45–6.

NIRENSTEIN, Fiamma 1986 "Ebbene dico sí a Oriana – lei sí che mi piace", Noidonne 41.6, June: 37.

OCCHIUZZI, Franco 1977 "Laurea dell'Università di Chicago alla scrittrice e giornalista Fallaci. Oriana dottoressa (ad honorem) del bestseller", Corriere della Sera, 9 June.

OSTELLINO, Piero 1990 "Oriana Fallaci: è l'ora di Insciallah", Supplemento del Corriere della Sera, exact source unknown.

PACILEO, Giuseppe 1979 "Un uomo eroe", Il Mattino, 9 Aug.

PANDINI, Giancarlo 1974a "Oriana Fallaci intervista la storia", Gazzetta di Parma, 5 Sept.

—— 1974b "Uomini che fanno il mondo presente", in *L'Avvenire*, 29 Aug.

PAREKH, Bikhu 1992 "The Cultural Particularity of Liberal Democracy", *Political Studies*, Special Issue, 40: 160–75.

—— 1994 "Superior People: The Narrowness of Liberalism from Mill to Rawls", *Times Literary Supplement*, 25 Feb.: 11–13.

PASOLINI, Pier Paolo 1992 *Petrolio*, Turin: Einaudi.

PASSERINI, Luisa 1993 "The Women's Movement in Italy and the Events of 1968", in CICIONI and PRUNSTER (eds) 1993: 167–82.

PATTAVINA, G. 1984 *Alekos Panagulis, il rivoluzionario don Chisciotte di Oriana Fallaci: saggio politico-letterario*, Roma: Edizioni italiane di letteratura e scienza.

PAVONE, Claudio 1992 *Una guerra civile. Saggio storico sulla moralità nella Resistenza*, Turin: Boringhieri.

PEDELTY, Mark 1995 *War Stories: The Culture of Foreign Correspondents*, London: Routledge.

PELCOVITS, N. A. 1991 "What Went Wrong?" in McDERMOTT and SKJELSBAEK (eds) 1991: 37–79.

PERMOLI, P. 1974 "Mille rabbie mille interrogativi", *La Fiera Letteraria*, 2 June: 12–13.

PETCHESKY, R. P. 1980 "Reproductive Freedom: Beyond 'A Woman's Right to Choose'", *Signs: Journal of Women in Culture and Society* 5.4: 661–85.

—— 1987 "Fetal Images: The Power of Visual Culture in the Politics of Reproduction", *Feminist Studies* 13.2: 263–92.

PETERSON, V. 1966 "A Personal Exploration of Tomorrow's World", *Chicago Tribune*, 30 Oct.: 3.

PHILLIPS, J. A. 1987 "Bluegill", in *Fast Lanes*, New York: Washington Square Press.

PICKERING-IAZZI, R. 1989 "Designing Mothers: Images of Motherhood in Novels by Aleramo, Morante, Maraini and Fallaci", *Annali d'Italianistica* 7: 325–40.

PORZIO, Domenico 1961 "Rapporto sulla felicità femminile – Oriana Fallaci tira le somme di un suo lungo e interessante viaggio intorno alla donna", *Oggi*, exact source unknown.

—— 1965 "A Cape Kennedy il sole non muore", *Oggi*, No. 43.

POZZATO, Maria Pia 1979 "Liala", in ECO *et al.* 1979: 95–122.

PRANDIN, Ivo 1975 "Per una goccia di vita", *Il Gazzettino*, 8 Oct.

PRISCO, Michele 1974 "Diciotto mostri sacri con le spalle al muro", *Oggi*, 22 May.

—— 1976 "Nota introduttiva", pp. i–vi in O. Fallaci, *Penelope alla guerra*, Milan: Rizzoli BUR, 1976.

PROPP, Vladimir 1975 *Morphology of the Folktale* (1928), trans. L. Scott (1958), 2nd edn revised and ed. by L. A. Wagner (1968), Austin and London: Texas University Press; paperback edn.

QUINE, W. V. O. 1960 "Translation and Meaning", pp. 26–79 in *Word and Object*, Cambridge (Mass.): MIT Press.

RAVAIOLI, Carla 1962* "L'altra faccia della terribile Oriana", source unknown, Mugar Box 11/F9.

RAVERA, Lidia 1979 *Bambino mio*, Milan: Bompiani.

REGGIANI, Stefano 1965 "Penelope tra i cosmonauti", *Arena*, 6 July.

REICH, Robert B. 1991 *The Work of Nations: Preparing Ourselves for Twenty-First Century Capitalism*, New York: Alfred A. Knopf.

RELIGIONI E SOCIETÀ 1991 *L'Islam in Occidente: identità, etnicità, religione*, 6.12, July–Dec., Turin: Rosenberg and Sellier.

La *REPUBBLICA* 1977 19 June: report on contempt conviction against Fallaci.

RICAUMONT, J. de Review of *Le Sexe inutile*. Source unknown – Mugar Box 11/F9.

RICOEUR, Paul 1981 "Narrative Time" (1980), pp. 165–86 in W. J. T. Mitchell (ed.), *On Narrative*, Chicago and London: University of Chicago Press.

ROSA, Giovanna 1982 "Il nome di Oriana", in SPINAZZOLA (ed.) 1982: 57–80; also in SPINAZZOLA (ed.) 1985.

ROSENFELD, Arnold 1966* "With Fire", *The Houston Post*, 13 Nov.

ROSSELLINI, Isabella 1980* "Duetto", *Amica*, No. 28.

ROSSI, Luigi 1961 Review of *Il sesso inutile*, in *La Notte*. Precise source unknown.

ROSSO, Francesco 1974 "Tanti ritratti per la storia", *La Stampa*, 24 May.

—— 1979 "Trenodia per Alekos", *La Stampa*, 6 July.

ROTA, Ornella 1976 "Perché vende questa Fallaci", *Tuttolibri – La Stampa*, 6 March.

SABELLI FIORETTI, C. 1979* "Il ritorno di Oriana", *Panorama*, 22 May: 216–33.

SAGAN, Françoise (pseud. of F. Quoiret) 1954 *Bonjour, tristesse!*, Paris: Julliard.

—— 1956 *Un certain sourire*, Paris: Julliard.

—— 1959 *Aimez-vous Brahms?*, Paris: Julliard.

SAID, Edward W. 1978 *Orientalism*, New York: Pantheon Books.

—— 1993 *Culture and Imperialism*, London: Chatto and Windus.

SAID, E. W. and Christopher HITCHENS (eds) 1988 *Blaming the Victims. Spurious Scholarship and the Palestinian Question*, London – New York: Verso.

SANFORD, David 1975* "The Lady of the Tapes", *Esquire*, June: 102–5, 154, 158, 160.

SANTINI, Aldo 1990a "Scrive con il sangue e dice cretino ai cretini", *Oggi*, 25 July: 50–6.

—— 1990b "Quando Oriana diventò castigamatti dei potenti", *Oggi*, 1 Aug.: 48–53.

—— 1990c "In Messico Oriana ebbe il suo battesimo del fuoco", *Oggi*, 8 Aug.: 38–42.

—— 1990d "Cosí Oriana si innamorò del suo grande eroe greco", *Oggi*, 15 Aug.: 37–41.

SAPORI, Alvise 1989 *Star 2: Dive, divi, divismo nella Hollywood degli anni Quaranta*, Padua: Marsilio.

SARO-WIWA, Ken 1994 *Sozaboy – A Novel in Rotten English* (1985), Harlow, Essex: Longman.

SCARFE, A. and W. SCARFE (eds) 1994 *All That Grief. Migrant Recollections of Greek Resistance to Fascism, 1941–1949*, Sydney: Hale and Iremonger.

SCHALKÄUSER, H. 1983* "Oriana Fallaci", *Cosmopolitan* (Milan), 11 Aug.: 98–100.

SCHEER, Robert 1981* "Playboy Interview: Oriana Fallaci", *Playboy*, Nov.: 77–108.

SCHELL, Jonathan 1974 "The Village of Ben Suc", in MILLS (ed.) 1974: 73–80.

SCHIPPISI, Ranieri 1979 "Un uomo (e una donna)", *Libertà* (Piacenza), 12 July.

SCHWEICKART, P. P. 1989 "Reading Ourselves: Toward a Feminist Theory of Reading", in SHOWALTER (ed.) 1989a: 17–44.

SEDGWICK – see KOSOFSKY SEDGWICK

SHAW, Irwin 1948 *The Young Lions*, New York: Random House.

—— 1960 *Two Weeks in Another Town*, New York: Random House.

SHEEHAN, Neil 1988 *A Bright Shining Lie: John Paul Vann and America in Vietnam*, New York: Random House.

SHEPARD, Alan and Deke SLAYTON 1994 *Moon Shot – The Inside Story of the Race to the Moon*, London: Hodder Headline.

SHOWALTER, E. (ed.) 1989a *Speaking of Gender*, New York – London: Routledge.

—— (ed.) 1989b *The New Feminist Criticism*, London: Virago Press.

SILVESTER, C. (ed.) 1993 *The Penguin Book of Interviews. An Anthology from 1859 to the Present Day*, Harmondsworth: Viking.

SKACHKOV, M. 1928 "Jaroslav Hašek", *Revolyutsia i Kul'tura*, 19–20: 112–19.

SMITH, Sidonie 1993 *Subjectivity, Identity, and the Body: Women's Autobiographical Practices in the Twentieth Century*, Bloomington: Indiana University Press.

SMITH, Sidonie and Julia WATSON (eds) 1992 *De/Colonizing the Subject: The Politics of Gender in Women's Autobiography*, Minneapolis: University of Minnesota Press.

SMYTH, E. J. (ed.) 1991 *Postmodernism and Contemporary Fiction*, London: Batsford.

SNELL, David 1966 "A Florentine girl and the spacemen", *Life*, Oct.–Nov.: 122.

SPINAZZOLA, V. 1979 "Cosí si seduce un pubblico di massa", *L'Unità*, 6 Dec.

—— (ed.) 1982 *Pubblico 1982 – Produzione letteraria e mercato culturale*, Milan: Milano Libri Edizioni.

—— 1984 *La democrazia letteraria: saggi sul rapporto fra scrittori e lettori*, Milan: Edizioni di Comunità.

—— (ed.) 1985 *Il successo letterario*, Milan: Unicopli.

—— (ed.) 1987 *Pubblico 1987*, Milan: Milano Libri Edizioni.

—— 1990 *L'offerta letteraria: narratori italiani del secondo novecento*, Milan: Morano Editore.

—— 1992 *Critica della lettura*, Rome: Editori Riuniti.

SQUIER, S. M. 1991 "Fetal Voices: Speaking for the Margins Within", *Tulsa Studies in Women's Literature*, Spring, 10.1: 17–30.

STAJANO, Corrado 1969 "Una giornalista nel Vietnam", *Tempo*, 13 Dec.

STANZEL, Franz Karl 1984 *A Theory of Narrative* (1979, 1982), Cambridge University Press.

STURROCK, John 1993 *The Language of Autobiography*, Cambridge University Press.

SULEIMAN, Susan 1983 *Authoritarian Fictions: The Ideological Novel as a Literary Genre*, New York: Columbia University Press.

SUTHERLAND, John 1981 *Bestsellers. Popular Fiction of the 1970s*, London: Routledge and Kegan Paul.

SUYIN – see HAN

TANI, Stefano 1990 *Il romanzo di ritorno. Dal romanzo medio degli anni sessanta alla giovane narrativa degli anni ottanta*, Milan: Mursia.

THAKUR, Ramesh 1991 "UN Authority and US Power", in McDERMOTT and SKJELSBAEK (eds) 1991: 101–28.

TODOROV, Tzvetan 1970 *Introduction à la littérature fantastique*, Paris: Seuil.

TOMALIN, Nicholas 1966 "The General Goes Zapping Charlie Cong", in WOLFE and JOHNSON (eds) 1973: 197–203.

TORELLI, Giorgio 1961 "La 'strega di Piazza Carlo Erba' ha messo nel sacco i peccati di Hollywood", *Candido* 32–5. Precise details unknown.

TOYNBEE, Philip 1980 "Princes of the trenches", review of Robert Wohl, *The Generation of 1914*, in *The Observer*, 16 March.

TUROLDO, D. M. 1990 "Viaggio nel vulcano *Insciallah*", *Corriere della Sera*, 2 Aug.

VALLI, Bernardo 1990 "La piccola *Iliade* di Oriana", *La Repubblica*, 29–30 July.

VERNY, Thomas 1981 *The Secret Life of the Unborn Child*, New York: Summit Books.

VIGORELLI, Giancarlo 1970 "Oriana mette tutte in ombra", *Tempo*, date and number unknown, p. 86.

—— 1990 "Guerra e amore nel 'suo' Libano", *Il Giorno*, 7 Aug.

VILLANI, Silvano 1975* "Storia di donna sola – Recensione-intervista con Oriana Fallaci autrice di *Lettera a un bambino mai nato*", in *Supplemento del Corriere della Sera*, 7 Sept.: 16.

VLACHOS, Helen 1970 *House Arrest*, London: André Deutsch.

VRYONIS, S. (ed.) 1991 *Greece on the Road to Democracy: From the Junta to PASOK 1974–1986*, New Rochelle, New York: Aristide D. Caratzas.

WARD, Graham 1994 "In the Name of the Father and the Mother", *Journal of Literature and Theology* 8.3: 311–32.

WARHOL, Robyn R. and D. P. HERNDL (eds) 1991 *Feminisms: An Anthology of Literary Theory and Criticism*, New Brunswick, New Jersey: Rutgers University Press.

Die WELTWOCHE 1967 "Penelope auf dem Kriegspfad", review signed "br", 7 April.

WERTH, Paul 1976 "Roman Jakobson's verbal analysis of poetry", *Journal of Linguistics* 12.1.208: 21–73.

WILLIAMS, Raymond 1974 "Observation and Imagination in Orwell", in R. Williams (ed.), *George Orwell. A Collection of Critical Essays*, Englewood Cliffs: Prentice Hall. First published in

R. Williams, *Orwell*, London: Fontana Collins, 1971, pp. 41–53.

WOLF, Naomi 1994 *Fire with Fire. The New Female Power and How It Will Change the Twenty-First Century*, London: Chatto and Windus.

WOLFE, Tom 1972 "Why They Aren't Writing the Great American Novel Any More. A Treatise on the Varieties of Realistic Experience", *Esquire,* Dec.: 152–8, 272. Repr. in WOLFE and JOHNSON (eds) 1973: 23–36.

—— 1979 *The Right Stuff*, London: Jonathan Cape.

—— 1989 "Stalking the billion-footed beast: a literary manifesto for the new social novel", *Harper's Magazine.*

WOLFE, Tom and E. W. JOHNSON (eds) 1973 *The New Journalism, With an Anthology*, New York: Harper and Row.

WRIGHT, Robin 1992 "Islam, Democracy and the West", *Foreign Affairs*, Summer: 131–45.

W. T. 1975 "Oriana Fallaci e Adele Faccio (Sibilla Aleramo). L'aborto visto con occhi di donna", *Corriere d'Informazione*, 9 Oct.

YOUNG, Kenneth 1969 *The Greek Passion: A Study in People and Politics*, London: J. M. Dent.

ZANIBONI RIVIECCIO, Maria 1975 "Il libro della Fallaci", *Il Mattino*, 18 Oct.

Index